Jonathan Freedman

Proust's

Latin

Americans

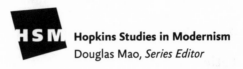

Hopkins Studies in Modernism
Douglas Mao, *Series Editor*

Proust's

Latin Americans

Rubén Gallo

Johns Hopkins University Press
Baltimore

© 2014 Johns Hopkins University Press
All rights reserved. Published 2014
Printed in the United States of America on acid-free paper
9 8 7 6 5 4 3 2 1

Johns Hopkins University Press
2715 North Charles Street
Baltimore, Maryland 21218-4363
www.press.jhu.edu

Library of Congress Cataloging-in-Publication Data

Gallo, Rubén.
  Proust's Latin Americans / Rubén Gallo.
    pages cm.—(Hopkins studies in modernism)
  Includes bibliographical references and index.
  ISBN 978-1-4214-1345-7 (hardcover : alk. paper)—ISBN 978-1-
4214-1346-4 (electronic)—ISBN 1-4214-1345-0 (hardcover : alk.
paper)—ISBN 1-4214-1346-9 (electronic)   1. Proust, Marcel,
1871-1922—Friends and associates.   2. Novelists, French—20th
century—Biography.   3. Latin Americans in literature.   4. Latin
Americans—France—Paris—History—20th century.   I. Title.
  PQ2631.R63Z6113 2014
  843'.912—dc23   2013036941

A catalog record for this book is available from the British Library.

*Special discounts are available for bulk purchases of this book. For
more information, please contact Special Sales at 410-516-6936 or
specialsales@press.jhu.edu.*

Johns Hopkins University Press uses environmentally friendly book
materials, including recycled text paper that is composed of at least
30 percent post-consumer waste, whenever possible.

For Marjorie Perloff

Contents

Acknowledgments ix

Introduction 1

1 **Reynaldo Hahn: Proust's Latin Lover** 25

    Paperolle No. 1. Proust's Mexican Stocks 73

2 **Gabriel de Yturri: An Argentinian in Paris** 90

    Paperolle No. 2. Proust's Peruvians 128

3 **José-Maria de Heredia: A Cuban Conquistador** 134

    Paperolle No. 3. Proust's Mexican Painter 176

4 **Ramon Fernandez: Proust's Mexican Critic** 185

    Paperolle No. 4. Proust's Spanish 211

Epilogue 216

Notes 219
Index 253

Color illustrations follow page 118

Acknowledgments

The publication of this book was made possible through a generous grant from Princeton University's Committee for Research in the Humanities and Social Sciences. Additional funds for translation were provided by the Program in Latin American Studies.

I am deeply grateful to Leo Bersani, who read the manuscript and offered invaluable advice and suggestions, and to Doug Mao and Matthew R. McAdam, who accepted this book for the Hopkins Studies in Modernism series. Annette Becker, Serge Gruzinski, Philippe Gumplowicz, Elisabeth Ladenson, and Jean-Yves Tadié read previous versions of the book and generously shared their expertise on French literature.

In the Paris archives, I received assistance from Pierre Vidal, director of the Opera library at the Palais Garnier. Xavier Mathieu provided images of La Gandara's paintings from his family's collection. Count Armand-Ghislain de Maigret allowed access to the Montesquiou family archives. Ralph Brauner shared his knowledge of the Montesquiou papers. In Argentina, María Tereza Carbonell provided access to Gabriel de Yturri's correspondence. Fernando Acosta Rodríguez brokered the purchase of Yturri's letters, now part of the Manuscripts Collection at Princeton's Firestone Library. Back in Paris, Dominique Fernandez made available several unpublished letters from Reynaldo Hahn in his private collection. Susan Stewart helped me understand Wallace Stevens's "The Idea of Order at Key West" in a new light. Dr. Reiner Speck and the Marcel Proust Gesellschaft in Cologne, Germany, allowed me to reproduce a Proust letter. In Brazil, Mario Sergio Conti, Proust's Portuguese translator, shared his insights on Proust's Brazilian doctor and the relevant bibliography.

At Princeton, Michael Glassman assisted me with the preparation of the

manuscript. Lorna Scott Fox translated passages from French with Proustian elegance.

As always, Terence Gower gave me boundless moral support as I struggled
with the ups and downs of a research project that led me to new fields. Since
the beginning of my academic career, Marjorie Perloff has been a constant
source of intellectual energy, fresh ideas, and collegial advice. I dedicate this
book to her.

Introduction

A few years ago I was reading a biography of Marcel Proust and came across a detail that caught my eye. When he was in his twenties, the novelist became the boyfriend of Reynaldo Hahn, a Venezuelan musician and composer who was three years his junior. The biographer mentioned Hahn's nationality in passing, without giving much thought to its larger cultural meaning. I, however, was fascinated by the idea of Proust having had a Venezuelan boyfriend and by imagining the conversations they must have had about South America, about Latin American culture, and about the experience of being a foreigner in belle-époque Paris. Most readers imagine Proust living in the world of aristocratic salons and elegant soirées described in his novel, but this little-known detail led me to an altogether different Marcel: one who fell in love with a Latin American, who spent time in a household that was bilingual and multicultural, and who must have heard endless accounts of the political turmoil that led the Hahns to emigrate from South America.

Under the spell of this new, *tropicalized* Proust, I began writing a book about Reynaldo Hahn (it was going to be called *Proust's Latin Lover*), but soon I discovered several other Latin Americans in Proust's circle: poets, writers, and critics who were well known to Proustian scholars but whose nationality and cultural background had never sparked the interest of critics. There was Gabriel de Yturri, an attractive young man born in the Argentine town of Tucumán to a modest family. He made his way to Paris, became the lover and secretary of Robert de Montesquiou—one of the most celebrated dandies of his time—and became a good friend of Marcel. There was José-Maria de Heredia, the Cuban poet who rose to fame as one of the key figures of the Parnassian movement, who became the first Latin American to be inducted into the Académie française, and whom the

young Marcel considered a model for the type of writer he hoped to become. There was Ramon Fernandez, a Mexican critic who became a star in
French letters during the 1920s, spent many hours at the novelist's bedside
during his final days in 1922, wrote one of the first philosophical analyses
devoted to Proust's work, and died in disgrace after collaborating with the
Germans during World War II. These Latin Americans were close to Proust,
corresponded with him, and taught him about the experience of foreigners
in France at the turn of the nineteenth century.

I set out to write a biography of Reynaldo Hahn but instead found myself
writing a book on Proust's Latin Americans. I became especially interested
in the question of what it meant to be a foreigner in belle-époque Paris, a
world with values extremely different from those of our time. Today, cultural
difference is one of the most discussed subjects in American universities, and
it has become one of the leading topics in literature departments, as well
as in sociology, anthropology, history, and philosophy. Most campuses now
have departments of Latino Studies, Asian Studies, Jewish Studies, and African American Studies devoted to examining diversity in American society.

Proust's France, in contrast, had radically different views of cultural identity. At the end of the nineteenth century, Paris counted a large number of
foreigners among its residents, but most sought to assimilate to the point
where their origins would be forgotten. They embraced French culture—
from fashion and gastronomy to poetry and opera—and felt proud to be
part of a city that Walter Benjamin famously described as "the capital of
the nineteenth century." Many of these foreigners seemed completely integrated, but the French rarely forgot their origins. Reynaldo Hahn arrived in
Paris when he was three years old, spoke French like a native, studied at the
country's most prestigious schools and conservatories, and prided himself
on advancing the French musical tradition. Yet critics lambasted his first
opera as an exotic, foreign work and derided the composer as a Venezuelan
intruder into the Parisian musical scene. [1] Heredia became one of the most
widely read French authors—school children had to learn his poems by
heart as part of the curriculum—yet his colleague and fellow academician
François Coppée once referred to him as "un beau créole de la Havanne" (a
handsome Creole from Havana). [2] And Montesquiou's friends never ceased
to mock Yturri—who emigrated to France in his late teens and spoke French
with a strong accent—as a *rastaquouère*: a vulgar, unsightly, and often wealthy
Latin American, which the dictionary of the French Academy associates
with "exoticism" and "bad taste." [3]

Rubén Darío, who lived in Paris during this period, noted that the term *rastaquouère* seems to have originated from the Spanish expression *rasca cueros,* or *arrastra cueros,* used by leather merchants, and that it denoted an individual marked by "a lack of culture: or, to be more precise, the lack of good taste."[4] Darío attributed the popularity of the term to the journalist Aurélien Scholl, who created a character named Don Iñigo Rastacuero, marquis of the Saladeros, a rich South American who parades around Paris covered in jewels and dressed in bright colors. "When he was broke, Rastacuero would take a little trip to South America; he would return a few months later with two million francs in his wallet. It was said that he had gone to kill someone in the Andes that he would bring back the spoils. Before leaving, he made sure to leave his address: poste restante in Buenos Aires or poste-restante in Valparaíso."[5]

Foreigners thus found themselves caught in a double bind: they lived in a culture that demanded assimilation but made it almost impossible to assimilate. Their only option was to speak, write, and love in French, yet they were constantly reminded that they were "exotic," "strange," or "foreign." Most of them entered the French cultural canon, but their origins were entirely disavowed. Today, Hahn is remembered as a French composer, Heredia as a French poet, and Fernandez as a French critic.

Despite this constant tension between assimilation and exclusion, these foreigners loved the new life they had found in Paris and embraced French culture. In *Strangers to Ourselves,* Julia Kristeva suggests that there are two types of foreigners: those who experience living in a foreign culture as a melancholic experience marked by loss and anxiety and those who take pleasure in reinventing their identity in a new context. It would seem that life in the twenty-first century has produced mostly melancholic foreigners —and thus recent critical literature counts numerous studies devoted to exile, displacement, and postcolonial malaise—while nineteenth-century France generated more joyful transplants. Proust's Latin Americans—Hahn, Yturri, Heredia, and Fernandez—are all examples of the kind of foreigners that Kristeva describes as expressing "a passion [. . .] for another land, always a promised one."[6]

Foreigners in Proust

Among the hundreds of books devoted to Proust and focusing on subjects as diverse as religion, architecture, sexuality, philosophy, and even banking, there is one topic that has been conspicuously absent: foreigners.

This is the first book-length study dealing with a specific type of foreign-ers—Latin Americans—in Proust's work, and I hope that in the future other scholars will study the place of Germans, Romanians, Russians, Norwegians, and Africans in the novel.[7] Though the main characters—from Charlus to the Verdurins—are all French, there are plenty of foreigners in *À la recherche du temps perdu*: a Norwegian philosopher whose efforts to avoid making mistakes in French render his speech halting and painfully slow, an anony-mous Peruvian guest at Madame Verdurin's salon (a character I explore in depth in paperolle number 2), a Singhalese man on exhibit at the Colonial Exhibition at the Jardin d'Acclimatation (though he is mentioned only in-directly, in an anecdote told by Odette),[8] and a regiment of African soldiers parading through Paris during World War I. There is also a handful of foreign dignitaries: the Count d'Argencourt, a Belgian diplomat; Princess Scherbat-off, who speaks French with a thick Russian accent; the Austrian Princess d'Orvilliers; as well as a German minister bearing the inordinately long name of Prince von Faffenheim-Munsterburg-Weinigen. These royal highnesses cannot be considered truly foreign, since—as the narrator well knows—aristocrats are at home wherever they go. Proust, however, plays on the tension between these characters' foreignness and their arrogant sense of belonging.

Proust himself would not have known what it felt like to be a foreigner. He did not speak any foreign languages—he famously translated John Ruskin without knowing English, working from a literal translation prepared by his mother—never lived abroad, and only left France on a handful of occasions for short visits to Germany, the Netherlands, and Italy, places where French was spoken readily and French customs were the norm. Unlike the Norwe-gian philosopher at the Verdurin salon, Proust never had to struggle in a foreign language or find his way in a strange society governed by unknown codes.

But even if Proust was never a foreigner in the strict sense of the term, he knew well what it felt like to be an outsider. His entire life oscillated between the experiences of belonging and not belonging—a state of being that emerges as one of the central themes of the novel. It is easy to think of Proust as a child of privilege who lived in the mainstream—he was wealthy, came from a respected family, counted many aristocrats among his friends, and moved in powerful circles—but Marcel understood from an early age that he never fully belonged in any of these worlds and that his identity—half-Jewish, homosexual, and bourgeois—rendered him marginal three times

over. Proust was an *étranger à soi-même,* to borrow the term coined by Julia
Kristeva to describe the psychic experience of being an outsider. Playing
on the double meaning of the French word *étranger*—which translates as
"foreigner" but also "stranger"—Kristeva argues that from a psychoanalytic
perspective we are all foreigners: "foreignness is with us" since "the other
is my [. . .] unconscious." [9] According to this perspective, "we are our own
foreigners," and we carry within us the experience of not belonging.

Kristeva explains that the encounter with a foreigner can produce an
uncanny experience. Like all instances of the *Unheimlich,* the foreigner reminds us of something archaic that has been repressed from memory—in
this case, our inner foreignness. "The foreigner is within us. And when we
flee from or struggle against the foreigner, we are fighting our unconscious
—that 'improper' facet of our impossible 'own and proper.'" Playing on the
French translation of Freud's concept of *Unheimlich*—*l'inquiétante étrangeté*
(literally, disturbing strangeness)—she concludes that only the realization
that we are all *étrangers à nous-mêmes,* "strangers to ourselves," can dispel
xenophobic fears in favor of a position of empathy and hospitality.

Kristeva stresses that Proust's narrator is someone who belongs and does
not belong in the world of *À la recherche.* He is "Inside and out, at the center
of the clan [. . .] and at its periphery" [10] —a borderline position that prefig-
ures Freud's reflections on the uncanny. And it is precisely the experience
of not belonging fully, of always feeling different from those around him,
that animates the narrator to observe, as if he were looking at them through
a magnifying glass, the almost imperceptible quirks that betray someone's
status as an outsider. Proust, as Kristeva concludes, "never ceases to disturb
those who wish to be 'one of them' [en être]." [11]

Proust was the ultimate "stranger to himself." As a neurotic, homosexual,
hypochondriac, Jewish bourgeois, he was as foreign in the salons as the
Norwegian philosopher at Madame Verdurin's dinner party—except that his
sense of nonbelonging was not inscribed in his speech. He could pass, but—
like most characters in his novel, from Bloch to Charlus—he was always on
the verge of being found out and exposed.

Even though there are relatively few true foreigners in Proust's novel,
it is full of characters who are strangers to themselves, who try but fail
to belong (*en être* is the expression favored by the narrator). Bloch might
be French by birth, but he is as out of place in the salons as the Norwe-
gian philosopher; Swann might be rich and charming, but his marriage to
Odette turns him into a pariah; and even Charlus, the most snobbish and

aristocratic of all Proustian figures, finds himself excluded from Madame Verdurin's salon—to which he desperately wants to belong so he can be close to the young violinist Charlie Morel.

Proust's Foreigners

Despite the paucity of foreigners in his novel, Proust the author was surrounded by friends and acquaintances who were born abroad. Antoine and Emmanuel Bibesco were Romanian; Marie Nordlinger, Hahn's cousin who helped him translate Ruskin, was English; and Ilan de Casa Fuerte was born in Naples to an old Spanish family. Apart from Hahn, Yturri, Heredia, and Fernandez, his Latin American friends included acquaintances like Lucio Mancilla, Roberto Guzmán Blanco, Enrique Gómez Carrillo, Max Daireaux, and Antonio La Gandara.[12] Proust befriended this eclectic bunch briefly after the term *Latin America* was coined in France to further the ideal of a pan-Latin unity among European and American countries. During his ill-fated attempt to gain control of Mexico in the 1860s, Napoleon III promoted the notion of an America that was also Latin—and thus linked to France by linguistic and cultural ties.[13]

At the turn of the nineteenth century, many Latin Americans living in France found themselves in a position similar to that of assimilated French Jews: they had often grown up in France (some, like Fernandez, were born in Paris but did not have French citizenship), spoke French without an accent, and had become fully integrated into their adoptive country. Most were *criollos* who were ethnically European, and many of them, like Hahn and Heredia, devoted their lives to promoting French culture. And yet, like Jews, Latin Americans found their acquired identity to be extremely fragile: their sense of belonging could be shattered at any minute by a scornful remark about *rastaquouères* or *metèques*. If episodes like the Dreyfus Affair unleashed intense anti-Semitic sentiment, events like Napoleon III's Mexican Campaign or the Panama Affair sparked a peculiar form of anti-Latin Americanism.

Latin Americans in French Literature

Though Latin American characters had appeared in French literature since at least the 1840s, the figure of the Latin American has received scant attention. (Scholars, most notably Sylvia Molloy, have focused on the reception of Latin American literature in France.)[14] One of the first works to feature a Latin American was Honoré de Balzac's *La cousine Bette* (1846), in which we find a Brazilian millionaire named Henri Montès de Montéjanos who is as rich as he is foolish.[15] The narrator compares him to Othello and describes him as "a magnificent specimen of the Portuguese race in Brazil,"[16] a "child of Rio," and a "beautiful jaguar." He is the typical *rastaquouère*—fabulously rich and loves to dress the part; he wears a large diamond "costing a hundred thousand francs, and shining like a star over his sumptuous blue silk necktie."[17] The narrator paints in detail "the foreign nobleman's superb waistcoats, his impeccably polished boots, his incomparable walking-sticks, his much-coveted horses, his carriage driven by completely enslaved, well-beaten negroes"[18] Montès makes only a few quick appearances in the novel, and his furtive presence serves mainly to provide comic relief.

In 1863, the Théâtre du Palais Royal presented *Le Brésilien*, a one-act comedy by Henri Meilhac and Ludovic Halévy in which a character impersonates a Brazilian prince named Acapulco and exclaims in pseudo Portuguese: "Quo resta buena avatas."[19] Some critics believe the term *rastaquouère* originated in this play. Gaston Jollivet recalls that on the night of the first performance the actor Brasseur came on stage dressed as the fake Brazilian prince and began to improvise a declaration of love: "Astaquer, Bonastaquer, Rastaquère." Upon hearing this last word, with its rolling *r*s and sonorous ending, the audience broke out laughing. As they left the theater, "the attendees, men and women, spread the use of this strident word in restaurants and cafés." Jollivet recounts that a day later a group of bona fide Brazilians attended the performance, booed Brasseur, and convinced their embassy to file a protest at the ministry of foreign affairs. But by then "it was too late. The term 'rastaquouère' had already become part of our slang."[20]

Three years later the same authors collaborated with Jacques Offenbach on the operetta *La vie parisienne* (1866), which features a nameless Brazilian who is rich, gaudy, and the epitome of the *rastaquouère*. When he first appears on scene, he sings a fast-paced aria vaunting his fabulous wealth (see plates 1 and 2):

Je suis Brésilien, j'ai de l'or,
Et j'arrive de Rio-Janeire
Plus riche aujourd'hui que naguère,
Paris, je te reviens encor!
Deux fois je suis venu déjà,
J'avais de l'or dans ma valise,
Des diamants à ma chemise,

Combien a duré tout cela?
Le temps d'avoir deux cents amis
Et d'aimer quatre ou cinq maîtresses,
Six mois de galantes ivresses,
Et plus rien! ô Paris! Paris!
En six mois tu m'as tout raflé,
Et puis, vers ma jeune Amérique,
Tu m'as, pauvre et mélancolique,
Délicatement remballé![21]

(I am Brazilian, I have gold
and I come all the way from Rio
richer today than ever before
Paris, here I come back to you.
Twice have I been here already;
I had gold in my suitcase,
diamonds in my shirt-front,
how long did it all last?
Time enough to have two hundred friends
and to love four or five mistresses;
six months of amorous raptures
and then nothing, O Paris, Paris!
Within six months you had bled me dry
and then back to my young America
you delicately packed me off,
a poor and melancholy wretch!)[22]

Like Balzac's Montès, Offenbach's Brazilian is a caricature, a minor character designed to elicit laughter from the audience. The operetta plays on the stereotype of the rich foreigner with a taste for Parisian luxury who squanders his fortune and is forced to return home penniless. Offenbach's Brazilian is more resilient than other ruined foreigners, and the libretto shows him returning to Paris "twenty times as rich as before" after obtaining more funds from home.[23]

The playwright Georges Feydeau—an acquaintance of Proust's—created another memorable Latin American in *Un fil à la patte* (1896), a comedy featuring General Irrigua, a South American official who has gambled away the funds entrusted to him by his government to purchase a fleet of warships. Exiled from his country for this misdeed, he now spends his time in Paris chasing after attractive women. He is introduced as a "rastaquouère" and speaks a comical mixture of Spanish and French. "Ah! Caramba! Caramba! [. . .] Dans mon pays yo l'étais ministre de la Gouerre!" he tells the other characters, who marvel at his strange patois.[24] Balzac and Offenbach's Brazilians are caricatures—one-dimensional characters designed to amuse the audience—but Irrigua reflects an important aspect of nineteenth-century political reality. Many disgraced Latin American politicians, including Venezuelan ex-president Antonio Guzmán Blanco and Mexican dictator Porfirio Díaz, settled in Paris to live a life of luxury, often financed by ill-gotten wealth.

The most eloquent, sympathetic, and detailed portrait of Latin Americans in Paris was written by Valery Larbaud (1881-1957), a writer, translator, editor, and cultural impresario who was also an acquaintance of Proust. As a teenager, Larbaud studied at the Collège Sainte-Barbe, a boarding school that counted many wealthy Latin Americans among its students. Larbaud was so fascinated by these cosmopolitan classmates, with their ability to switch between languages and cultures, that he made them the central characters of his novella *Fermina Marquez* (1910).[25] Larbaud's novella is set in a fictional boarding school, "a curious little cosmopolitan world," where Latin American boys have the upper hand and Spanish is the main language spoken: "These sons of Montevideo ship owners, of guano merchants from Callao, of hat makers from Ecuador, felt themselves to be the descendants of the Conquistadors to the cores of their being and at every moment of their lives." These boys are wealthy; unlike Balzac's or Offenbach's Brazilians, they have names—Santos Iturria, Zuniga, Montemayor—as well as complex personalities. They are intelligent, cultivated, proud of their culture, and at one point they teach French boys to admire Latin American history. As the narrator recalls, "It was with the memories of one of the most renowned of all nations that we grew up there; Castile was our second country and for years we considered the New World and Spain as being other Holy Lands where God, through the agency of a race of heroes had put his marvels on display." In this cosmopolitan realm, it is the French boys who seem the odd ones out. As Fermina—an attractive Colombian girl who becomes the object of all the boys' desires—tells one of them, "You Frenchmen are so difficult to understand . . . I think you must be the most peculiar of all foreigners."[26]

Of all the French writers who became interested in Latin America, Larbaud was the most engaged with its culture and its literature. He learned Spanish, befriended Latin American writers living in Paris, and worked actively to make their work accessible to French readers. An indefatigable cultural promoter, he wrote prefaces for the French translations of works by Mariano Azuela, Jorge Luis Borges, and Alfonso Reyes. (He also disseminated the work of other foreign writers, including Walt Whitman and James Joyce.) As Sylvia Molloy has written, "Larbaud was one of the few French writers who sought to have a panoramic view of Latin American literature" and who was fascinated by Latin American cosmopolitanism.[27]

Latin Americans in À la recherche du temps perdu

Proust would have been familiar with the long history of Latin American characters in French literature, and he would have been especially attuned to the works of Valery Larbaud, a writer he respected and admired (as he acknowledged in the autographed copy of *Pastiches et mélanges* he sent him).[28] Proust, too, included in his novel several references to Latin America and Latin Americans that attest to his interest in the dialectics of belonging and not belonging.

The first references to Latin American appear in the first drafts of *À la recherche,* where South America and Central America are given as examples of far-away, exotic cultures. In one passage, a minor character called Penhoët, who did not make it into the final version of the novel, tells other characters: "Partez donc pour l'Amérique du Sud [. . .] vous verrez que vous n'en reviendrez pas." (Leave then for South America . . . you will see that you will not come back.)[29] In earlier drafts, Proust had originally written "Algérie," but then crossed out this word before replacing it with "Amérique du Sud." The comment is ambiguous: the hypothetical traveler would never come back, either because he would find a paradise on earth where he would live happily ever after or because he would be killed or imprisoned by hostile natives.

Elsewhere in the novel, Central America appears as an example of a land that is exotic and yet familiar. When the narrator is finally invited to a soirée at the Guermantes', he is shocked to discover that the world he has idealized for so long is, in reality, inhabited by rather ordinary people. In a passage full of irony, the narrator expresses his disappointment by using the analogy of a French traveler to Central America who discovers that the inhabitants of this far-away land are not that different from Europeans.

> j'éprouvais [. . .] le même étonnement qu'un voyageur, après avoir tenu compte, pour imaginer la singularité des mœurs dans un vallon sauvage de l'Amérique

centrale ou de l'Afrique du Nord, de l'éloignement géographique, de l'étrangeté des dénominations de la flore, éprouve à découvrir, une fois traversé un rideau d'aloès géants ou de mancenilliers, des habitants qui (parfois même devant les ruines d'un théâtre romain et d'une colonne dédiée à Venus) sont en train de lire *Mérope* ou *Alzire*.[30]

(I felt the same astonishment that an explorer does, after he has taken into account, in order to visualize the singularity of the native customs in some wild valley of Central America or North Africa, its geographical remoteness, the strange names of its flora, and then discovers, once he has made his way through a screen of giant aloès or manchineels, inhabitants (sometimes indeed among the ruins of a Roman théâtre and beneath a column dedicated to Venus) are engaged in reading *Mérope* or *Alzire*.)[31]

The hypothetical traveler is disappointed to find out that Central Americans are not as foreign as he had imagined. Whereas he expected the people to be as exotic as the landscape in this imaginary voyage—dotted by giant aloes and trees—he instead discovers that they are thoroughly conversant with high French culture and spend their time reading Voltaire—just like his fellow citizens. In a typically Proustian ironic twist, the Central Americans read Voltaire's *Alzire,* a play set in colonial Peru that recounts the clash between the Spaniards and the Incas. The scene becomes a game of mirrors —a Frenchman witnesses a group of Latin Americans reading a French book about Latin America—suggesting that in the nineteenth century the destinies of France and Latin America had become enmeshed and that Latin Americans were closer to France than most Europeans imagined.

Proust's narrator invokes this episode to express his disappointment at discovering that the Duchesse de Guermantes lives in a world that is less exotic than he had imagined. Like the traveler, he had expected to find a strange new world, and, like the traveler, he is disappointed to discover a group of ordinary people who are not much different from himself. The narrator thus establishes an analogy between the Guermantes and Central Americans and suggests that their elegant salon is, as it were, the Central America of the Faubourg Saint-Germain. In Proust's world, Central America is in the eye of the beholder.

In another passage, Proust invokes South America as an example of political instability. During a discussion of the Dreyfus Affair at Madame de Villeparisis's salon, Ambassador Norpois exclaims, "France, thank God, is not some replica of South America, and no one has yet felt the need for a military *pronunciamento*."[32] The diplomat places France and South America at opposite extremes of the political spectrum: in contrast to French stability, South American countries are volatile, prone to revolutions and *pronunciamientos,* and at the mercy of caudillos and strongmen who can overturn governments at will. Here, Proust might have been thinking of Reynaldo Hahn's family history. Carlos Hahn, Reynaldo's father, had been close to the Venezuelan president Guzmán Blanco, enjoying a political friendship that translated into lucrative business contracts. But after a coup d'état in 1877, the Hahn family lost its privileged position and left the country along with the deposed ruler.[33] When visiting Reynaldo, Proust must have often heard the Hahns decry the political instability in Venezuela and the coups and revolutions that drove them to leave the country.

In addition to these general evocations of South and Central America as exotic landscapes and sites of political instability, Proust's narrator makes specific references to Argentina, Chile, Guatemala, Panama, and Peru. Proust's Latin America is a curious geographical construct: it includes the Southern Cone (Argentina and Chile), Central America (Guatemala and Panama), and a tiny piece of South America (Peru). Cuba does not figure in this imaginary landscape, and neither did Mexico or Venezuela. In one of the drafts for the novel, the narrator marvels at the beauty of the Bay of Querqueville in Normandy and exclaims, "Je suis au bord du golfe d'opale qui a semblé à Whistler digne d'être immortalisé à côté de Valparaiso" (I am standing by the opalescent bay that Whistler deemed worthy of being immortalized next to Valparaiso).[34] Proust, who never left Europe, discovered this Chilean port through Whistler's Valparaiso landscapes, which he saw in a 1905 Paris exhibition.[35] When Proust visited Querqueville, the misty seascape of the Normandy coast triggered a recollection of the painting . . . and an image of the Chilean port. This experience is the opposite of the impressions received by the French traveler in Central America: Proust visited a French town, but instead of a familiar sight, he discovered a landscape that reminded him of the colors of an exotic port at the other end of the world, in a country he had never visited and knew only through an exhibition he had seen in his hometown. The familiar becomes foreign, the foreign familiar, and the French narrator, a stranger to himself.

But there was more to Latin America than exotic landscapes. Proust makes several references to the most important political event in Franco-Latin American relations: the Panama Affair. This failed project to build a transoceanic canal in Panama financed by French capital unraveled into one of the worst financial scandals in nineteenth-century history and is discussed at length in chapter 3. In the novel, the faithful servant Françoise loses all the money she inherited from Aunt Léonie after she invests it in Panama bonds. In a passage Proust rewrote at least three times, the narrator notes that Françoise lost her small inheritance "in the Panama."[36] If the Dreyfus Affair fueled anti-Semitism, the Panama Affair filled newspapers and magazines with graphic accounts of a dangerous tropical country where French workers perished, victims of the harsh climate and terrifying tropical maladies. Even those who never left France, like Françoise, found their lives turned upside down by the "scandal" of Panama.

In a draft of the novel, Proust mentions the class of well-to-do Latin Americans with a passion for Parisian luxury. At one point, the Duke de Guermantes laments that certain foreigners are treated better than Frenchmen, and he points to a Latin American diplomat as an example.

[. . .] entre nous, il est certain qu'on peut se demander pourquoi notre faubourg se met à plat ventre devant des étrangers, qui ne valent pas souvent la corde pour les pendre quand nous sommes si peu accueillants pour tant de Français, même pour des parents de province que nous avons plus de peine à faire recevoir au club que le ministre du Guatemala.[37]

(Between us, it is certain that we can ask why our Faubourg bends itself over for foreigners, when we offer so little hospitality to so many Frenchmen, even for some of our relatives from the country, whom it is harder to have received at the club than the Minister of Guatemala.)

Proust's contemporaries might have recognized the duke's comments as a jab at Enrique Gómez Carrillo, the Guatemalan diplomat and socialite who became one of the most important Latin American writers in Paris and was the epitome of the elegant, worldly foreigner who had became a fixture in the salons.[38] The duke's remarks echo the anti-Semitic statements often heard during the Dreyfus Affair—and later during World War II—and illustrate the anti-Latin Americanism that went hand-in-hand with the anti-Semitism and xenophobia that dominated Parisian salons.

Rich Latin Americans also make an appearance at the Grand Hotel in Balbec. Servants, the narrator observes, can be divided into two groups according to their attitude toward money: there are naïve servants who are awed by money, and there are others, more sophisticated, who are attentive to social stature. The narrator exalts those who are "more responsive to the reasonable gratuity from an old nobleman [. . .] than to the reckless largesse of some foreign money-bags [*rastas*], who thereby betrayed a lack of breeding that was referred to as generosity only to his face."[39]

Here the narrator invokes the most common insult hurled against rich Latin Americans: "rasta," short for *rastaquouère*. Rastas are introduced as the opposite of aristocrats; in contrast to representatives of history, tradition, values, and culture, these newly rich foreigners are rootless transplants whose only value is money. The narrator is as repelled by them as he is fascinated by the Guermantes, though in real life Proust acted like a *rasta*, handing out large tips everywhere he went.

But it was not only Latin Americans who moved to Paris who were eyed with suspicion. Frenchmen who traveled to the Americas in search of fortune —thus exchanging culture and history for money—were also suspect. In one passage, the sharp-tongued Madame Verdurin, marveling at an impressive display of fresh fruit, maliciously suggests that the Baron de Charlus, who belongs to one of the oldest families in France, must have "an uncle or a nephew in the Americas" in order to have access to such ripe pineapples. The narrator then reveals that the fruits are presents from a telegraph boy whom Charlus seduced and then recommended for a job "in the Colonies," thus putting an end to the speculation.[40] Madame Verdurin introduces the specter of a "Latin American" relative as one of her multiple efforts to discredit Charlus to her guests—a family member who emigrated to the Americas in search of fortune would be a stain on Charlus's otherwise impeccable genealogy.

The narrator perceives Latin Americans not only as rich and gaudy but also as driven by powerful sexual urges. In a passage set at the hotel in Balbec, Jewish and Latin American guests prowl the hallways at night in search of amorous adventures. Especially conspicuous is Monsieur Nissim Bernard, a rich Jew whose insatiable libido is presented as an "oriental atavism" driving him to wander through the nooks and crannies of the hotel. In one of this character's fantasies—which appears in Proust's sketch for the Balbec hotel scene but did not make it into the novel—he imagines surprise visits to his hotel room by "a lady with a passion for baccarat who lost too much during the week" and also by a "bankrupt Peruvian." In this hypothetical encounter, "both [visitors] would have pretended to have entered the wrong room, but M Nissim Bernard would have invited them to stay, and would have dined with him or her in front of the lapis lazuli windows."[41] Nissim Bernard does not discriminate: either a ruined lady or a bankrupt Peruvian man can satisfy his erotic need. The scene suggests that sexual favors will be traded for hard money: both guests visit the rich Nissim Bernard in the hopes of raising some funds. The bankrupt Peruvian belongs to a long line of fictional Latin Americans—from Offenbach's Brazilian to Feydeau's General —who gamble away their fortunes in French casinos. But unlike Offenbach's Brazilian, who keeps returning to South America for more money, the anonymous Peruvian must turn to prostitution as his last financial hope.[42]

Another mischievous Peruvian appears in one of the soirées given by Madame Verdurin. Described only as "a young Peruvian," he becomes incensed when he realizes that he has been excluded from the guest list of a future party and, in order to take his revenge, vows "to play all sorts of disagreeable hoaxes" on the offending hostess. This Peruvian is one of the most intriguing of Proust's Latin Americans, and his case is analyzed further in paperolle number 2.[43] The passage reveals that Madame Verdurin is acquainted with some of the Latin Americans living in Paris, and she invites at least one of them to her home—which makes her salon the only one in the novel that admits Latin Americans.

In addition to the imaginary scene involving Nissim Bernard and the bankrupt Peruvian, there is another episode in which debauched Latin Americans make an appearance in Balbec. Aimé, the Grand Hotel's headwaiter, reveals that when he was younger, rich guests from Latin America and other far-away countries often propositioned him. The narrator tells us that Aimé "always arrived punctually at the rendez-vous set by Persians or Argentineans, because he loved his wife and children and took life seriously." The consummate host, Aimé is willing to do anything to please his guests and is dismayed to see that a younger employee, an elevator boy, would not make himself available to important personages, despite Aimé's pleas.[44]

In these passages the narrator suggests a kinship between "Orientals" (a code word for Jews), Persians, and Latin Americans: all of these exotic guests are driven by an unusually strong libido. The comparison of Jews and Latin Americans reappears in other passages in the novel, as we will see in paperolle number 4, devoted to the Verdurins' private language.

Of these Latin Americans, the one who has the closest contact with the narrator is a Brazilian doctor who proposes to cure his asthma with medicinal plants. The narrator, horrified by this "absurd" suggestion, dismisses him a charlatan and, in an effort to assert his expertise in medical matters, boasts that he knows the illustrious Doctor Cottard, to which his interlocutor responds by suggesting that Cottard might want to present a paper on this experimental treatment at the Academy of Medicine.[45] Commenting on this episode, a Brazilian critic suggested that the scene might have been inspired by a real consultation with a South American doctor and by Marcel's horror at the thought that his terrible asthmatic crises could be treated with simple plants. "Let us consider the gravity of the situation: A Brazilian doctor, with his 'absurd inhalations,' could have gone as far as to kill Proust. A Brazilian could have thus sabotaged the publication of that monument of artistic genius that is *A la Recherche du temps perdu*."[46]

As this overview shows, Proust's Latin America is a continent of exotic and beautiful landscapes; a land marred by political instability, frequent revolutions, and strong-armed generals; a promised land for *rastas* who live ostentatiously, squandering fortunes made during revolutions or *pronunciamientos*. Latin Americans are also governed by passions: they prowl hotel hallways in search of tawdry midnight trysts and explode into a rage if they are slighted. Proust's novel invokes many of the stereotypes that we have seen in Balzac and Offenbach, but it also goes beyond them. In addition to the one-dimensional, nameless characters like the bankrupt Peruvian and Madame Verdurin's guest, the novel includes an elaborate, original meditation on the kinship between Latin Americans and Jews as special groups of *others* that seem fully integrated into mainstream French culture—until an involuntary gesture gives away their alterity. (This theme is explored in detail in paperolle number 4.)

Theories of Cosmopolitanism

Three of the Latin Americans in Proust's circle—Reynaldo Hahn, Gabriel Yturri, and José Maria de Heredia—had similar biographies. They were born in Latin America, arrived in France at an early age, and spent the rest of their lives in Paris. With the exception of Yturri, they never returned home. They devoted their lives to French culture and wrote exclusively in French, though they continued to speak Spanish with friends and family. All three died in France and are buried in Paris.

Recent critical theories have analyzed the experience of foreigners who —like Hahn, Yturri, and Heredia—find themselves living in a foreign culture. Postcolonial studies, as well as theories of displacement, exile, cultural imperialism, and transculturation, offer a set of tools to explore this phenomenon. Theorists from Homi Bhabha to Edward Said present displacement as a traumatic experience as they analyze figures who have lost their homelands, have been driven to exile, and live in a state of melancholic longing. In general, the type of subject envisioned by postcolonial studies corresponds to the first type of foreigner theorized by Kristeva: the subject who experiences transplantation as a loss, is plunged into a state of mourning, and has trouble adapting to a new culture. Said, for instance, has written about writers who "bear their past within them—as scars of humiliating wounds."[47] Theories of exile and displacement tend to emphasize the same traumatic terms: "scars," "wounds," "pain." In *Reflections on Exile* (1971), Said writes about "the uprooting and dislocation that has made [so many individuals] into exiles and expatriates" and stresses that exiles "feel the pain of recollection" and engage in a "desperate search for adequate (and usually unfamiliar) expression."[48]

But the figures studied in this book had an altogether different experience as they left Latin America to settle in France. For them, moving to a new country was not a traumatic experience but, on the contrary, a joyful one. All three had a passion for France, its culture, and its history, and they embraced their Parisian life with open arms. Their sense was not of loss but of gain: they acquired a new country, a new language, a new social circle, and a new life. Starting a new life in Paris was a rebirth that allowed all three to thrive to a degree that might not have been possible in their home countries. Hahn, Yturri, and Heredia were not exiles, refugees, outcasts, or victims of geopolitical conflict, and they were not traumatized by their experience. All three moved easily across countries and languages, and their lives were marked by intellectual curiosity and openness to other cultures. They were, in brief, cosmopolitan figures.

Cosmopolitan—a neologism that incorporates the Greek terms for *world* (κοσμοσ) and *city* (πολισ) became an important concept during the Enlightenment. In their *Encyclopédie,* Denis Diderot and Jean le Rond d'Alembert defined "cosmopolitain ou cosmopolite" as "un homme qui n'a point de demeure fixe, ou bien un homme qui n'est étranger nulle part" (a man who has no fixed residence, as well as a man who is not a foreigner—or a stranger—anywhere).[49] A cosmopolitan subject could make himself at home anywhere in the world.

Philosophers considered cosmopolitanism to be one of the building blocks of an enlightened world governed by democratic values. Kant believed it held the secret for world peace: he envisioned a future "League of Nations" governed by "the highest purpose of nature, a universal *cosmopolitan existence.*"[50] Elsewhere, he called for the creation of a "cosmopolitan constitution" based on hospitality that would codify "the right of a stranger

not to be treated with hostility when he arrives on someone else's territory."[51] Kant suggests that cosmopolitan subjects have a complex understanding of identity as open and malleable and are thus more likely to treat
foreigners with kindness than those who have never had the experience of
being others in a different land. Kristeva has argued that Kant's theory of
cosmopolitanism is especially pertinent for our multicultural world, dominated by debates about cultural difference and assimilation. Anthony Appiah has underlined the importance of cosmopolitan experience as a key
component of modern ethics.[52] And recently, literary scholars have praised
cosmopolitanism as a model for multicultural reading in an increasingly globalized world. Like Diderot's cosmopolitan, the modern, enlightened reader
is now required to cross the borders of different literary traditions and make
himself at home in cultures different from his own.[53]

Philosophers from Kant to Appiah have been chiefly concerned with
cosmopolitanism as a political doctrine, and in recent years there has been
an explosion of interest in cosmopolitanism as a guiding principle of international relations.[54] These thinkers extrapolate the original definition of the
cosmopolitan—one who can make his home anywhere—to a geopolitical landscape that would allow every individual to become a citizen of the world, crossing boundaries, traveling across cultures, and feeling at home everywhere.
The only way to live in our increasingly globalized world, these thinkers
conclude, is as a cosmopolitan citizen.

The figures studied in this book, however, invite us to conceive of a
different theory of cosmopolitanism: one that focuses on individual experience. Such a theory would help explain why Hahn, Yturri, and Heredia
embraced their adopted culture so wholeheartedly and why this experience
was such a positive one. The key element in such a theory of cosmopolitan subjectivity would be love. In contrast to exiles and refugees, who experience geographical displacement as a trauma, cosmopolitans are driven
by love: love for a country, for its language, history, and literary tradition.
Freud explained that love functions by incorporation: the subject takes the
loved object and installs it within himself. In the end, the object fuses with
the subject's ego. Proust's Latin Americans took France as an object, idealized it, introjected it, and fused it with their egos. France, as it were, became
an integral part of themselves. Freud once described a successful analysis
as allowing the subject to "love well and work well." For these cosmopolitan Latin Americans, their fascination with French culture played the role
of a good analysis: all of them loved France and worked well within its

traditions. And as only happens in rare cases, love and work became fused. They demonstrated their love of France through their work as composers and writers, and their productivity was fueled by a passion for their new homeland.

Readers might object that most of the Latin Americans in this book—and most of those who settled in Paris in the belle époque—came from a world of privilege that enabled them to experience little conflict or trauma when they moved to France. But not all the figures in this book came from wealthy families. Gabriel de Yturri was born to extremely modest parents in the Argentinean provinces, and he managed to move to France—and to find himself an aristocratic lover—through his own efforts. And Paris was full of rich transplants—including the deposed Mexican president Porfirio Diáz—who, despite their wealth, privilege, and family connections, lived their new lives overwhelmed by a sense of loss.[55] The cosmopolitan experience of love requires much more than money. It requires a special psychic disposition, an openness to others, and a willingness to reshape one's experience.

Proust's Latin Americans, World Literature, and Cosmopolitanism

In addition to foregrounding the experience of five little-known figures in Proust studies, this book is also an invitation to rethink the boundaries of comparative literature. For several decades now, the discipline has been torn in opposite directions: Should it devote itself to canonical authors —Dante, Proust, Joyce? Or should it open itself up to other literary traditions—from Africa to Latin America—in the name of diversity? These culture wars have often pitted European against non-European authors, leading professors and students to choose between the Western canon and new authors whose work seems more in tune with our cultural preoccupations. Should one read James Joyce or Salman Rushdie, Balzac or Maryse Condé, Cervantes or Rigoberta Menchú? In the mid-1990s, the inclusion of Rigoberta Menchú's autobiography in a "great books" course at Stanford sparked a heated controversy. Dinesh D'Souza objected that such a minor book had no place in a serious curriculum, while John Beverly and others defended Stanford's move as one that forced us to rethink the very notion of a canon.[56] Some worried that rethinking the canon was a fine idea but that this move meant that Proust, Joyce, or Goethe had to be dropped from the syllabus to make room for Menchú, since there were only a limited number of readings in the course.

Since the Stanford controversy, critics have sought a way out of these culture wars that does not force us to choose between the European canon and cultural diversity. David Damrosch has argued that the mission of comparative literature today is to study "world literature," an open, all-inclusive category that "could include any work that has ever reached beyond its home base"[57] and that does not pit Western against non-Western works. For Damrosch, the study of world literature is a cosmopolitan enterprise. If the cosmopolitan subject is at home everywhere, the cosmopolitan reader can turn his attention to literature produced anywhere.

Damrosch argues for opening up the canon by including more authors from other traditions. In this book, I propose another model. It is also possible to study the canon with an eye for cultural diversity and to show that it is possible to read authors like Proust—or Joyce or T. S. Eliot—in the context of a cosmopolitan experience that extends well beyond Europe's boundaries. We do not have to choose either Proust or Latin American authors; we can read Proust *with* Latin American authors and think of the French novelist's relation to these cultural others. It is possible to read canonical authors *alongside* authors from non-European traditions and to think of this relationship as one of complementarity rather than one of opposition. This is a cosmopolitan model in which critic and reader make themselves at home in different cultural traditions, crossing linguistic and national boundaries.

Reading Proust with Latin America in mind is an example of what Said called "contrapuntual reading." Despite the differences between postcolonial studies and my own approach, Said's perceptive readings—especially their attention to the historical and political context in which works of literature were created—stand out as one of the most important influences on my work. In *Culture and Imperialism,* Said urged the public to "read the great canonical texts, and perhaps also the entire archive of modern and pre-modern European and American culture, with an effort to draw out, extend, give emphasis and voice to what is silent or marginally present or ideologically represented [. . .] in such works."[58] In the case of Proust, it was Latin Americans—along with the entire history of Franco-Latin American historical and political relations—who were both "marginally present" and "ideologically represented" in his writings, as I argue in this book.

A User's Guide

This volume consists of four chapters, each devoted to one of the Latin Americans in Proust's life: Reynaldo Hahn, Gabriel de Yturri, José-Maria de

Heredia, and Ramon Fernandez. Each chapter has three aims: first, to pro- vide a brief biographical sketch, emphasizing how each of these Latin Amer- icans negotiated the vicissitudes of cultural alterity while asserting a cosmo- politan identity; second, to analyze their correspondence with Proust, with an eye to locating passages that might shed light on the novelist's reflections on foreignness and *étrangeté*; third, to consider each of these figures in the larger context of a transatlantic cultural history, with particular attention to their place in aesthetic and political debates that occurred in France and Latin America.

These four chapters are punctuated by *paperolles*: shorter meditations on minor characters or events that illuminate Proust's interactions with Latin America and Latin Americans. Proust was an obsessive editor of his own texts, and he never ceased revising and making lengthy additions to his novel. Whenever his insertions filled the margins of his notebooks, he would extend the page by gluing on strips of paper on which he could con- tinue writing. These *paperolles,* as he called them, turned his pages into texts that radiate in all directions. I, too, have extended the chapters on these Latin Americans with shorter meditations on related topics that function as *paperolles* of sorts, devoted to Proust's Mexican stocks, Proust's Peruvians, Proust's Mexican painter, and Proust's Spanish, respectively.

Of all the Latin Americans Proust met in Paris, Reynaldo Hahn—the sub- ject of chapter 1—was the one closest to his heart. He was Proust's first boyfriend, the Latin lover who taught him much about the experience of being a foreigner in France. This chapter begins with an overview of their friendship—which lasted until Proust's death in 1922—and then proposes a detailed analysis of the letters exchanged by the two friends over more than two decades. Reynaldo's foreignness is one of the main concerns in the correspondence: Proust found many ways—inventing a private language, drawing likenesses of Reynaldo—to comment on his friend's experience of alterity. Hahn was a consummate cosmopolitan; he spoke Spanish, French, and German fluently and spent his life moving effortlessly across boundar- ies, conducting and performing in France, Germany, England, and Egypt. He would pay tribute to and poke fun at the cosmopolitan experience in *Ciboulette,* his most famous operetta.

Paperolle number 1, "Proust's Mexican Stocks," explores a little-known facet of the novelist's life: his passion for playing the stock market. After his parents died, Proust inherited a considerable fortune that in today's money would be worth many millions of dollars. He proceeded to lose much of it

in risky investments that included gold mines in Africa, oriental carpet companies in Russia, and rubber plants in Malaysia. He also bought a number of
Mexican stocks that plummeted in value after the eruption of the Mexican
Revolution in 1910. In his letters to his stockbroker, the novelist followed
the ups and downs of Mexican politics, including the rise of caudillos and
the assassination of presidents Madero and Huerta, though his main interest always remained the value of his portfolio. Proust has been studied as a
novelist of World War I; these letters reveal him as an unlikely chronicler of
the Mexican revolution. They also show us another kind of cosmopolitanism. Even though Proust rarely left France, he traveled with his imagination by buying stocks in foreign companies (and, as his biographers have
shown, by reading railway schedules in bed): he was an armchair—or even
a bedridden—cosmopolitan.

Chapter 2 examines the life and writings of Gabriel de Yturri, an Argentinean born in the northern province of Tucumán, who arrived in Paris in the
1880s to become the secretary—and lover—of Count Robert de Montesquiou, a celebrated dandy whose extravagant costumes, apartments, and
parties inspired Huysmans to write *Against the Grain*. Unlike Hahn, Yturri
came from a modest, provincial family; he was a self-made cosmopolitan. As
a poor student, he found an ingenious way to flee from the oppressive, conservative world in which he was born, and he made his way to Paris, where
he devoted himself to organizing Montesquiou's parties and social activities. Yturri was one of Proust's few friends who had come from a humble
background, and he taught the novelist much about the experience of being
an outsider in Parisian salons.

Paperolle number 2, "Proust's Peruvians," examines how a minor character
—an anonymous guest at Madame Verdurin's salon—sparked a lively debate
among Peruvian scholars who sought to uncover the model for this mean-
spirited guest. Even though this character appears and disappears in a single
paragraph, he has inspired critics to write several articles discussing his possible identity as well as the political significance of his presence in the novel.
Proust's Peruvian is a frivolous cosmopolitan: he can travel across countries
and languages, but the only use he finds for his transcultural mobility is to
frequent salons, receptions, and parties.

Chapter 3 focuses on José-Maria de Heredia, a Cuban-born writer who
rose to fame as one of the poets of the Parnassian movement and was
elected to the Académie française. He was also one of the earliest models
for the type of writer the young Proust hoped to become. Heredia attained

an important place in French letters, but literary histories rarely mention that he was born in Cuba, an omission that places him in the company of the many foreign-born artists and writers—Eugène Ionesco, Samuel Beckett, Pablo Picasso, Tzvetan Todorov, Julia Kristeva—who came to embody French culture despite their foreign origins. Ironically, in the process, their cultural difference was entirely forgotten. As Kristeva notes in *Strangers to Themselves,* "when your otherness becomes a cultural exception—if, for instance, you are recognized as a great scientist or a great artist—the entire nation will appropriate your performance, will assimilate it along with its own better accomplishments, and give you recognition better than elsewhere."[59] Heredia is a case in point of such an appropriated cosmopolitan.

Paperolle number 3, "Proust's Mexican Painter," focuses on Antonio de La Gandara, a little-known society painter who was born in Paris to a Mexican father and an English mother. La Gandara knew Proust, and he painted portraits of several Latin Americans: Yturri, Hahn's sister Maria, and the Chilean ambassador to France. Though La Gandara was born in Paris, he was considered an exotic foreigner; critics referred to him as a "Spaniard," and Montesquiou once called him an "Aztec." Like many of the characters in Proust's novel, he was caught in the double bind of *en être*; he belonged . . . without ever fully belonging.

Chapter 4 examines Ramon Fernandez, a Mexican critic who became one of the most influential intellectuals in Paris during the 1920s and 1930s. Fernandez studied with Henri Bergson and published one of the first philosophical studies of Proust's work. He was an editor of the *Nouvelle Revue française* and was widely acknowledged as one of the most brilliant critics of his generation. Despite his interest in foreign literature—he helped publish T. S. Eliot and George Meredith in French—he never expressed interest in Mexican or Latin American letters, even after the Mexican poet Alfonso Reyes met him in Paris and urged him to write for Mexican journals. During World War II, Fernandez collaborated with the Nazis and embraced their cultural program. He would have landed in prison had he not died, prematurely, in 1944 before the liberation of Paris. Fernandez was a paradoxical cosmopolitan if there ever was one; he displayed an extreme openness to some foreign cultures but remained closed to others.

Paperolle number 4, "Proust's Spanish," examines the only passage in the novel that discusses the Spanish language. In *La Prisonnière,* the narrator reports a conversation between Monsieur and Madame Verdurin but stops short when the two pronounce a word in a private language that he cannot

understand and that he compares to the "Spanish words" used in assimilated Latin American families. The mysterious word becomes a shibboleth,
a sign of cultural alterity that reveals the Verdurins, who until now seemed
fully French, as marked by a distant, foreign origin.

The critic Charles Augustin Sainte-Beuve believed that a work of literature is always an extension of the author's personality and that literary criticism should concern itself with the author's life. Proust disagreed. One of his
first projects was a book called *Contre Sainte-Beuve* that argued for reading
literature as an independent creation separate from the author's biography.
The present study falls between these two critical extremes. Some chapters—
including the one on Proust's Peruvians—are concerned chiefly with passages
in the novel; others—those devoted to Hahn, Yturri, and Heredia—focus on
Proust's correspondence and interactions with his Latin American friends.
This mixed approach—studying the novel alongside the author's life—has
been the standard practice in Proust studies for the past decades. Proust's
life and work bear the same relationship as the carafes plunged in the
Vivonne depicted in a famous passage of the novel: the carafe contains the
water but is also contained by the river. Proust's life and work are also *con-
tenantes et contenues.*[60]

1 Reynaldo Hahn
Proust's Latin Lover

"Everything I have done in my life," Proust confessed in 1904, "has been thanks to Reynaldo."[1] Of the Latin Americans studied in this book, Reynaldo Hahn (1874–1947) was the closest to Proust and the one who left the deepest mark in his life and work (fig. 1.1). Born in Venezuela to a South American mother and a German-Jewish father, he emigrated to Paris when he was three and quickly rose to fame as a singer and composer. By fifteen, he had gained fame as the child prodigy who set to music Victor Hugo's verses "Si mes vers avaient des ailes." By seventeen (fig. 1.2), he was studying under Jules Massenet at the conservatory, where Erik Satie was a classmate, and he premiered his first opera in Paris at twenty-four. He went on to have a brilliant musical career conducting and performing from London to Bucharest.[2]

Marcel was twenty-three and Reynaldo twenty when they met at a Parisian salon in the summer of 1894. The two had an instant intellectual connection, bonded over their shared passion for literature and music, and immediately began an epistolary exchange that would continue until Marcel's death. The future novelist was no doubt dazzled by Reynaldo's cosmopolitanism: Marcel did not speak any foreign languages and had barely traveled out of France; Reynaldo, in contrast, was fluent in Spanish, German, English, and French, had lived on two continents, and traveled across Europe to visit family or perform at concert halls.

The two became inseparable. They saw each other in Paris, spent weekends in the country—at the château de Réveillon owned by Madeleine Lemaire, a rich hostess who would become one of the models for Madame Verdurin—and even went on a honeymoon of sorts. In 1895 they spent several weeks traveling in Brittany in what was then a remote area of the French countryside. (In a letter to Suzette Lemaire, reproduced in figure 1.3, Reynaldo complains that the region is so rough that his writing paper has

Figure 1.1. Nadar, portrait of Reynaldo Hahn, June 6, 1898. Ministère de la culture / Média-thèque du Patrimoine, Inv. NA23815439. Distributed by RMN / Art Resource, New York.

been covered by fly droppings!) Reynaldo and Marcel each found his way into the other's work. Marcel dedicated one of his first stories, "La mort de Baldassare Silvande," to "Reynaldo Hahn, poet, singer, and musician."[3] And Reynaldo wrote a series of melodies to accompany Marcel's "Portraits de peintres," which the two friends performed together on several occasions[4] and which were later included in *Les plaisirs et les jours* (1896), Marcel's first book.[5] Marcel also paid homage to Reynaldo in his first novel, *Jean Santeuil,* which he began writing around the time they met (and which remained un-published during his lifetime). One of the main characters is a young aristo-crat named Henri de Réveillon, whose initials are an inversion of Reynaldo Hahn's. Years later, when he published *À la recherche du temps perdu,* Marcel would also pay tribute to his friend by having Doctor Cottard appear at the Verdurin salon during the war wearing a uniform that resembled a coronel from Reynaldo Hahn's opera *L'île de rêve.*[6]

When they first met, Reynaldo was already a successful composer, but Marcel had not published much beyond a few articles in newspapers and journals. Over the years, Reynaldo's fame grew as he premiered operas, cre-ated works for the Ballets Russes, published books, and performed around Europe. Marcel, in contrast, was an aspiring and unrecognized writer and

Figure 1.2. Otto Wegener (1849-1922), portrait of Reynaldo Hahn at seventeen. Bibliothèque Musée de l'Opéra, Ph. No. 34, Bibliothèque Nationale de France, Paris.

would not be recognized as an important author until the publication of *Swann's Way* in 1913, almost two decades after their first meeting. Only then did the two friends seem to be on an equal footing, though that lasted only a few years: Marcel's fame surpassed Reynaldo's after he won the Prix Goncourt in 1919.

Marcel and Reynaldo were lovers for only a few years, but they remained close friends—Reynaldo was one of last visitors Proust received on his deathbed—and exchanged playful, flirtatious letters until Proust's death. In many ways, the two had parallel lives: they were both gay and half-Jewish; they were both born to wealthy, bourgeois families; they both chose creative careers; they were both fascinated by the world of Parisian salons; and

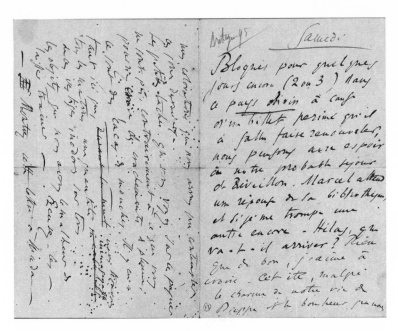

Figure 1.3. Letter from Reynaldo Hahn to Suzette Lemaire, Brittany, 1895. Harvard, bMsFr 219.1 (18).

they both lived with their mothers and lost their fathers at a young age—Reynaldo at twenty-four and Marcel at twenty-nine.[7]

Despite his passion for French culture, Reynaldo's legal status as a foreigner prevented him from achieving many of his goals. During his years at the conservatory, he was excluded from the Prix de Rome because he was not a French citizen. When *L'île de rêve* premiered in 1898, chauvinistic critics lamented the fact that a French institution, the Opéra Comique, would present the work of a Venezuelan composer—one reviewer called him an "exotique inconnu."[8] (Other reviewers wondered why a composer born in the tropics did not infuse his music with more "local color.")[9] Reynaldo was naturalized in 1908, and during World War I he enlisted and fought against the Germans. This experience must have been especially difficult for him; his father had been born in Germany, and his sisters and extended family still lived in Hamburg. At the front he was the victim of anti-Semitic attacks,[10] but despite these setbacks he distinguished himself as an exemplary soldier, and by 1918 he had accumulated an impressive list of decorations: the Légion d'honneur, the Croix militaire, and a promotion to the rank of corporal.[11]

After Marcel's death, Reynaldo's career continued to flourish, and he became a successful composer of operettas, that very French genre that had
been refined by Jacques Offenbach in the nineteenth century. During the
1920s and 1930s, Reynaldo composed some of his most memorable works,
including *Ciboulette* (1923) and *Ô mon bel inconnu* (1933)—operettas that remain in the repertoire of French theaters. By then Reynaldo was widely
recognized as one of the most important figures in French music.

Despite his success, Reynaldo was the target of right-wing music critics
like André Cœuroy and Lucien Rebatet, who sought to discredit his music
and its place in the French tradition by pointing to his triple alterity—Latin
American, Jewish, homosexual.[12] He was baptized, raised Catholic, and always considered himself a Venezuelan living in Paris,[13] but when the Nazis
occupied Paris in 1940, they blacklisted him as a Jewish musician and out-
lawed the performance of his works. Reynaldo fled to the south of France
and then to Monaco, where he spent the war years directing the Monte
Carlo Orchestra. He lost several family members and close friends, including a former classmate from the conservatory, Fernand Ochsé, who was
deported and died in a German concentration camp.[14] After the liberation,
Reynaldo returned to Paris, and Charles De Gaulle's government appointed
him director of the Paris Opera—a position he held until his death in 1947.

Music, Nationalism, and Cultural Identity

Since his arrival in Paris as a child, Reynaldo had embraced French culture, and soon he mastered the baroque social codes of French salons. At
the conservatory he devoted himself to the French musical canon: as a student of Massenet, he saw himself as working within a line of French composers stretching from Jean-Baptiste Lully to Offenbach to Camille Saint-
Saëns. While he was still in his teens, he took part in a lively debate about
the relation between music and national identity that revolved around the
figure of Richard Wagner. France had had a complicated relationship with
Wagner since the 1861 premiere of *Tannhäuser* at the Paris Opera, when
loud protests forced the composer to withdraw his opera after only three
performances. Since then France had been divided into two enemy camps:
Wagnerians and anti-Wagnerians. The first group, which included Baudelaire and Théophile Gautier, championed the composer as a revolutionary
whose theory of the *Gesamtkunstwerk* charted the future of opera.[15] Anti-
Wagnerians—including Jean Cocteau—on the other hand, argued that
Wagner's music was too Germanic and thus incompatible with the cultures

of Latin nations like France.[16] The debate grew so intense that some critics spoke of a "Wagnerian commotion,"[17] and others decried "Wagnerian
theology."[18]

A few years before meeting Proust, Reynaldo took sides on this divisive
issue. Despite being a foreigner himself, he supported musical nationalists
and argued that Wagner's Germanic compositions were alien to the French
soul. He was only eighteen, but he expressed his views passionately in his
letters to Édouard Risler, a conservatory classmate who would go on to become a famous pianist.[19]

"What is so ugly about Wagnerism," Reynaldo wrote to Risler, "is the
colossal affectation of it, that frightful hypocrisy constantly mixed into
the question of art." He explained that his criticism was directed at Wagnerians, not at the composer: "I am not speaking of Wagner himself, but,
quite frankly, of three-quarters of those who go to Bayreuth: those who
go merely to have been there, as Alphonse Kaas would say."[20] Reynaldo admired *Parsifal* and *Die Meistersinger,* but he despised critics who preached a
Wagnerian orthodoxy. "What I detest most in the world," he told Risler, "are
bêcheurs (harsh critics) and Wagnerians."[21] Ironically, Reynaldo, who was
still a Venezuelan citizen, adopted a nationalist, essentialist position that
pitted Germany against France. Germans, he wrote, were heavy—"their
bodies, their souls, their laughter, their gestures, their food"—as opposed
to the French, marked by lightness, warmth, and sensuality. German composers could have impressive techniques but they lacked grace; they were
like "elephants dancing skillfully on a tightrope." To put it bluntly, Reynaldo
told his friend that France and Germany were as different as "champagne
and beer."[22] The French were drawn to Wagner because they found his German tonality exotic, and Reynaldo worried that "in the end [this] exoticism
will kill French art."[23] He was not alone in his view. In 1900, an influential
critic lamented that "modern music had succumbed to Wagner's tyranny,"[24]
and others complained that French composers were being forced to adopt
Germanic models that were ill suited to the national character. As a young
man, Reynaldo acquired a reputation as a "notorious anti-Wagnerian."[25]

Marcel was more receptive to the German composer's ideas and enthu-
siastic about his music. In a letter to Suzette Lemaire written in May 1895,
Marcel explains that his disagreement with Reynaldo had to do less with the
place of Wagner in the musical tradition than with the role of language and
narrative in opera. Marcel praised music as a higher art form whose expressive powers surpassed those of literature.

[J]e crois que l'essence de la musique est de réveiller en nous ce fond mystérieux (et inexprimable à la littérature et en général à tous les modes d'expression finis, qui se servent ou de mots et par conséquent d'idées, choses déterminées, ou d'objets déterminés—peinture, sculpture—) de notre âme, qui commence là où le fini et tous les arts qui ont pour objet le fini s'arrêtent, là où la science s'arrête aussi, et qu'on peut appeler pour cela religieux.[26]

(I believe that the essence of music is to bestir in us the mysterious depths (inexpressible by literature and more generally by all finite modes of expression, which use either words and hence ideas, determinate things, or determinate objects—painting, sculpture) of our soul, which begin where the finite, along with all of those arts whose objective is the finite, ends, and where science stops likewise, and which may for that reason be called religious.)

Marcel's letter alludes to the nineteenth-century theories of Schopenhauer, who posited music as the most perfect of the arts because of its nonrepresentational stance. Marcel explained to Suzette that Reynaldo, in contrast, could only conceive of music in relation to language.

Reynaldo, au contraire, en considérant la musique comme dans une dépendance perpétuelle de la parole, la conçoit comme le mode d'expression des sentiments particuliers, au besoins de nuances de la *conversation*. Vous savez qu'une symphonie de Beethoven [. . .] l'ennuie beaucoup. Il est bien trop artiste pour ne pas l'admirer profondément, mais ce n'est pas cela qu'est pour lui la musique et cela au fond, ne l'intéresse pas.[27]

(On the contrary, Reynaldo, who regards music as inherently dependent upon words, conceives it as the expressive mode of particular feelings, of *conversational* nuances if need be. You know how bored he is . . . by a Beethoven symphony. He is too much of an artist not to admire it profoundly, but to him that's not what music is, and ultimately it holds no interest for him.)

Marcel's letter was an accurate reflection of his friend's ideas. In a letter to Risler, Reynaldo confessed that, for him, the highest musical emotions always involve lyrics.

Je n'ai jamais ressenti, entends-tu, *jamais* une *émotion intérieure* en entendant une *œuvre symphonique quelle qu'elle soit,* même de Beethoven, même de Mozart. Je ne suis ému *qu'au théâtre,* ou lorsqu'il y a des *paroles*! C'est un phénomène inexplicable mais certain; et de là vient que je préfère la "symphonie" de Saint-Saëns à celle de Schubert! Devant une œuvre purement instrumentale, je n'éprouve que de *l'admiration,* mais je ne m'y *mêle* pas. Une phrase musicale me charme et me ravit, mais ne *m'émeut jamais*; il n'y a que les *sentiments* qui m'émeuvent.[28]

(I have never, I tell you, *never once* felt the least *inner emotion* upon hearing *any symphonic work at all,* even Beethoven's, even Mozart's. I am only moved when at the *theater,* or when there are *words*! It's an inexplicable but incontrovertible phenomenon; and that's why I prefer a "symphony" by Saint-Saëns to one by Schubert! Faced with a purely instrumental work, I am filled with *admiration,* but do not *merge* with it. A musical phrase can enchant and delight me, but it never *moves me*; only *feelings* move me.)

Reynaldo favored musical forms like *chansons* and operas precisely because they allowed him to combine words and music. As he told Risler, he considered the voice, with its ability to give a musical inflection to words, the most perfect musical instrument.

La voix! La voix humaine, c'est plus beau que tout! Instrument naturel, organique crée par Dieu, il est le plus méprisé des instruments. Alors qu'il les contient tous! Instrument prodigieux, qui parle!!! La musique est devenue abstraite purement— à cause de l'abolition de la *voix*!!! . . . *Je reviendrai et pour toujours à la divine Voix!*[29]

(The voice! Nothing is as beautiful as the human voice! This natural, organic instrument, created by God, is the most despised of all the instruments. And yet it contains every other! A prodigious instrument with the power of speech!!! Music has become purely abstract—because of the abolishment of the *voice*!!! . . . *I shall return, and forever more, to the divine Voice!*)

Marcel and Reynaldo disagreed not only about words and music but also about the relation between music and national culture. Marcel defended pure music, while Reynaldo, by insisting that music be accompanied by words, tied it to a specific linguistic and cultural tradition.

Marcel's interest in these questions led him to compose a short piece, "Mélomanie de Bouvard et Pécuchet" (1894)—one of his very first texts, written in one of his favorite genres, the pastiche—in which the Flaubertian characters argue about Wagner, nationalism, and music.[30] Marcel wrote this playful text in a letter to Reynaldo and described it as "a modest exercise on Bouvard and Pécuchet for you and about music."[31] Bouvard heralds Wagner, while Pécuchet champions French musicians (and the values of "order, tradition, and country," as Mireille Naturel has argued);[32] eventually their discussion leads them to the music of Reynaldo Hahn, "the object of their liveliest debates." Bouvard criticizes the young musician's debt to Massenet, while Pécuchet lauds him as an example of French "clarity."

> [Pécuchet], partagé entre les sonorités tudesques du nom de Hahn et la désinence méridionale de son prénom Reynaldo, préférant l'exécuter en haine de Wagner plutôt que l'absoudre en faveur de Verdi, il concluait rigoureusement en se tournant vers Bouvard: "Malgré l'effort de tous vos beaux messieurs, notre beau pays de France est un pays de clarté, et la musique française sera claire ou ne sera pas, énonçait-il en frappant sur la table pour plus de force . . ."[33]

> (Pécuchet, torn between the Teutonic sounds of the name Hahn and the southern cadences of his first name Reynaldo, and preferring to execute him in hatred of Wagner rather than absolving him in favor of Verdi, concluded sternly as he turned towards Bouvard: "Despite all your efforts, messieurs, our beautiful France is a land of clarity, and French music will be clear or it will not be at all," he said, as he pounded on the table to give more force to his words.)

This passage plays on both Reynaldo's identity and on his place in the debate about music and nationalism, and it stresses that in France he was more of a foreigner than the German composer. Wagner is simply German, but Reynaldo occupies an ambivalent position between North and South: he is "divided" between the "Teutonic" sounds of his last name and the "southern cadences" of his given name. (In a 1901 letter, Marcel made a similar play on his friend's exotic name by rhyming *Reynaldo* and *Heraldo*—the name of a Latin American newspaper).[34] In writing this dialogue, Marcel was exposing the great irony inherent in Reynaldo's passionate anti-Wagnerian stance: he, a foreigner, had become more nationalistic about French music than many Frenchmen.

"Mélomanie" concludes with a parody of Reynaldo's nationalist view of Wagner as foreign to the French spirit. "I'm not surprised," Pécuchet argues, "that the *Walkyria* is liked in Germany . . . But to the French ear it will always be the most infernal of punishments—and the most cacophonic." Mocking the notion of a national music, the text argues that the *alouette,* an "eminently French" bird, should be set to music, while the dark *chauve-souris* should not (a minor jab at Montesquiou, who had published *Les chauves-souris* in 1893). Proust included an expanded version of "Mélomanie" in his first book, *Les plaisirs et les jours* (1896), where it appears alongside "Portraits of Painters" and "Portraits of Musicians," pieces written in collaboration with Reynaldo.[35]

The debate on Wagner found its way many years later into *À la recherche*. *Swann's Way* includes an unnamed pianist, a regular at the Verdurin's salon who plays for the guests, just like Reynaldo did at Madame Lemaire's. Verdurin's pianist, unlike Reynaldo, does not sing—his music is the kind of pure musical composition favored by Proust. And the "little phrase" from Vinteuil's sonata—the composition that so enraptures Swann—is another example of the pure, nonrepresentational music Marcel claimed as his ideal. The narrator spends pages describing the phrase, but rather than attempting to depict its form, he describes the affects and memories it awakens in Swann. This exaltation of the musical sublime is the clearest expression of *À la recherche*'s Wagnerian bent and illustrates the novel's rejection of Reynaldo's musical nationalism.

Despite his passionate defense of the French musical tradition, Reynaldo was not a cultural chauvinist. He championed French music but not all French composers, and he found plenty to dislike in his Parisian peers, including his classmate Erik Satie, whose experimental compositions he abhorred, as he wrote Risler in one of his most candid letters.

> Ce soir . . . Satie doit nous jouer son opéra "Le fils des Etoiles." Ça va être effrayant. Tout le monde va se rouler par terre et mordre le parquet, ou s'arracher mutuellement la barbe et les sourcils et l'exaspération arrivera au point suivant: tout le monde commencera à pisser, chier, vomir, jouir, cracher, pleurer, baver, péter ensemble, il y aura des fleuves de toutes sortes d'immondices et Satie jouera toujours. Puis, on s'arrachera les doigts, et on brisera les meubles, on jettera tout par terre, on incendiera la chambre et on se jettera dans les flammes et Satie continuera à jouer pendant l'incendie et quand tout sera brûlé, que la maison sera plus qu'un tas de décombres, Satie continuera à jouer sur les cendres du piano, des accords faux, jusqu'à ce que, vaincu par la force de sa musique, il mourra lui-même d'extase. Voilà ce qui se passera chez Duras ce soir.[36]

(Tonight . . . Satie is to play us his opera "The Son of the Stars." It will be dreadful. Everyone will be rolling on the floor, biting the parquet or tearing out each other's beards and eyebrows, and irritation will reach a pitch as follows: everyone will set to pissing, shitting, vomiting, ejaculating, spitting, weeping, dribbling and farting as one; amid streams of all kinds of disgusting effluvia, Satie will play on. Then people will start pulling off their fingers and smashing the furniture and throwing everything onto the floor, they will set fire to the room and cast themselves into the flames and Satie will play all through the fire and when everything has burned, and the house is no more than a heap of rubble, Satie will continue playing on the ashes of the piano, out of tune now, until overcome by the power of his own music he expires in ecstasy. That's what will happen at Duras's tonight.)

The night of the opening, Reynaldo's fears were confirmed, as he reported to Risler a few days later.

> L'autre soir, chez Duras, nous avons entendu *Le Fils des Étoiles* de Satie. Franchement, c'est trop. Ou bien ce garçon est sincère et convaincu, et alors il faudrait le faire voir par un aliéniste; (2) ou bien il se fout de nous et alors on devrait le trouver mauvais et lui ficher son pied au cul. On ne doit pas plaisanter avec la musique de cette façon indigne. [O]u bien, il y a une troisième solution: c'est un art nouveau qui naît, mais qui n'est pas "la Musique." C'est un art indépendant comme la sculpture l'est de la peinture, etc.[37]

> (The other night, at Duras's house, we heard Satie's *Son of the Stars*. Really, it's too much. Either the lad is sincere and means it, in which case he ought to be seen by a psychiatrist; (2) or else he is pulling our legs, in which case we should find him to be no good and administer a kick up the backside. Music should not be so ignominiously trifled with. Or else, here's a third solution: a new art is being born, but it is not "Music." It's an independent art, just as sculpture is independent from painting, etc.)

Satie was French, but Reynaldo saw him as the enemy of the French musical tradition he defended with such passion: "Erik Satie," he fumed, "appears to me to have sunk to the lowest degree possible of artistic prostitution. May he prove to be the rubber that bounces us back into the purlieus of Honor."[38] With the years, Reynaldo became more tolerant. He met Satie a few times and even discussed music with him. By 1893 his judgment was much less severe; he considered Satie, above all, an eccentric. "He could be very sweet if he wished. But for that he would have to compose less and wash more!"[39]

Reynaldo also crossed paths with Igor Stravinsky during his years at the conservatory and was equally unimpressed. "He is a pretentious, unmusical fool, all in all insipid and cold," he wrote Risler.[40] Could Reynaldo's reaction have something to do with Stravinsky's status as a foreigner living in France? *Cold* was a word Reynaldo had applied to German music and culture. Years later, he reviewed *The Rite of Spring* for one of the Paris papers and gave it a negative review: "It seemed to me that the show as a whole betrayed a perpetual search for the bizarre, a bid for 'ugliness.'" And, in a more direct jab at the composer, he wrote, "Here, Mr. Stravinsky was seeking to express such amorphous things, such rudimentary sentiments [that] his score was more disjointed even than is usual with him, becoming almost unintelligible at times."[41] Marcel read the review with a mixture of amusement and shock and told Reynaldo, "Vous avez été terrible pour le *Sacre du printemps*" (You were ferocious about the *Rite of Spring*).[42]

Reynaldo denounced Wagner's influence in French music, but he did the same with Satie, a Frenchman, and with Stravinsky, a Russian. Could it be that Reynaldo objected primarily to avant-garde experimentation? What Reynaldo considered "French music"—a tradition that, as he explained in other letters, was represented by Massenet and Saint-Säens—excluded the kind of radical experiments favored by Wagner in the nineteenth century and by Satie and Stravinsky in the twentieth. Just as the last two decades of the nineteenth century had seen the rise of Wagnerism, the first decades of the twentieth brought a new wave of radical experiments in musical composition: Satie composed pieces in the shape of a pear and devised a mechanical ballet; Stravinsky caused an uproar with his *Rite of Spring,* and the Italian Futurist Luigi Russolo stunned audiences with his futurist performances of an "art of noise." Reynaldo expressed little interest in any of these attempts to devise a new music and remained faithful to his "two masters"—Massenet and Saint-Saëns—the standard bearers of the French musical tradition.

Except for their disagreement over Wagner, Reynaldo's traditionalist aesthetics generally aligned with those of Marcel. The two friends preferred the past to the present, and both remained aloof to the aesthetic revolutions that swirled around them. Marcel lived through the launching of the first Futurist manifesto, the invention of cubism, and the creation of *calligrammes*; he overlapped with Guillaume Apollinaire, James Joyce, Pablo Picasso, and Filippo Tommaso Marinetti. But he was more interested in the duke of Saint-Simon, Giotto, Madame de Sevigné, and thirteenth-century cathedrals than in any of his contemporaries.

Marcel was a perfect example of the class of artists William Marx has described as "arrière-garde": figures who introduced modernist innovations while working with models from the past.[43] "We need only think," writes Marx, "of Ezra Pound and T. S. Eliot in the English-speaking world, or Jacques Rivière and the *Nouvelle Revue Française* in France: the same Eliot who had revolutionized Anglophone poetry with 'The Waste Land' was soon after to proclaim himself, in a famous profession of faith, as 'classicist in literature, royalist in politics, and Anglo-Catholic in religion.' [. . .] In just a few years, the appeal to tradition had switched sides."[44]

Is Reynaldo Hahn, like Proust, a figure of the *arrière-garde*? We have already seen his passion for French tradition, but at least one of his creations belongs to the history of the avant-garde: *Le dieu bleu,* performed at the Théâtre du Châtelet in 1912, was a project for the Ballets Russes, the company Serge Diaghilev brought to Paris in 1910. It was a collaboration between Reynaldo, who composed the music, and two young artists— Fréderic de Madrazo and Jean Cocteau—who designed the sets. Léon Bakst created the costumes (see plate 3), and Vaslav Nijinski danced the lead role (fig. 1.4). This work was Reynaldo's most experimental project, and it added another twist to his musical nationalism: at the same time he was writing passionate defenses of the French musical tradition, he created a foreign ballet. *Le dieu bleu* is set in India, and the sets and costumes evoke a dreamy orientalist landscape. The narrative tells the story of a young man who is about to be inducted into the sect of the Brahmans, but his lover interrupts the ritual, calling on him to return to her. The priests condemn the woman to be thrown into a pit of monsters, but she prays to the Blue God, who decides to spare her life. The god rises from a lotus flower—"the god emerges: his body is blue all over, with silver lips and nails"—rescues the girl, and reunites her with her lover.[45]

Despite its exotic setting, *Le dieu bleu* fits within a well-established French cultural tradition: orientalism. The Orient became an obsession amid turn-of-the century French artists and intellectuals, and music, art, and literature overflowed with the imaginative depictions of India, China and Japan that Edward Said has studied in *Orientalism.*[46] Just a few years before Reynaldo composed his first opera, Léo Delibes presented one of the greatest orientalist fantasies of all times—*Lakmé*—at the Opéra Comique. Reynaldo's first opera, *L'île du rêve* (1898), fits squarely within this tradition. The libretto was based on a story by Pierre Loti, one of the most prolific orientalist authors, and the story, set in Tahiti and described as a "Polynesian Idyll," featured characters named Mahénu and Tsen Lee.[47] Orientalist fantasies had become so engrained in French culture that by setting an opera in Tahiti or a ballet in India, Reynaldo was actually inscribing his work within a French cultural tradition.

Orientalist compositions like *L'île du rêve* and *Le dieu bleu* reflected Reynaldo's cosmopolitanism: he was a Venezuelan who embraced French culture to the point of adopting its fantasies about an imaginary Orient. Marcel, in contrast, was a Frenchman who was never seduced by the exoticist vogue. In

Figure 1.4. Lucien Waléry, Vaslav Nijinksi in Reynaldo Hahn's *Le dieu bleu* (1912). Album Kochno, *Dieu bleu* 4, 1912. Département de la Musique, Bibliothèque Nationale de France, Paris.

his novel he poked fun at this bourgeois obsession by having the frivolous Odette decorate her house with Japanese lanterns and kakemonos. In these early years, Reynaldo's aesthetics—anti-Wagnerian and orientalist—were the exact opposite of Marcel's.

Language Games

Marcel's correspondence with Reynaldo offers readers a privileged glimpse into the novelist's perception of his friend's status as a Francophile foreigner. There are more than one hundred letters, covering the period from their twenties to their forties, and they reveal a little-known side of the novelist: a mischievous Marcel who invents pet names for Reynaldo, who devises an imaginary private language, and who executes countless portraits of his friend. These letters and drawings reveal much about their relationship and also about the novelist's perception of his friend's identity as an assimilated foreigner. In them we find a polymorphously perverse Marcel who alludes, in code, to his erotic games; a mischievous Marcel who debunks religion and high culture; and a playful Marcel who remains, until the end, an eternal adolescent.

Marcel wrote many of his letters to Reynaldo in what he called "*langasge*" or "*langasge moschant,*" a pidgin French in which words have been altered to sound Germanic, grammar has been stripped down to the basics, and verbs appear in the infinitive.[48] Marcel warned Reynaldo that it was meant as a private language: "Don't show anyone our bininulseries," he wrote, "which I assure you would only serve to make us appear ridiculous, even to the most kindly disposed."[49] The primary function of the *langasge* was not to convey a specific message. Most of the letters Marcel wrote to Reynaldo have no pragmatic function—they ramble on about his health, repeat sweet nothings, and, in one striking case, apostrophize Reynaldo's dog; they operate on the level of what we might call the *affective* signifier.[50] The two friends continued to write in *langasge* until the end; even the letters written in their forties make use of these linguistic games.

Many Proustian critics have expressed little interest in these language games. William C. Carter writes that "the affectionate nonsense found in the exchanges between Proust and Hahn exceeds even the tolerated bounds."[51] But as Marjorie Perloff has shown in her numerous readings of authors from Gertrude Stein to Kenneth Goldsmith, the skillful critic can find much sense in what appears, at first sight, to be linguistic "nonsense." A few examples give an insight into the peculiarities of the *langasge*. In a letter written in 1906, Marcel inquires after Reynaldo's health in a type of baby French, even while he continues to use the formal *vous* to address his friend:

> Cher Binchnibuls,
> . . . c'est trop moschant qu'écrivant lettereh si gentille ne disiez pas si toussez, si voix pas enrouée, si malaise, si fièvre [. . .] si grippe de Moschant es guersie.[52]

> (Dear Binchnibuls, It's too noshty that writing so kind leheter no say if coughing, if voice not hoarse, if dizzy, if fever [. . .] if Noshty influentsa cured.)

Marcel addresses Reynaldo as Binchnibuls, a made-up pet name that agglutinates the Germanic-sounding particles *Binch, Nib,* and *Buls* and alters

French words to make them sound Germanic: *méchant* (naughty) becomes
"moschant," a term that also evokes *Boche,* a pejorative term for Germans;
and *lettre* (letter) becomes "lettereh," substituting the very French silent *e*
for a hard *h.* This unorthodox spelling introduces the equivalent of a foreign
accent into the written text: soft French words are exoticized through a
profusion of *sh* and *h* sounds, and Marcel's letters read as if he were speaking French with a thick German accent. There are many such Germanic
twists in the correspondence; the clearest is in a letter from January 1914 in
which Marcel addresses Reynaldo as "Petit Boschant," playing on *Boche.*[53]
These language games constitute an example of the type of imitation Gérard
Genette defines as "xenism"—a play on the Greek term for foreigner—and
which consists of a "translinguistic replication" that effectively pastiches the
style, intonation, and grammatical structure of another language.[54]

In addition to this Germanization of individual words, Marcel also alters
the syntax of his letters to make them sound foreign by stripping language
down to its most basic elements: his skeletal phrases recall the speech of
a foreigner struggling to make himself understood in another tongue. We
can see how much is missing from Marcel's *langasge* if we rewrite the above
passage by filling in the missing terms:

> Cher Binchnibuls,
>
> [. . .] c'est trop moschant qu'[en] écrivant [une] lettereh si gentille[,] [vous] ne
> [me] disiez pas si [vous] toussez, si [votre] voix [n'est] pas enrouée, si [vous avez
> une] malaise, si [vous avez une] fièvre [. . .] si [la] grippe de Moschant es
> guersie.
>
> (It's too noshty that [in] writing so kind [a] leheter [you do] not say if [you're]
> coughing, if [your] voice [is] not hoarse, if [you feel] dizzy, if [the] fever [. . .] if
> [the] Noshty influentsa [has been] cured.)

Marcel drops punctuation, articles, pronouns, and prepositions to create
a telegraphic French that retains only nouns and verbs, the basic building
blocks of syntax. Particles like *en, une,* and *votre* are not essential to the
meaning of the phrase, but it is these un-signifying parts of speech that
allow a native speaker to play with the tone, register, and style, and to sur-
pass the purely communicative function of language.

Marcel's "langasge" reads like a foreigner's broken French but also like
the babblings of a little boy. In a letter to Reynaldo written when he was
forty-five, Marcel seems to have trouble saying goodbye.

Asdieu mon petit bunibuls, je ne veux pas de [la duchesse de] Rutland. Adieu mon hibuls, adieu mon hibuls, adieu mon hibuls, j'ai reçu de ma tante la lettre la plus stupide qu'on puisse imaginer. Mais vous êtes un genstil, asdieu mon gentil, bonjour mon petit, bonsjour bonne nuit.[55]

(Byebye my little bunibuls, I don't want no [Duchess of] Rutland. Goodbye my hibuls, goodbye my hibuls, goodbye my hibuls, I got the stupidest letter you could imagine from my aunt. But you're a shweetie, goodbye shweets, hello my boy, good day good night.)

Marcel repeats *adieu* five times and the phrase "adieu mon hibuls" three times, as if he could not bring himself to close his letter to Reynaldo. Near the end, he suddenly writes *bonjour* twice, as if he were starting a letter and not closing it. Finally, after all these hesitations, Marcel is able to end his letter by writing *bonne nuit.* Lacan once called repetition "one of the four fundamental concepts of psychoanalysis" and claimed it was the main mechanism at work in most neuroses.[56] Marcel's made-up language is both infantile and neurotic, and the letter reads as if it were written by a hysterical child, caught in the pangs of separation anxiety and unable to part with his best friend.

Philippe Sollers observes that in his letters to Reynaldo Marcel seems to "regress" to an "eternal adolescence."[57] He stops being a forty-something-year-old to become, once again, a little boy who, like the narrator in *À la recherche,* has trouble saying good night and struggles to express his thoughts in a language he has not yet mastered. Freud remarked that children have more direct access to the unconscious than adults, since they have not fully undergone the processes of repression required by socialization, and in these letters we see Marcel regaining his lost infancy by playing with words, free associating, and giving free rein to his linguistic imagination.

The letters play on Reynaldo's identity as a foreigner by engaging in a delirious naming game. In the letters discussed above, Marcel addressed Reynaldo as "Bunchnibuls" and "Funinuls"; in others, he calls him "Genstil," "Hibuls," "Buncht," "Burnuls," and "Muninuls." Almost every letter introduces a new nickname, as we can see from the following compilation of all the salutations found in the correspondence:

Monsieur de Binibuls, Mon cher petit Birninuls, Mon cher Genstil, Cher Binibuls, Cher Binchnibuls, Mon cher Hibuls, Mon cher Binunuls, Cher Guncht, Mon petit Buninuls cheri, Mon cher Marquis de Bunibuls, Burnuls, Bom bon Buncht, Mon cher cher cher cher cher petit Buncht, Mon petit Binibuls, Mon cher Irnuls, Muncht, Mon cher Bunchnibuls, Mon petit Buninuls, Cher Cormouls, Mon Bunchtbuls, Hirnuls, Binchturbuls, Ounl' Reh Ni Buls, Bi Ninuls, Mon cher petit Bunchtnibuls, Mon pauvre petit Birnechnibus, Mon cher petit Buncht, Mon cher MMM. . . . mm . . . Muninuls, Mon cher Monsieur de Bunchtnibuls, Mon cher Mintchniduls, Mon petit Bunchtniduls, Monsieur le petit Binibuls ou même Nur-nols, Mon petit Funinels, Mon petit Bugnibuls, Mon Tuninels, Mon cher petit Kunibuls.

Vincht, Mon cher Funinels, Mon petit ami Bugnibuls, Mon cher petit Vinchtnibuls, Mon cher petit Bunchtniguls, Mon vieux petit Bugnibuls, Mon petit Guninuls, Petit Gunimels, Monsieur mon Bunibuls, Cher petit Gunimels, Petit Bi gni guls, Mon Bugniguls, Mon petit Guminuls, Mon cher petit Bi_ni_mels, Gi-ni-nuls, Mon cher petit Gunimels, Mon cher petit Ginibuls, Cher Minibuls, Cher Gueninuls, Petit Boschant.

Most of these names play on Reynaldo's last name by echoing the sounds of real German words: "Birnibuls" sounds like *Birne* (pear); "Guncht" and "Muncht" like *Wunscht* (wish). Other pet names read like parodies of German patronymics. Marcel liked to imagine Reynaldo as a nobleman (in *Jean Santeuil,* Henri de Réveillon, the character inspired by Reynaldo, is a marquis). One of the pet names for his friend was "Marquis de Bunibuls," and a name like "Bom bon Buncht" evokes the particle *von* found in most aristocratic names. "Von Buncht" sounds like a plausible family name, but "Bom bon" brings all aristocratic pretentions crashing down to earth by turning the name into a bonbon, a piece of candy. Names like "Birnechnibuls" turn Reynaldo into a *Birne,* a fruit, while others like "Buncht" make him into a *Bund,* a truss.

All of these made-up names play on the idea of Reynaldo as a Germanic foreigner. The intention behind this linguistic game appears clearly in a greeting Marcel sent Reynaldo on the eve of World War I addressing him as "Petit Boschant," a neologism that agglutinates *Boche* and *méchant*— a word that is also inscribed in the name of the *langasge moschant.*[58] Marcel saw Reynaldo as a naughty German, and he told him so in the dizzying profusion of pet names with which he began his letters.

These letters could not be more different in tone, style, and syntax from *À la recherche du temps perdu.* Proust's novel is written in the register of high literature, and its long, labyrinthine phrases are famous for their syntactic complexity. The letters, in contrast, use an infantile language characterized by short sentences and a bare-bones syntax. This telegraphic prose has much in common with a very different literary project launched in Paris as Marcel was writing his letters to Reynaldo Hahn: Marinetti's *Parole in libertà*. After the bombastic publication of the 1909 "Manifesto of Futurism" in *Le Figaro,* Marinetti composed a series of instructions on how to write avant-garde literature. In his "Technical Manifesto of Futurist Literature" (1912), he gave specific recommendations to would-be Futurist poets: "We must destroy syntax," he urged. "We must use the verb in the infinitive [. . .] We must abolish the adjective [. . .] We must abolish the adverb [. . .] No more punctuation."[59] Even though Futurism was born in Paris and its fame spread around Europe and the world in the same years as Proust was writing *À la recherche,* there is no indication that the novelist ever read Marinetti or expressed interest in his poetic revolution. And his novel— which as we saw belongs squarely in the tradition of the *arrière-garde*— could not be further removed from the Futurist celebration of noise, machines, and the chaos of urban life.

Marcel's letters to Reynaldo, in contrast, would be entirely at home in an anthology of Futurist writings. They seem to follow Marinetti's prescriptions to the letter, as they abolish adjectives and adverbs, eliminate punctuation, and place all verbs in the infinitive. The *langasge* is Germanic, neurotic, and infantile; it is also an example of Futurist prose. Like the compositions of Marinetti, Velimir Khlebnikov, or the Mexican Estridentistas, these letters reproduce, through their destruction of traditional syntax, the linguistic fragmentation produced by telegraphs, radio transmitters, writing machines, and other inventions of the modern era. But if Marinetti used his "parole in libertà" to put poetry at the service of Italian nationalism, Proust's *langasge* was a form of linguistic hospitality: it welcomed Germanic sounds and turns of phrase into French. And if Marinetti's words-in-freedom were public, designed to spark a poetic revolution, Marcel's linguistic experiments were private, written with only one reader in mind.

Do the similarities between Marinetti's words-in-freedom and Marcel's *langasge moschant* mean that Proust should be considered part of the historical avant-garde? Should literary histories of the twentieth century include a chapter on Proustofuturism and list it as the queerest (and sexiest) of all avant-garde movements? While it is true that Marcel's language experiments are confined to the private sphere of his personal communications with Reynaldo and that they constitute a private language—one marked by a joyful complicity—between the two friends, these language games are too important to be ignored. If Marcel's published work belongs to the *arrière-*

garde, as William Marx has suggested, then his private letters to Reynaldo fit squarely within the literary aesthetics of the avant-garde. Reynaldo led Marcel into a space of linguistic freedom and syntactic experimentation we do not find anywhere else in his writing.

Drawing Reynaldo

Many critics have expressed disappointment at how little information we have about the erotic aspects of Marcel and Reynaldo's relationship. Marcel's letters give us a general idea of the ups and downs of their court-ship, but they reveal little about their sexual life. Reynaldo, likewise, re-mained tight-lipped in his published *Journal* and even in his correspondence with Risler. Some critics have wondered if later in life Reynaldo might have discarded the letters that were too intimate. (We are missing, for instance, most letters written between 1897 and 1903.)[60] Marcel had a habit of asking his friends, including Reynaldo and Suzette, to burn missives deemed too compromising—"Brûlez cette lettre!" he would often demand—and Rey-naldo might have been happy to oblige. Or perhaps the two lovers were simply too shy and too fearful that their correspondence might be discov-ered by their parents or relatives and thus avoided mentioning anything that could compromise them.

Although Marcel's letters to Reynaldo disclose little about his sexual life, the drawings that accompanied these letters are more revealing. Marcel was an avid draftsman, and his notebooks are full of doodles and sketches: some depict elegant women draped in flowing robes and coiffed with baroque hats, while others form phallic shapes. In his letters to Reynaldo, Marcel would often include sketches at the end of the letter below his signature or on a separate sheet. About 160 of these drawings have survived, and only a small number of these have been published or analyzed.[61]

In one drawing from 1907 (fig. 1.5), Marcel pictures Reynaldo seated at a grand piano, playing before a group of seated figures; the word "semplicis-simo" hovers above him.[62] This scene evokes the Parisian salons where the two friends met, and where Reynaldo sang and played for an audience that often included Madeleine and Suzette Lemaire, the Daudets, and some of the Latin Americans discussed in this book. The drawings go hand-in-hand with the *langasge moschant.* Many of the letters written in Marcel's faux-German are accompanied by drawings, and the language games find a coun-terpart in his eccentric sketches—odd compositions, marked by the graphic equivalent of a foreign accent. The drawing of Reynaldo at the piano, for

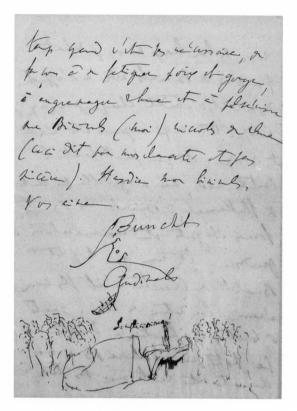

Figure 1.5. Marcel Proust to Reynaldo Hahn, December 31, 1907. *Corr.,* 7:327-28. A facsimile of the letter showing the drawing is reproduced in Reiner Speck, *Sur la lecture II* (Cologne: Marcel Proust Gesellschaft, 1996), 74.

instance, is part of a letter, addressed to "Mon cher Buncht," that includes the following passage:

> . . . je vous ai téléphoné pour vous demander si sortiez, si vouliez faire petite promenade avec Gudimels pour la fin hannée. [. . .] Et que Genstil ne s'enrhume plus si moschamment et ne tousse pas tout le temps quand n'est pas nécessaire, de façon à se fatiguer voix et gorge, à engrenager rhume et à pulvériser sur Bunninuls (moi) microbes de rhume (ceci dit par moschanceté et pas sincère). Hasdieu mon bininuls, vous aime, Buncht GUDIMELS.[63]

> (I telephoned you to ask if going out, if little walk wanted to do with Gudimels for yearsend. [. . .] And Genstil must stop getting noshty colds and always cough-

ing when unnecessary, so that he strains voice and throat, entrenches cold and sprays Bunninuls (me) with cold germs (this said noshtily and not meant). Farehwell my bininuls, love you, Buncht GUDIMELS).

Here Marcel establishes a specular identification with Reynaldo: Marcel is the sickly one, but he imagines Reynaldo suffering from various illnesses, coughing, and infecting him with "microbes de rhume." Marcel's pseudo-Germanic language follows a similar logic: it is Reynaldo who is half German, but Marcel Teutonizes his French to sound like his friend. These projections and identifications create a specular game. If Marcel is ill, Reynaldo will be ill too; if Reynaldo is German, Marcel will be German too.

Several drawings link Reynaldo to one of Marcel's passions—French medieval architecture. As is well known, Marcel discovered John Ruskin around 1899 and translated *Sesame and the Lys* and *The Bible of Amiens*. Less known is Marcel's engagement with Émile Mâle, the author of *L'art religieux du XIIIème siècle en France* (1902), an erudite study of religious iconography in French cathedrals. Along with Ruskin, Mâle's book became one of the most important sources for Marcel's understanding of medieval art and for the meditations on gothic architecture that punctuate *À la recherche*.[64] Around 1900, Marcel sent Reynaldo a special present: a drawing of the Amiens cathedral, accompanied by a short text written in *langasge moschant* (fig. 1.6). The sketch depicts the west façade, with its three doorways, round stained-glass window, and two towers. The caption reads:

ABZIENS (KASTHEDRALCH)
(Facadch wwwouest)
Aspect général de la cathédrale d'Amiens en négligeant justement ce que je sais (porche ouest) bien que ce soit la façade ouest mais de mémoire très vague. *Je n'irai plus gare*.[65]

(ABZIENS (KASTHEDRALCH)
(vvvuest fatsade)
General view of Amiens Cathedral precisely omitting what I know (west porch) although this is the west façade but very vaguely recalled. *Shan't go there again*.)

This drawing continues the elaborate commentary on Reynaldo's foreignness Marcel had begun in his letters. Writing to Reynaldo awakens a series of associations related to Germany and the German language, and here Marcel coins a new series of pseudo-Germanic terms. But this time he takes his cultural play a step further. In addition to making French words sound

Figure 1.6. Marcel Proust, undated drawing of the Amiens Cathedral. Philip Kolb, *Lettres à Reynaldo Hahn,* 117, and Philippe Sollers, *L'œil de Proust,* 42.

foreign, he Germanizes the cathedral of Amiens, one of the foremost icons of French history. *Amiens* becomes "Abziens," and the French *cathédrale* gives way to a Teutonic "Kasthedralch." In this game of cultural translation, French cathedrals are projected into a world of Germanic fantasies.

There are many parallels between the *langasge moschant* and the drawings. They are two versions—one textual, the other pictorial—of a private language Marcel used only with Reynaldo, both versions have an infantile dimension and read like the creations of a child who is learning to speak or draw, both serve to affirm the tight bonds of intimacy and complicity shared by the two friends, and both are used to comment on Reynaldo's foreignness. Marcel also uses the drawings to project Reynaldo into the realm of medieval architecture he discovered through Mâle and Ruskin. One sketch (fig. 1.7), for instance, shows a bearded Reynaldo (identified by the initials *R* and *H* inscribed on his feet) ensconced in a niche, wearing a long robe and holding a scroll bearing the title of one of his operas, *La Carmélite.*[66] Marcel traced this drawing—as he did with most portraits he sent Reynaldo—from Mâle's book on religious art (fig. 1.8). He copied Mâle's reproduction of a

Figure 1.7. Marcel Proust, undated drawing of Reynaldo Hahn, "Prophète de Reims." Philip Kolb, *Lettres à Reynaldo Hahn,* 105.
Figure 1.8. "Un prophète," from Émile Mâle, *L'art réligieux du XIIIème siècle en France,* 194.

statue in the Rheims cathedral, added a mustache, and inscribed the title of the opera on the scroll. With these simple additions, Mâle's prophet was transformed into Marcel's Reynaldo.[67]

These "medieval drawings"—as critics have called them—establish a curious dialectic between the sacred and the profane. On the one hand, they desacralize medieval iconography by replacing religious figures with Marcel's boyfriend; on the other, they bring about a playful canonization of Reynaldo, elevating him to a kind of architectural sainthood. (See, for instance, the drawing from 1909 reproduced in figure 1.9, where Marcel depicts Reynaldo as an angel whcse open wings are inscribed with the titles

Figure 1.9. Marcel Proust, undated drawing of Reynaldo Hahn. Philippe Sollers, *L'œil de Proust*, 39.

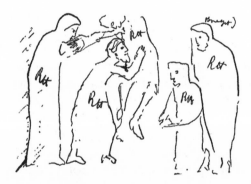

Figure 1.10. Marcel Proust, undated drawing, "Descente de la croix." Philip Kolb, *Lettres à Reynaldo Hahn*, 81, and Philippe Sollers, *L'œil de Proust*, 83.

of his operas.)[68] This double movement is most apparent in "Esquisse d'une descente de croix (Prieuré Le Bourget)" (fig. 1.10), where the dead Christ being lowered from the cross in a relief found in the Priory of Le Bourget (fig. 1.11) has been replaced by a figure marked with Reynaldo's initials.[69] In a blasphemous move, Marcel has eliminated Christ and replaced him with Reynaldo, and he does the same with the Virgin and the saints: all of these religious figures are substituted by characters identified as "RH." In Marcel's private religion, there is only one god, and his name is Reynaldo.

Figure 1.11. "Descente," from Émile Mâle, *L'art réligieux du XIIIème siècle en France,* 269.

A number of drawings play on the image of Marcel as a pony. Early in their correspondence, Reynaldo began calling his friend "pony."[70] At first Marcel was surprised. "Why 'Marcel the pony'?" he quipped. "I don't like this new thing. It sounds like Jack the Ripper or Louis the Headstrong." But he soon embraced this pet name and wrote back: "Don't forget it's not a nickname and that I am really and truly, Reynaldo, your pony Marcel."[71] Their close friends were in on the joke: Reynaldo often talked about "the pony and I" in his letters to Madeleine Lemaire, and he once closed a letter to Pierre Lavallée by urging him "Ecrivez à mon poney" (write to my pony).[72] From that moment on, Marcel refers to himself as a pony and repeatedly portrays himself as an animal: he asks to have his head petted,[73] writes about going back to his stable,[74] and demands a veterinarian.[75] He mused on the vagaries of the "language of ponies and of humans,"[76] and described himself as having an animal instinct.[77]

Critics have puzzled over Marcel's insistence on calling himself a pony. William C. Carter suggested that the French *poney* was merely a term of endearment and noted that "another common term of affection [. . .] is *rat,* which is generally used for a child or a woman."[78] Sybilla Laemmel believes that this animal appellation is merely a playful reference to Reynaldo's address—he lived on rue du Cirque, a street named after a circus that certainly included ponies in its menagerie.[79] Philippe Sollers, in contrast, has a more perverse reading of Marcel's pet name:

> ... on est en pleine régression assumée, fluide, surnoms, petits noms, animalisations, scènes intimes [. . .] Proust est son "poney." Qu'est-ce qu'on fait d'un poney? On le flatte, on le bouchonne, on le pomponne, on lui fait faire le beau, mais on peut aussi l'éperonner, l'étriller, le cravacher, le chevaucher, le *monter*. Inutile de faire un dessin plus précis, la coulisse se comprend sans peine.[80]

> (. . . here is a fluid, fully embraced regression, complete with pet names, nicknames, animal disguises, and intimate scenes. [. . .] Proust is his "pony." What do we do with ponies? We stroke them, rub them down, braid their manes, teach them tricks, but we can also spur them, curry them, whip, mount, *ride* them. No need to spell it out: the implication is clear.)

Following Sollers's insight, we can see that the friendship between the two young men is colored by sadomasochistic overtones. Marcel plays the pony, calls Reynaldo "my master," and makes numerous allusions to being dominated, as we can see in two drawings. The first (fig. 1.12), "Le maître et le poney (Lyon)" depicts Marcel as a pony and Reynaldo as his master. The caption reads: "Le poney fumse. Le maître lève les bras en signe de découragement et dit 'pauvre petit poney'!'" (The pony shmokes. The master throws up his arms helplessly and says "Poor little pony!")[81] Marcel portrays himself in animal form, performing the ritual that consumed a good part of his days: "fumsing," or burning Legras powders to fill his room with his preferred anti-asthma remedy, while Reynaldo "the master" raises a hand and adopts the threatening posture of a rider about to beat his horse.[82] Marcel traced this drawing from Mâle's image of a stained-glass window at the Lyon cathedral showing a young woman and a unicorn (fig. 1.13). Once again, Marcel indulges in a debasement of religious iconography: the young woman, a symbol of virtue, is transformed into an image of Reynaldo riding Marcel, an allegory of rough play.

Marcel traced another drawing, "Orgueil et son petit Chevalch ND de Paris" (fig. 1.14) from Mâle's illustration of a stained-glass window at Notre Dame, where pride is represented by a knight on a runaway horse approaching a ditch (fig. 1.15). As Sollers and other critics have noted, the horse here is almost identical to the pony in other letters, and the image can be read as yet another depiction of Reynaldo riding Marcel.[83] But unlike "Le maître et le poney," which shows a docile Marcel-pony inhaling Legras powders, this

Figure 1.12. Marcel Proust, undated drawing of "Le maître et le poney." "Le poney fumse. Le maître lève les bras en signe de découragement et dit 'pauvre petit poney'!" Philip Kolb, *Lettres à Reynaldo Hahn,* 30, and Philippe Sollers, *L'œil de Proust,* 47. Figure 1.13. "La jeune fille et la licorne," from Émile Mâle, *L'art réligieux du XIIIème siècle en France,* 56.

composition features a dangerous, wild pony, threatening to hurl Reynaldo off a precipice. If the earlier drawing depicts a scene of domestic bliss, this one evokes the darker, more violent undercurrents of the relationship. The original image was part of a series of windows illustrating the vices and warning Christian viewers against the dangers of pride; Marcel's version, in contrast, celebrates a different "vice"—the bedroom equivalent of rough riding—that had brought the two friends together.

These drawings express Marcel's sadomasochistic fantasies: he pictures himself as an animal, as a pony that could be ridden, beaten, and controlled by Reynaldo the master. The aggressive content of these images becomes clearer in another sketch showing two figures—"toi-même" (yourself) and "ton poney" (your pony)[84]—where the pony adopts a human stance, standing on two legs and walking away as the other character, a towering,

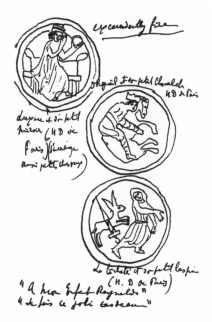

Figure 1.14. Marcel Proust, untitled drawing. Philippe Sollers, *L'œil de Proust,* 86.

Figure 1.15. "L'orgueil," from Émile Mâle, *L'art réligieux du XIIIème siècle en France,* 150.

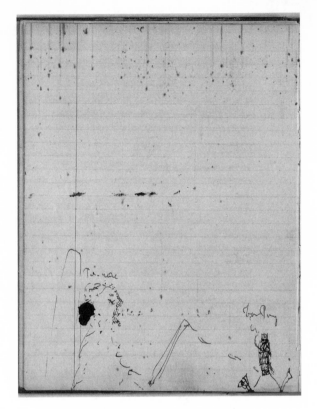

Figure 1.16. Marcel Proust, cahier 16684, pp. 7–8. Fonds Marcel Proust, Département de Manuscrits, Bibliothèque Nationale de France, Paris.

amorphous blob, threatens it with a whip (fig. 1.16). Claude Gandelman has pointed out that this drawing and another showing a lion tamer (fig. 1.17) recall the scene of Charlus being whipped at Jupien's brothel in *Time Regained*.[85]

Marcel's drawings point upward, toward the heavenly concerns of religious art; they also point downward, toward perverse pleasures and sexual games. They simultaneously elevate Reynaldo—placing him high on a niche, in a stained-glass window, in an altar—while they stage a debasement of the religious iconography that inspired them. Saints are replaced by boyfriends, horses by ponies, and pious messages by indecent proposals. Christian cathedrals are transformed into perverse temples devoted to the pleasures of the flesh and adorned with erotic statues, suggestive stained-glass windows,

Figure 1.17. Marcel Proust, cahier 16643, p. 47. Fonds Marcel Proust, Département de Manuscrits, Bibliothèque Nationale de France, Paris.

and explicit paintings. In this imaginary cathedral of worldly pleasures, Reynaldo emerges as the only god of Marcel's private religion.

By turning cathedrals into the settings for his sadomasochistic fantasies, Marcel is effectively sullying these sacred spaces. As in the scenes of profanation that abound in his life and work—Mademoiselle Vinteuil hurling insults at the photograph of her late father as she embraces her lover; Marcel sullying the photograph of his mother at Le Cuziat's brothel—these forms of debasement render erotic pleasure more intense. Taken together, these drawings form a perverse comic strip: they tell the story of Marcel being ridden by his master Reynaldo inside a cathedral, surrounded by stained glass windows, and religious sculptures.

Marcel's drawings also express less violent scenarios, including a long-standing fantasy that one day he and Reynaldo could live together. At various points in their friendship, Marcel invited Reynaldo to move into his apartment on boulevard Haussmann, but Reynaldo—the more realistic of the two—never took up the offer. Marcel first mentioned the project of living together in 1912. Reynaldo had just lost his mother and now had to leave the family apartment. Marcel proposed, only half in jest, that they find an old house in the country to share.

> Est-ce que tu ne conviens pas que nous achetions un hôtel historique où tu te représenterais dans un étage et moi l'autre. Il me semble que dans l'ancien hôtel des Archevêques de Sens ou des Bénédictins anglais ta prélature et ma vermine feraient un contraste assez sanctifiant.[86]

> (Don't you think we ought to buy an historic country house where you could occupy one story and I the other. I daresay that in the former pile of the Archbishops of Sens or the English Benedictines your prelature and my vermin would form a holily edifying contrast.)

A few months later Marcel conjured up a different scenario and invited Reynaldo to live with him in Paris.

> Mon cher Genstil, je voudrais bien que vous veniez demeurer chez moi. Je ferais arranger ma salle à manger qui est très grande, sans que vous vous en rendiez compte, en chambre à coucher pour vous. Je ferais mettre double porte au petit salon qui serait votre salon et où vous feriez musique aussi fort que vous voudriez. Vous auriez salle de bains et cabinet de toilette. Céline vous ferait la cuisine et ainsi vous n'auriez pas l'ennui d'avoir à faire des comptes, du ménage, etc. Et si meson vous déplaît je déménagerai et irons où vous voudrez. Qu'en pensez-vous?[87]

> (Dearest Shweets, it would be awful nice if you came to live with me. I would refurbish my dining room, which is very large, without you noticing, into a bedroom for you. I would put a double door on the little drawing room which would be all yours and you could play music as loud as you please. You would have bath room and toilet chamber. Céline would cook for you and so no bother with accounts, housework and such. And if haus you don't like I pack up and we go wherever you want. What say you?)

This plan sounded more feasible than finding an ancient monastery, but it was equally unrealistic, given Marcel's nocturnal schedule, combined with his intense phobias of noise, germs, and visitors.[88]

Marcel did not give up, and some weeks later he sent Reynaldo an even more insistent note from Cabourg—so insistent indeed that, in a rare move, he lapsed into the informal *tu*.

> . . . je ne t'écris qu'une ligne c'est pour te pourvoyer que je voudrais puisque tu n'as pas où te fourrer, *que tu ailles résider vite boulevard Haussmann.* Je t'y hospitalise jusqu'à ce que tu aies un bon logis. Et si tu n'en trouves pas et t'accoutumes, je ne te chasserai pas de chez moi mon genstil.[89]

> (. . . just a line to convey that I do wish, since you've nowhere to lay your head, *you'd come live at boulevard Haussmann quick.* I can hospitalize you until you find a proper home. And if you don't find one, and grow accustomed, well I shan't chase you out my shweet.)

Days later he reiterated the offer, though now using the formal *vous*.

> . . . je vous dis seulement que je voudrais que vous occupiez le boulevard Haussmann jusqu'à ce que vous trouviez appartement et que si ne trouvez pas je me [. . .] frotterai les mains. Et comme j'ai exilé Céline dans ses terres de Marizy, je vous ferai un cordon bleu qui vous fera oublier Paillard.[90]

> (. . . all I'm saying is I wish you'd move to boulevard Haussmann until you find an apartment and if you don't I shall [. . .] rub my hands in glee. And having banished Céline to her lands at Marizy, I'll produce a cordon bleu that will make you forget Paillard.)

Reynaldo never took up any of these invitations. He must have realized that Marcel could not have lived with anyone: he was too neurotic, too hypochondriac, too phobic, and too obsessed with the eccentric rituals of his daily routine to ever share his home with another person (except for servants and what we would now call personal assistants; at one point Marcel had four people, including a young man he had found at the Hotel Ritz, at his service). In the meantime another close friend, Prince Antoine Bibesco, invited Reynaldo to move into his apartment at 9, rue du Commandant Marchand. Reynaldo accepted the invitation, moved in over the summer, and stayed at the prince's for over a year.[91]

Marcel never realized his fantasy of living with Reynaldo, but he used pen and paper to draw an imagined life of blissful domesticity. The drawing known as "Petit projet de genstil vitrail" (fig. 1.18), for instance, depicts what could have been a typical day in their life together; they share an apartment and help each other in their daily tasks. As Marcel explained in the text that accompanies this sketch, their life would unfold in the following manner:

Petit projet de genstil vitrail
Executé avec beaucoup troubail
À gauche on voit Marie et Félicie
qui font lessive et dissent quelle scie.

À droite Buninuls ne peut ouvrir poudre Legras
Et Binchdinuls vient pour alumser
Buninuls s'aide de genou et de bras
Binchdinuls est par colonne gothique
                          en deux divisé
Tout ceci pour montrer à Binchdinuls quelque
                          jour qu'il fasse
Qu'il ne se passe pas jour sans que lui
                          envoie petit dessindicace.[92]

(Little sketch for shweet stained glass,
Made with plenty sweat and fuss
On left Marie and Félicie
Grumble as they do laundry.

Buninuls can't open Legras tin on right . . .
As Binchdinuls arrives to light it
Buninuls applies knee and arm with all his might
Binchdinuls by Gothic column is in two divided
All this to show my Binchdinuls that rain or shine
No day can pass without he gets a dedicadrawing of mine.)[93]

This imaginary stained-glass window celebrates the life Marcel and Reynaldo could have had together. On one end of the apartment, the maids Marie and Félicie wash clothes and complain about their workload. (The drawing seems to play on the fact that if the two friends were to live together, their two maids would have to move in together as well.)[94] At the other end, Marcel-Buninuls struggles to open a can of Legras anti-asthma powder as Reynaldo-Binchniduls arrives to assist him.[95]

Reynaldo's initials appear everywhere in this drawing: on the washbasin, on the clothes worn by one of the maids, at the foot of the table, on the legs of the two figures, and on the gothic arches that frame the drawing. They also appear in the lower right-hand corner of the drawing, on either side of the little table used for the fumigation, as if they were the artist's signature. But it is Marcel who created the drawings signed "RH": in another twist in the game of specular identification, he usurps his friend's signature and

Figure 1.18. Marcel Proust, untitled drawing ("Petit projet de genstil vitrail"). Philip Kolb, *Lettres à Reynaldo Hahn,* 74, and Philippe Sollers, *L'œil de Proust,* 85.

presents these sketches as works by Reynaldo. Neither authorship nor identity have clear boundaries.

The accompanying caption explains that Buninuls struggles to open the can of Legras powder while Binchdinuls comes to help, thus suggesting that Buninuls stands in for Marcel and Binchdinuls for Reynaldo. But since both Binchdinuls and Buninuls bear the initials "RH" on their bodies, we might be led to interpret both figures as likenesses of Reynaldo. We could also take them as two likenesses of Marcel, since both are shown inhaling the anti-asthma powders. Does the drawing show Reynaldo and Marcel, two Reynaldos, or two Marcels? Marcel's gloss does not resolve the question, and this specular game is further complicated by the fact that both friends used the same pet names to refer to one another. Marcel called himself "Buninuls" in one letter and, in another, used the same term to address Reynaldo. As Sollers wrote, "Proust est 'Binibuls,' 'Buncht,' mais Hahn aussi. Lui c'est moi, moi c'est lui. Reynaldo est une figure en miroir" (Proust is 'Binibuls' or 'Buncht,' but Hahn is, too. He is me, I am him. Reynaldo is a mirror image).[96]

In his caption Marcel explains that Binchdinuls has been "divided in two by a gothic column." Like the fantastic beings imagined by Aristophanes in Plato's *Symposium*, Marcel is cut in two, and yearns to be reunited with his missing half. The stained glass drawing presents a new version of the Aristophanic myth, with a happy ending: the two friends find their missing halves and reunite by moving in together. Marcel sent Reynaldo this elaborate textual-graphic game as part of his effort to entice him into what we would now call a domestic partnership.

There is one final drawing I would like to discuss that also sheds light on Marcel's fantasy of living with Reynaldo. In 1910 he sent his friend an elaborate drawing of a stained glass accompanied by an "explication of the window."[97] This was the most ambitious sketch he had ever done, an illustration of a gothic window composed of eighteen panes. As in the "petit projet de genstil vitrail" (fig. 1.19), the individual panels tell the story of the life the two friends could have led had they lived together. In the accompanying text, Marcel explains that the narrative opens with Marcel-Buncht lying in bed, listening to music, while Reynaldo-Bunibuls plays Wagner on the piano and the maid Céline prepares dinner. Reynaldo-Bunibuls suddenly throws a tantrum and leaves; Marcel-Buncht, "touched by Bunibul's kindness, weeps [and] he brings a handkerchief to his eye." Marcel-Buncht continues his daily routine, receiving visitors, telephoning his brother Robert, and even "washing his little hooves [*pattes*]." He stays up all night reading and falls asleep at dawn. In bed, Marcel thinks of Reynaldo-Bunibuls and blows him a kiss. Out of nowhere, a bespectacled "docteur-médekin" appears to tell Marcel-Buncht he is going to die. The story ends with a depiction of "Buncht's grave, covered by flowers, trees, hawthorns, and, above, the sun, which can no longer harm him. And Bunchtnibuls, wearing a top hat, arrives at the little cemetery to say farewell to Buncht."[98]

This elaborate window imagines the life the two friends could have led as a couple in belle-époque Paris. Servants cook and friends come to visit while Reynaldo-Bunibuls plays the piano in another room. (Marcel, with a touch of irony, has him play Wagner.) Unlike the previous sketches, this one is more realistic and anticipates the ups and downs, the frictions and problems that could mar their cohabitation. Reynaldo-Bunibuls throws a fit and storms out of the apartment, leaving Marcel-Buncht alone. The drawing is largely accurate in its depiction of Marcel's odd hours and daily schedule. Most of the action—and the drama—takes place late at night; Marcel-Buncht goes to bed at dawn and sleeps all day. Continuing the dou-

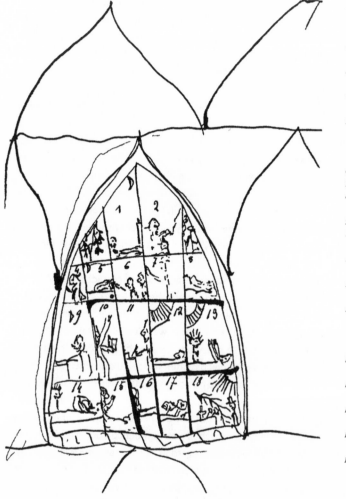

Dessin d'un vitrail que Philip Kolb, dans son édition de la *Correspondance*, date du troisième trimestre 1910. Il illustre la mort de Buncht (Marcel Proust) et est accompagné d'une lettre où chacune des scènes se trouve expliquée à Bunibuls (ou Bunchtnibuls), c'est-à-dire à Reynaldo Hahn.

Figure 1.19. Marcel Proust, untitled drawing. Philippe Sollers, *L'œil de Proust,* 92.

ble theme of sublimation and debasement we have seen in other drawings, Marcel-Buncht represents himself as an animal—he has hooves instead of legs—but transforms Reynaldo-Bunibuls into a spiritual being capable of appearing, as if by magic, at his bedside. This is yet another variation on the figures of Saint Reynaldo and Marcel-the-pony found elsewhere in the correspondence.

The story ends with the death of Marcel-Buncht. The "docteur-médekin aux lunettes," the only evil character in the story and the one who embodies Marcel's phobia of doctors, delivers a death sentence. Marcel-Buncht dies (but not without some humor—the caption explains that the glass pane depicting this final scene has been "badly damaged" [a beaucoup souffert], as if the window could reflect Marcel's suffering). Death brings him all the things he could not tolerate in life because of his allergies and phobias—sun, trees, flowers, hawthorns—as well as his dear Reynaldo-Bunchtnibuls dressed in a top hat. Like dreams in Freud's theory, this drawing brings about, in fantasy, the fulfillment of a wish.

This composition would turn out to be an accurate prediction of Marcel's last moments. In October 1922, at age fifty-one, he fell ill with a pneumococcal infection. According to Céleste Albaret, his maid at the time, the only person Marcel allowed to visit in these last months was Reynaldo Hahn.[99] Marcel's health deteriorated rapidly but he refused to be seen by a "docteur-médekin." Reynaldo wrote him a long letter pleading him to seek treatment: "Mon petit Buncht," Reynaldo wrote, "Je sais que personne n'a de poids sur vos décisions et que je ne puis rien pour ce que je considère comme raisonnable et souhaitable pour mon ami le plus cher, pour une des personnes que j'aurais le plus aimées dans ma vie." (I know that nobody can influence your decisions and that I'm helpless to bring about what I regard as sensible and desirable for my dearest friend, one of the people I have loved most in all my life.)[100] But Marcel did not heed his advice and died, in great pain, a few days later.

As my readers have surely noticed, there is something missing from Marcel's elaborate play on Reynaldo's foreignness: Latin America. In his letters and drawings, Marcel finds a thousand ways to comment on Reynaldo's German background, but Reynaldo was only half German—German-Jewish, to be exact—and Marcel does not seem to comment on his friend's Latin American identity (other than his early allusion to the "southern" cadences of his given name). This is a striking omission, given that Reynaldo was born in Venezuela, spent the first three years of his life in Caracas, and continued to identify himself as a South American living in France. So why would Marcel's elaborate commentary on his friend's identity neglect the most important part of his background?

We have seen how Reynaldo engaged in a passionate defense of French music against the Germanic influence of Wagnerism. He viewed French and German cultures as antithetical and argued that Wagner had no place in the French tradition. Marcel used his letters and drawings to poke fun at Reynaldo's musical nationalism; he made his friend, a notorious Germanophobe— at least when it came to music—into a caricature of Germanic identity, into a "petit Boschant" who spoke with a German accent. In the stained glass window, Marcel depicted Reynaldo as a Wagnerian—he plays *Die Mestersinger* on the piano—an identity that could not be further from the composer's own self-perception. When it came to cultural questions, Marcel had great fun turning his friend's identity on its head and making a Francophile Latin American into a Germanic Wagnerian.

Marcel's drawings establish a playful dialectic between religious iconography and sexual imagery, between the sacred and the perverse, and also between French and foreign cultures. Echoing the numerous plays on belonging and not belonging that appear in the novel, Marcel pays tribute to Reynaldo as a liminal figure, as someone who is, at once, saint and devil, sacred and profane, immaculate and perverse, French and German. Marcel learned quite a bit about the experience of being a foreigner in France by watching—and drawing—Reynaldo.

Cultural Cross-Dressings

A few years before Marcel's death, Reynaldo met a seventeen-year-old singer and actor named Guy Ferrant (fig. 1.20) who was a fan of his work; it was an encounter that would transform his life and his music. The two met in 1919 in Monte Carlo, where Reynaldo was directing a production of *Nausicaa*. They fell in love and later began working together in Parisian theaters.[101] One of their first collaborations came on May 11, 1923, when they performed at La Folie Saint James: Guy sang Reynaldo's "Le souvenir d'avoir chanté" while Reynaldo played the piano.[102] Over the years, Guy acted in many of Reynaldo's productions, including the operetta *Ô mon bel inconnu* (1933), the film version of *Ciboulette* (1932), and the 1936 production of the opera *La Carmélite*. He also had a successful film career and played minor roles in various films, including Cavalcanti's *La p'tite Lili* (1927) and Jacques Feyder's *Les nouveaux messieurs* (1928).

Figure 1.20. Reynaldo Hahn and Guy Ferrant, at sea, en route to Egypt, 1938. Bibliothèque de l'Opéra, Ph. 38, Bibliothèque Nationale de France, Paris.

After meeting Guy, Reynaldo's music underwent a radical transformation. He was known as a composer of serious works and long operas like *L'île
du rêve* and *La Carmélite,* but in 1923 he tried his hand at operetta—a genre
that critics derided as "musique légère" or "light music." Reynaldo accepted
an invitation from Robert de Flers, a childhood friend who had also been
close to Marcel, to collaborate on a new operetta to be called *Ciboulette.*
Robert and Francis de Croisset worked on the libretto and Reynaldo on the
music, but in the end the narrative was a collaboration among the three
friends, and the story is colored—as we will see—by Reynaldo's own experience. *Ciboulette* premiered on April 7, 1923, at the Théâtre des Variétés
and was an instant success. The audience loved it, the critics applauded it,
and it quickly became Reynaldo's most popular work. Even today Reynaldo
is chiefly remembered as the composer of *Ciboulette,* the only one of his
works to be performed regularly.

Ciboulette presents a lighthearted narrative punctuated by comic arias.
It tells the story of a girl who sells vegetables at a market in Paris and falls
in love with Antonin, a rich but naive aristocrat who holds the title of Vice-
count of Mourmelon. A market official serves as go-between and helps the

couple overcome numerous obstacles—including Ciboulette's eight fiancés
—so that they can get married. The action starts at a rowdy tavern, then
moves to the Parisian market of Les Halles before shifting to the drab suburb of Aubervillers, where Ciboulette lives with her aunt and uncle. The
story ends with a lively scene back in Paris, at the salon hosted by the
musician-socialite Olivier Métra, where Ciboulette, disguised as a Spaniard,
stuns the audience with a virtuoso (and campy) performance of boleros and
Iberian dances.

Ciboulette can be thought of as lighter version of À la recherche du temps
perdu, written in a parodic register. Both Ciboulette and Marcel's novel are
set in Paris during the Second Empire.[103] Both explore the effects of time on
love—Ciboulette's freshness fascinates the older Duparquet, whose nostalgic arias convey his own search for lost time—and both paint a vivid
portrait of Parisian salons. Ciboulette presents Olivier Métra's atelier as a
world frequented by artists, singers, and socialites: an operatic version of
the Guermantes salon. Even Proust's Duchesse de Guermantes finds a perfect counterpart in the operetta—the Comtesse de Castiglione, who makes
an appearance in the fourth scene of Act III, accompanied by a waltz. (Her
first words upon arriving at Métra's studio are, "Ah, Monsieur Métra, vos
valses! Vos valses!")[104]

Ciboulette can also be read as a biographical sketch of Reynaldo, though
one written in code. It reveals more about his life than any of his compositions or publications; de Flers and de Croisset must have been inspired
by their Venezuelan friend's life story as they composed the libretto. The
main theme of this operetta is the vitality of young love and its rejuvenat-
ing effects on older characters. Ciboulette has just turned twenty-one, and
her life seems to be in perfect synchrony with the arrival of spring. "It is
the first day of spring / Birds are moving in together," the script announces.
Ciboulette's youth not only transforms the life of her older lover (Antonin
is twenty-eight but behaves like an old man) but also infects the characters
around her with a sense of lively optimism. Reynaldo's lover Guy Ferrant
turned twenty-one the year Ciboulette premiered, and like Ciboulette he
was attractive and young; like her, he met a successful older man; like her,
he sang and performed for elegant audiences. Antonin's story parallels Reynaldo's own life; the character has lived a melancholy existence until he
meets a younger lover who brightens his life.

After meeting Guy, Reynaldo's music changed drastically. Most of his earlier compositions had a melancholic air about them. One of his first projects—in 1893, when he was nineteen—was setting Verlaine's *Chansons grises* to music, and "grey" is a perfect description of the mood conveyed by these pieces, languorous melodies tinged by a certain sadness. *Ciboulette,* in contrast, is airy and light, and the dances and repartees move in a dizzying *prestissimo.* It is one of Reynaldo's brightest works—a quality that explains the operetta's extraordinary success. Reynaldo had fallen in love again in his middle age, and he rediscovered a lost vitality that infused his music with new tempos and melodies.

Another central theme in *Ciboulette* is the experience of foreignness. The story sets up a series of oppositions between aristocrats and plebeians, the city and the countryside, Frenchmen and foreigners. Like Proust's narrator, Ciboulette inhabits a borderline state; she lives between the city and the country, between aristocrats and plebeians, and—as we discover in Act II—between France and Spain. As part of Duparquet's elaborate scheme to get the couple married, Ciboulette disguises herself as a Spanish singer called "Conchita Ciboulero." The girl's transformation from French peasant to Spanish diva is recounted in the following dialogue, accompanied by the rhythms of a Spanish-sounding bolero:

> Duparquet: Il n'y a plus de Ciboulette!
> Chœur: Plus d' Ciboulett'?
> Duparquet: En guis' de châle, un boléro! . . .
> Chœur: Un boléro?
> Duparquet: Plus d' carrot's, des castagnettes! . . .
> Chœur: Des castagnettes?
> Duparquet: Il n'y a plus d' Ciboulette!
>   C'est Conchita Ciboulero!
> Chœur: C'est Conchita Ciboulero!
>
> (Duparquet: She is no more, our Ciboulette!
> Chorus: No more our Ciboulett'?
> Duparquet: In place of her scarf, a bolero! . . .
> Chorus: A bolero?
> Duparquet: Instead of carrots, castanets! . . .
> Chorus: Castanets?
> Duparquet: She is no more, our Ciboulette!
>   Behold Conchita Ciboulero!
> Chorus: Behold Conchita Ciboulero!)

At the beginning of the opera, Ciboulette appears as a peasant rooted in French tradition. She lives in the country, harvests her own vegetables, and sells them at the Parisian market of Les Halles. Like Françoise in Proust's novel, she represents the salt of the earth, the authentic French peasant. But in Act II, Ciboulette trades the symbols of her cultural rootedness for exotic equivalents: a shawl for a bolero, carrots for castanets, and the simple name "Ciboulette" for the very exotic "Conchita Ciboulero."

Invoking the stereotype of the Spanish femme fatale, Duparquet and Ciboulette narrate Conchita's long and complex love life: her long string of seductions turn her into a feminine version of Don Juan—a Doña Juana of sorts.

> Duparquet: Elle naquit à Grenade,
>   De l'amoureuse incartade
>   D'une duchesse et d'un torero.
> Chœur: C'est Conchita Ciboulero.
> Duparquet: A treize ans, elle leva . . .
> Ciboulette: Le duc de Calatrava.
> Tous DEUX: A quatorze, au clair de lune,
>   Le comte de Pampelune.
> Duparquet: A quinze ans, elle affola . . .
> Ciboulette: Le p'tit marquis d'Alcala.
> Tous DEUX: A seize, elle ouvre sa mantille
>   Devant l'gouverneur de Castille.
> Duparquet: Enfin, couronnant sa campagne,
>   Sous le manteau, incognito,
>   Et subito,
>   Elle rend marteau . . .
> Chœur: Qui donc?
> Duparquet: Le roi de toutes les Espagnes.
> Chœur: Ollé!
> Tous DEUX: Voilà ce qu'elle fit à seize ans.
> Chœur: Ollé!
> Tous DEUX: Jugez de c' qu'elle f'ra maintenant.
> Chœur: Viv' Conchita!
>   Ollé
>   Viv' Conchita Ciboulero![105]

(Duparquet: She was born in Granada
   After indiscreet palaver
   Between a duchess and a torero.
Chorus: That's Conchita Ciboulero.
Duparquet: At thirteen, she gave her favor . . .
Ciboulette: To the Duke of Calatrava.
Both: At fourteen, by the light of the moon,
   To the Count of Pampelune.
Duparquet: At fifteen, she gave a kiss . . .
Ciboulette: In Alcalá to a marquis.
Both: At sixteen she removed her mantilla
   Before the governor of Castilla.
Duparquet: And lastly, crowning her campaign,
   Beneath a mantle, incognito,
   Not to mention quite subito,
   She was the anvil for a hammer with a name . . .
Chorus: Tell us, who?
Duparquet: The king of all the Spains.
Choris: Olé!
Both: At sixteen that's what she'd done.
Chorus: Olé!
Both: Just think where she'll go next for fun!
Chorus: Hurrah for Conchita!
   Olé!
   Hurrah for Conchita Ciboulero!)

Conchita appears as a hot-blooded southern woman who has slept her way to the top. She is also a stereotypical Spaniard: the daughter of a torero who uses mantillas to seduce her lovers, and is greeted with cries of "Ollé." Conchita seems to embody every conceivable received idea of Spanish culture.

The melody accompanying Conchita's appearance, a bolero, is a musical pastiche of George Bizet's *Carmen*. Both Reynaldo and Marcel had been close to Bizet's family. Marcel was a schoolmate of—and developed a crush on—Jacques Bizet, the composer's son. Geneviève Straus, Bizet's widow, held a salon where the two friends were frequent guests, and she later became one of the models for the Duchesse de Guermantes. During Reynaldo and Marcel's childhood, *Carmen,* reviled by critics during Bizet's life, became a spectacular success and one of the most popular operas in the history of music. Reynaldo also had intellectual reasons to admire this composer: in *The Case of Wagner*—translated into French by two of Marcel and Reynaldo's close friends, Daniel Halévy and Robert Dreyfus—Friedrich Nietzsche hailed Bizet as the perfect antidote to Wagner.[106] Reynaldo had grown up, literally, in the world of *Carmen*.[107]

In *Carmen*, Bizet used castanets and Andalusian melodies to paint a stereotypical Spain, inhabited by gypsies, femmes fatales, and treacherous villains. He also gave his characters made-up Spanish names—Lillas Pastia, Frasquita, Escamillo—and introduced Castilian words into his French libretto to create unusual rhymes: "Séville" and "seguidille," "Pastia" and "manzanilla."[108] Reynaldo uses similar strategies to evoke a Spanish atmosphere in his operetta, which features castanets, boleros, and Andalusian melodies, as well as arias peppered with French-Spanish wordplay: he rhymes "Ciboulero" with "torero," "Pampelune" with "lune," "Alcalá" with "affola," and "mantille" with "Castille."

After a lifetime of being tagged with all kinds of cultural stereotypes, Reynaldo agreed to work with de Flers and de Croisset on an operetta punctuated by the type of exotic, colorful music many had come to expect from a Latin American. It is not only Ciboulette who undergoes a transformation; it is Reynaldo himself who becomes, like Conchita Ciboulero, a purveyor of Spanish folklore through the operetta's music. After fifty years of composing like a respectable Frenchman, in the tradition of Massenet and Saint-Saëns, Reynaldo pastiched Spanish music to accompany this character in Latin drag, dressed in mantillas and donning a pair of castanets. If Ciboulette cross-dresses as a Spanish seductress, Reynaldo cross-dresses as a composer of boleros. But why would Reynaldo, who spent most of his life battling received ideas about Latin America, compose a work that plays on the stereotypes of Spanish culture? Is *Ciboulette* one more addition to the long list of French fantasies of an exotic Spain? Or, on the contrary, does the operetta offer a critical commentary on this history of cultural received ideas?

I would propose reading *Ciboulette* as a parody. Within the frame of the narrative, Conchita is not a real character but simply a fictional persona invented by Ciboulette. The operetta stages the construction and subsequent deconstruction of a false identity: Ciboulette's transformation into a Spaniard is immediately followed by a public unmasking that exposes the entire process as a charade. At the end of Act III, Conchita removes her wig and becomes, once more, Ciboulette, as the other characters exclaim: "Tout était faux! L'accent! Le nom! La mère" (All was false: the accent, the name, the mother!).[109] A perceptive audience might say the same about the Spanish types that had appeared in French culture from Balzac to Bizet: "Tout était faux!" This scene demonstrates that national stereotypes are—like the mantillas and castanets on stage—theater props that can be taken on or off at will. If *Carmen*'s Spain was a caricature, then *Ciboulette*'s Spain is a caricature of a caricature, a *mise-en-abîme* of the long history of French constructions of an exotic land next door.[110]

There is one more irony in Reynaldo's creation of Conchita Ciboulero. From the time he presented his first opera at age twenty-four, Reynaldo had been confronted with a French audience that assumed that he, as a Venezuelan, should be composing "exotic" music, even though he saw himself as defending and furthering the French musical tradition against the pernicious influence of Wagner and other foreign models. How are we then to explain his sudden turn away from French tradition in *Ciboulette*? The incorporation of Spanish musical genres like boleros and zarzuelas might seem like a departure from his lifelong commitment to a tradition that extends from Lully to Massenet.

Reynaldo's sudden embrace of Spanish music and Spanish stereotypes in *Ciboulette* is a strategy of resistance. Like the characters in Jean Genet's novels who respond to homophobic attacks by adopting the most feminine dress and demeanor, Reynaldo's revenge was to embody the stereotype that had been directed at him. Through the character of Conchita Ciboulero, he was giving back to French audiences the image of the exotic Spaniard that they had projected on him for decades. In *Ciboulette*, Reynaldo assumes the folkloric identity that he was always assumed to have; like the protagonist in *The Thief's Journal*, Reynaldo embraced the negative image his opponents projected on to him as an act of revenge.

But there is also another way to read *Ciboulette*'s appropriation of boleros and zarzuelas. Perhaps this was not so much a break with as a continuation of French musical tradition. The most canonical figures in the history of opera—from Offenbach to Bizet—had incorporated exotic rhythms into their compositions, and perhaps Reynaldo was simply inserting *Ciboulette* into this orientalist tradition. In the house of mirrors of cultural identity, there was no way to be more French than to incorporate exotic references into a musical composition. By creating a work that was also an homage to Bizet, Reynaldo had also found a more lighthearted expression to the anti-Wagnerian position he had espoused since his adolescence. In *The Case of*

Wagner, Nietzsche hailed Bizet as a composer of light, airy music that offered an alternative to the heavy and "brutal" Wagner.[111] *Ciboulette* thus inscribes itself in a tradition that is anti-Wagnerian by virtue of its humor and sensibility.

By the time *Ciboulette* premiered in 1923, Reynaldo's ideas about cultural nationalism had changed dramatically since he first debated the merits of Wagner's music in his letters to Edouard Risler. As a teenager, Reynaldo believed that Germany and France had distinct cultural identities—one was beer, the other champagne—and that Wagner was incompatible with the French musical tradition. His musical nationalism was an essentialist position —one that Marcel parodied in his letters and drawings over the years. Proust did not believe in essences, and he used his correspondence to try myriad identities on Reynaldo. In one letter he was a Germanic "Petit Boschant"; in another, a Catholic saint; a third would imagine him as a sadistic master, and a fourth as a Wagnerian roommate. It is as if Marcel were dressing and undressing his friend in different costumes, using each missive to give him different nationalities, religions, and sexual identities.

By the 1920s, Reynaldo came to adopt a view of cultural identity that was much closer to Marcel's. Like the imaginary Reynaldo in the letters and drawings, Ciboulette undergoes a series of transformations, as she mutates from French peasant to Spanish Diva and back to a Parisian bride. All she needs to acquire a new identity is a new costume, and the operetta stages not only the construction of these cultural traits but also their deconstruction. Identity—like gender, in Judith Butler's account—is a mere performance, one that can be exposed and unmade for the delectation of the audience.[112]

This antiessentialist view of cultural identity is closely linked to the cosmopolitan experience. Proust came to it after living as an *étranger à soi-même,* as a bourgeois, Jewish homosexual who straddled the borderline between different social positions and who did not fully belong in any of the worlds he frequented. Reynaldo, in contrast, became an antiessentialist after a lifetime of moving across languages, cultures, and borders as he traveled the world performing and conducting. He also learned the dangers of a monolithic conception of identity after experiencing the relentless attacks by xenophobes, homophobes, and anti-Semites that would haunt him until the end of his life.

Reynaldo's wartime experiences taught him the fundamental incompat-

ibility between cosmopolitan experience and totalitarian ideology. The cosmopolitan identity is characterized by an openness to other cultures and a
willingness to experience plurality and diversity. Reynaldo spoke Spanish,
French, German, and English; he was equally at home among aristocrats in
Paris or Jewish relatives in Hamburg; he was French and foreign, Catholic
and Jewish. Yet Nazi ideologues—and reactionary critics like Rebatet after
them—pigeonholed Reynaldo into a single category—Jewish. (It was not a
coincidence that the Nazis used the term *cosmopolitan* as a code word for
Jews.)

Despite the numerous setbacks he experienced during his life, Reynaldo
is a perfect example of the first type of foreigner discussed by Julia Kristeva
in *Strangers to Ourselves*: the one who embraces his new country with open
arms, develops a passion for its language and culture, and thrives in his professional and personal lives. In the end, he became one of those foreigners—
along with Beckett, Ionesco, and Cioran—who became representatives of
French culture and who led Kristeva to exclaim "one is nowhere *better* a
foreigner than in France."[113]

Paperolle No. 1

Proust's Mexican Stocks

Proust's friendship with Reynaldo Hahn taught him much about the lives of Latin Americans in Paris and about the elusive experience of assimilating into French culture. While visiting Reynaldo, Marcel would have heard the family discuss the vicissitudes of Latin American politics and the many upheavals and revolutions that led the Hahns to emigrate. Later in life, the novelist would learn his most important lesson about Latin American history and politics from an unusual source: the stock market.

Few people around him knew that Marcel developed a passion for investing and that he spent considerable time and energy trading Latin American stocks.[1] After the death of his parents—his mother died in 1905, two years after his father—Marcel inherited a considerable fortune that was invested in blue-chip stocks and bonds and was managed by Léon Neuburger, a family friend who worked for the Rothschild Bank. When the novelist began purchasing exotic financial products, Neuburger asked his nephew Lionel Hauser, who was almost the same age as Marcel, to take charge of his friend's portfolio.

Starting in 1906 and continuing though 1921, Proust wrote frequent, elaborate letters to Hauser. The style and form of these missives could not be more different from those he sent to Reynaldo Hahn. His notes to Hauser conveyed instructions to buy and sell stock, asked advice about possible investments, and often veered into extended meditations on life, politics, and literature. Proust treated Hauser not only as a financial advisor but also as a psychoanalyst and a guru of sorts; he seems to have been under the impression that his friend, given his line of work, could accurately predict the rise and fall of securities and the general tendency of the world markets. The two had met as children, and Lionel was one of the rare people whom Marcel addressed using the informal *tu*.

Hauser, for his part, was no ordinary broker. He was the scion of an illustrious banking family—several relatives worked for the Rothschild Bank—who had a passion for literature, philosophy, and the arts. His letters to Proust include long discussions of operas, novels, poems, and paintings. More intriguingly, Hauser was a theosophist, and some of his financial advice is intermingled with meditations on karma and the effects of greed on the chain of reincarnation. In 1920 he wrote a book summarizing his views. *The Three Levers of the New World: Competence, Probity, Altruism,* published by the London Theosophical Publishing House, called for the creation of a "league" of ethical professionals. "The member of the League who is a banker," he wrote, "must regard the interests of his clients as his own and never suggest an investment to them which he would consider too risky for himself."[2] He sent Marcel a copy, and a lively debate ensued as the two friends compared views on the best way to live an ethical life.

As an investor, Proust had a special interest in exotic securities. His purchases—or at least his intended purchases—included bonds issued by Holland, Spain, Serbia, Egypt, Turkey, Tunisia, Chile, Argentina, and the United States; railway stock in Switzerland, Pennsylvania, Kentucky, Argentina, Brazil, and Tunisia; gold, nickel, and diamond mines—including those exploited by De Beers; and oil and shipping companies from around the world (including the Port of Rosario, Argentina); as well as random securities, such as shares in Société de l'Azote, a nitrogen producer; Société Pop, a firm specializing in compressed air; Malacca Rubber, a company based in Malaysia; and Oriental Carpet, a Russian venture.

Scholars have offered different interpretations for Proust's puzzling obsession with the stock market. Philip Kolb—who first published the Proust-Hauser correspondence and wrote an article called "Marcel Proust, Speculator"—judged that "when he occupied himself with financial matters, Proust behaved less as a businessman than as a poet, with a particular imagination."[3] Jean-Yves Tadié adds that Proust

> belongs to the category of small-time speculators who buy high and sell low [. . .]
> It is not a matter of incompetence on Marcel's part, but of character traits: he sells
> when he feels bored or anxious, and buys to amuse himself. Speculating breaks
> for an instant his daily toil: and the more he works, the more the stock market
> [. . .] attracts him. The very name of the stocks casts a poetic spell on him, from
> the "pines of the Landes" to the "Railways of Mexico," from the "Gold mines of
> Australia" to the Tanganyika Railway": thus he conquers, in an imaginary voyage,

places he will never see. When he dreams of place names, stock charts serve the same purpose as railway timetables.[4]

Of all the stocks Proust bought and sold during his run as a speculator, his Mexican investments turned out to be the most unfortunate. Proust first invested in Mexico in 1906: a year after his mother's death, he purchased Mexican government bonds, paying 4 percent interest.[5] In 1908, he added shares of Mexican railways to his portfolio.[6] Hauser approved of this investment and told him that "Mexico is undoubtedly in the process of regenerating itself, and everything makes one suppose that one day it will enjoy a first-rate credit."[7] In 1910, Proust sought "some good, first-rate American investment, but more speculative" and briefly considered the Bank of Mexico before settling on a company that ran the tramway network in Mexico City.[8]

Mexico Tramways Company—as the firm was officially called (see plate 4)—was established in March 1906 by a group of Canadian investors in Toronto and soon became the largest and most important operator of tramways in the Mexico City metropolitan area. The company benefited greatly from president Porfirio Díaz's plans to modernize the country's infrastructure by contracting European and American companies to expand the rail network. A 1910 article published in *Brill Magazine* hailed the firm's strength and potential: "The electric railway system," the author enthused, "has been the chief factor in the expansion and improvement of the city and its suburbs, and is more closely related to the life of the citizens of Mexico than is the case in most cities. The cars are used by all classes in their daily life, for business and pleasure, for attending religious services and funerals, and for the transportation of building materials, merchandise, [and] household goods." The author applauded the Mexico Tramways Company for having "established a standard of service and equipment not exceeded by the most advanced in any part of the world, and this in the face of many abnormal conditions of customs, people, and language."[9]

In Paris, Mexico Tramways shares were promoted aggressively by financial analysts, including Arnaud Yvel in the pages of *Le Figaro*. On February 11, 1910, he touted the shares as "a deal that deserves to attract the public's attention" and explained that "the term of the concession, which will not expire until 1983, its range, which encompasses the capital and its suburbs, make 'Mexico Tramways' an investment whose profits could increase significantly."[10] Proust asked Hauser for his opinion, but the broker replied he "did not know the value of Mexico Tramways."[11] Proust purchased some shares

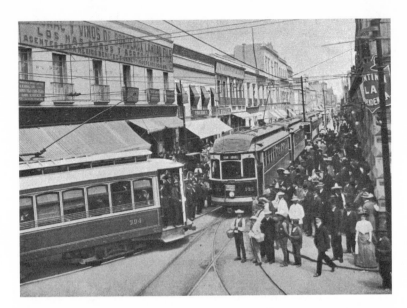

Figure P1.1. A tramway wagon, downtown Mexico City. From Mexico Tramways promotional materials, ca. 1910.

of the company anyway, leading Hauser to criticize his "thirst for speculative investments."[12]

Proust's investment in Mexico Tramways could not have come at a worst
time. He bought his first shares in early 1910, probably influenced by *Le Figaro*'s reports about the thriving Mexican economy. That year marked the
centennial of Mexico's independence, and President Díaz organized an extravagant celebration for heads of state and dignitaries from around the
world. Visitors were impressed by the modern metropolis, full of brand-
new buildings that included a palatial post office (figs. P1.1 and P1.2), a national theater, and a legislative palace. Many of these structures had been
designed by a team of international architects and were built out of the
highest-quality materials, including steel and marble. The capital had been
recently electrified, and streetlamps illuminated city streets filled with late-
model automobiles and shiny railway cars. On September 12, *Le Figaro*
reported on the banquet the president offered his foreign guests: "[Díaz]
said that he hoped the ambassadors would take with them good memories
of their stay in Mexico, and that once they return to their home countries,
they will do justice to the flourishing situation of Mexico, to its many ac-

Figure P1.2. Tramway wagons circulating by the Central Post Office, Mexico City. From Mexico Tramways promotional materials, ca. 1910.

complishments and advances, and to the welcome offered to all foreigners who come here looking for work and for fortune. Mexico, he added, will strive to be always a second home for them, and will offer them protection and support."[13]

Most visitors did indeed return home proclaiming the rebirth of Mexico as a wealthy, stable, and sophisticated country. But they had only seen Mexico City and missed the poverty, inequality, and social tensions that were festering in the countryside. On November 20, 1910 the Mexican revolution erupted; President Díaz was ousted and replaced by Francisco I. Madero, a young, reform-minded lawyer. French newspapers reported on the insurgency, but Le Figaro's financial writers sought to portray the revolt as a minor affair. "The measures taken by the government," wrote one optimistic journalist in 1910, "permit us to assure that these passing local troubles will have no repercussions."[14] Mexican stocks plunged, but Arnaud Yvel predicted that they would rise again "as soon as we realize the scant importance of the small uprising mentioned by the newspapers." He noted that "clever investors have taken advantage of this situation to buy Mexico Tramways."[15]

Despite the journalist's assurances, the value of Mexico Tramways stock followed the country's fortunes. The shares had been introduced in 1910 at 660 francs,[16] but by November 21, they had lost almost 6 percent of their value and were worth 621 francs. They continued to decline over the next two years, and by the end of 1912 they were trading at 560 francs.[17] Proust began to get nervous about his "considerable losses in the stock market,"[18] and Hauser, in turn, censured his friend's drive to speculate.[19]

The year 1913 would be a good one for Proust—he finally published the first volume of the novel he had been preparing for years—but it would prove catastrophic for Mexico. Madero was deposed and assassinated, Victoriano Huerta seized the presidency, and the country plunged into an unprecedented wave of chaos and violence that went down in history as "la decena trágica," or the "ten tragic days." By November, Mexico Tramway stock had plunged to four hundred francs.[20] In the first days of 1914, an article published in the British trade journal *The Tramway and Railway World* noted that "those concerned in tramway undertakings abroad in which British capital is invested have been a good deal perturbed since war and chaos descended on Mexico on the conclusion of the long and pacific domination of President Porfirio Diaz. Since that strong hand was withdrawn, revolutions and fighting have plagued the country, and for more than two years settled pacific government has been absent." Lest he scare potential investors away, the author conceded that "in the City of Mexico itself everyday life appears to have been comparatively little disturbed, as is shown by the fact that the revenues of the Mexico Tramways Company still go on increasing."[21]

The stock continued to fall, and in the summer of 1914 Proust began to panic. By July, it was clear that a war would erupt in Europe, and, as Reynaldo Hahn prepared to go to the front, Marcel wrote a contrite letter asking Hauser for help untangling his investments. He confessed that not only had he been speculating with foreign stocks but also he had indulged in some of the riskiest practices by buying on margin and investing in futures and other exotic derivatives. In addition to one hundred shares of Mexico Tramways, he had purchased one hundred future contracts of the same company. These securities were held at the Crédit Industriel, where he had cash and margin accounts that allowed him to purchase stock using borrowed money. Proust did not understand the complexities involved in these investments, but he did know that they were bleeding his portfolio and asked Hauser to help stop the hemorrhage. He realized he had acted recklessly and compared his situation to that of a remorseful Catholic: "never has a sinner at the confessional made such shocking revelations. I'm only telling you this for my own mortification because naturally one can no longer sell anything."[22]

Hauser—who had the patience of Job—spent the next several months trying to sort out his friend's financial affairs. He explained that by investing in futures, Marcel's losses had been compounded: he had to pay back the full amount borrowed to finance the initial investment, plus interest, and since the value of his shares had declined, even a rapid sale would leave him in the red. Marcel called his tramway adventure "disastrous" and complained that the banks issued constant margin calls that "made him double the deposit as the stock continued to decline."[23] To make things worse, the futures market had been suspended because of the threat of war, and Hauser advised him to "save what you might still be able to rescue."[24]

Marcel had also invested in Russian stocks, and he now worried that if Russia entered the war "the value of all these could come to naught."[25] For once he was right, and he managed to sell some of his holdings before the October Revolution wiped out the value of Russian securities. By then, his portfolio had taken a beating from three of the major conflicts of the twentieth century: the Mexican Revolution, World War I, and the Russian Revolution. Other speculators found ways to make money from these insurrections—trading gold, diamonds, and hard currency; Proust, in contrast, compounded his losses.

Ironically, Porfirio Díaz fled to Paris after being deposed by the Mexican Revolution in 1911. He lived there until his death in 1915, and during these four years Marcel could have potentially crossed paths with him on the street, at the theater, or at the home of one of the Latin Americans discussed in this book. If they ever met, Marcel would have quizzed the former president about Mexican politics . . . and about Mexico Tramways. A nostalgic Díaz might have seen Marcel as one of the many foreign investors who had supported his modernizing projects, and the former president would have been impressed to learn that a French writer who had never been to Mexico knew so much about the capital's tramway network.

The war raged in Europe, but Proust continued to worry about Mexico. In 1915, he considered selling all of his stock in Mexico Tramways and asked Hauser if "you, who know the secrets of the financial world, happen to know if Mexico's situation is likely to continue forever."[26] Hauser, of course, did not have an answer. The situation in Mexico worsened. The United States invaded in 1914 and seized the port of Veracruz for fear that German ships would dock there. In the same year, Carranza replaced Huerta as president; on October 30, 1915, *Le Figaro* reported a rumor—false, it would turn out—that the new head of state had been assassinated, and Mexican stocks plunged.[27] Proust lost his patience, and on October 31 he ordered his bank to "sell everything, including the 200 Mexico."[28] No buyers could be found, and the Mexican stocks lingered in his account.

As Hauser explained, Proust's portfolio produced a yearly income of thirty-two thousand francs, but he was paying twenty-two thousand a year in interest, leaving him with a real income of only ten thousand.[29] Hauser proposed transferring all Proust's investments—which were spread in multiple accounts at several banks—to his own firm so that he could perform a "deep cleaning."[30] A few weeks later, Hauser delivered more bad news. Mexico Tramways "has been delisted from the French stock exchange, and thus I don't know if these shares can be sold in Paris,"[31] though they could be sold through a London bank. Puzzled about these shares that could only be traded abroad, Proust wrote Hauser, "I trust your skillful initiatives for selling these tramways that, from what you tell me, one takes in London, and, since they are bound for Mexico, they represent a 'radius of action' comparable to that of the Deutschland." Proust joked that "a fall is a common accident when it comes to tramways. Unfortunately this time I fell from much higher than I had been used to." "In any case," he continued, "I am in the habit of missing the tramway and arriving late." His investments in tramways had always been unfortunate; another banker had "recommended a certain Tram, Licht [*sic*] and Power, which I neither took nor abandoned at the time I should have."[32]

Hauser hit another obstacle. It was indeed possible to sell the Mexico Tramways shares in London, but wartime financial restrictions required that the proceeds of the sale be reinvested in English bonds. And to make matters worse, the shares were trading for the equivalent of 150 francs apiece in England—a price that was well below the 240 francs last quoted in Paris and a small fraction of what Proust had paid back in 1910. Despite these unattractive conditions, Hauser advised Proust to go through with the sale: by unloading the Mexico Tramways he could save about seven hundred francs a year in interest.[33] Proust agreed and was so impressed with Hauser's resourcefulness that he baptized him "Duke of Mexico and of La Plata," thereby making him an honorary Latin American.[34] Finding a buyer took longer than anticipated, and Hauser began to grow impatient. They would sell one day, but "perhaps by then" he mused, "[Woodrow] Wilson will have proclaimed himself Emperor of Mexico, thereby increasing the value of the Tramways."[35]

On August 26, Hauser conveyed good news: a French bank had found a buyer for twenty-five Mexico Tramways futures at 230 francs, well above the going rate in London. Proust lost money on the trade, but Hauser sounded a bright note: "In any case, this makes 25 shares that will no longer decline in value."[36] "If there is a security for which any sale will be a good one," Proust responded, "it will be Mexico Tramways, an investment that could have been a very good one, but which I now consider ill-fated."[37] All these skillful maneuvers had given Hauser the reputation of being an expert on all things Mexican, and Proust reported that "the other day I was singing your praises to a certain figure [. . .] who, wanting to show me that he was well aware of your position, told me that you were above all a specialist in Mexican stocks."[38]

Three months later, Hauser had found no buyers for Proust's shares. He joked that the Mexico Tramways were "the Flying Dutchman of the Stock Exchange"; like the phantom ship in Wagner's opera, they seemed to be haunted.[39] (Elsewhere he called them "our Mexican sheep," a metaphor that turns the banker into the shepherd of this unruly flock.)[40]

In early 1917, Hauser reported more bad news. Proust still had 175 shares in his account, and the price had declined to 147 francs. The situation in Mexico had stabilized. "President Wilson," Hauser explained, "ordered the withdrawal of American troops from Mexico, and plans to ask his government to recognize General Carranza. It is possible that the Mexican situation will finally sort itself out, and that the value of your Tramways will profit from this."[41] Proust worried that the recovery would take too long: "It is possible that America will annex Mexico and that in ten years these Tramways will be worth as much as a Rolls Royce. But in ten years I will be dead."[42]

Still, no buyers were found, and it was now the end of March. "Your Mexico Tramways continue to worry me," Hauser wrote. "It is a gaping wound in your portfolio."[43] At this point, Proust wrote Hauser one of his most poetic letters, quoting the famous closing verses of José-Maria de Heredia's poem "Les conquérants."

Bien que les valeurs soient généralement comme les vieilles maîtresses et qu'on les aime précisément en raison des embêtements qu'elles nous ont causés, espé-rant toujours qu'un jour meilleur se lèvera, il y a beau temps que j'ai renoncé à voir luire sur la terre de Fernand Cortez un soleil d'or et se lever *Du fond de l'Océan des étoiles nouvelles. C'est donc avec joie que je bazarde ces saletés.* [44]

(Investments are like old mistresses, and one loves them precisely because of the problems they cause us as we wait for a better day to rise. It has been some time since I abandoned the hope of seeing a golden sun ray shine on the land of Hernán Cortéz and new stars rise from the depths of the ocean. I am glad to be rid of this junk.)

In early May, Hauser wrote with good news: another fifty futures had just sold at 130 francs. A day later, the remaining twenty-five futures were liquidated "at the fantastic price of 163." The Tramway stock had risen because of recent political developments: "The President of Mexico seems to have the intention of abandoning his friends in Berlin and placing the destiny of his country in the hands of the Americans—a report that sufficed to energize all the Mexican stocks."[45] Hauser was referring to the affair known as "the Zimmermann Telegram," which had been reported in French newspapers in previous months. In early 1917, worried that his country was losing the war, the German foreign minister, Arthur Zimmermann, asked his ambassador in Washington to approach the Mexican government with a proposal for a military alliance. In exchange, Germany promised to help Mexico reclaim the vast territories lost to the United States in the nineteenth century, including Texas, New Mexico, and Arizona. President Carranza declined the German offer, judging that it was not sensible to risk another war with the United States.[46]

Hauser congratulated Marcel on closing all his open futures positions. He still owned one hundred shares of Mexico Tramways in his cash account, but at least now he could cease to worry about margin calls and exorbitant interest rates. "Your situation," Hauser told him, "is evidently not comparable to that of Peru before its conquest by the Spaniards, but it is already a great accomplishment, especially in the times we live in, to know the exact value of your portfolio."[47] Proust was not in a hurry to sell the remaining Mexico Tramways shares. "We can set them aside until the resurrection of Hernan Cortez," he wrote Hauser,[48] noting that "the projects periodically attributed to President Carranza make the Tramways climb like simple funiculars when he is considered a germanophobe, but fall at full throttle when he is deemed germanophile."[49]

But by early 1918, he was again anxious to sell and asked Hauser for help: "I think I no longer have any investments on rue de la Victoire [the address of Hauser's office] except for Mexico Tramways. It is possible that passengers ride them without paying the conductor, since the said company does not pay interest. If you think the equity may be sold (and that it is advantageous to sell), and if you do not see on the horizon a surprise invasion of Mexico by the United States that would have favorable repercussions on the price of the Tramways, then perhaps [they should be sold]."[50] Hauser, who did not appreciate being treated like an oracle, replied, "In regards to the Mexico Tramways, since I'm not in direct communication with President Carranza, I find myself in the impossibility of informing you about the immediate future of this transportation company."[51]

In April 1918, Hauser learned that he might be drafted. He was a British subject, and the English had just expanded the draft to all men up to the age of fifty. As a precaution, he transferred Proust's Tramways stocks to the London County and Westminster Bank.[52] This was the third time the Mexican stocks had been transferred—a complicated process that involved locating the original stock certificates, finding a secure way to transport them to the new location, and linking the securities to a regular bank account.

The Tramways continued their downward turn and were now trading around one hundred francs. Proust decided to liquidate all his shares. On May 15, the London bank found a buyer, but the brokers canceled the sale because of wartime restrictions on international trades.[53] Proust changed his mind and decided to keep the shares, but the bank, confused by the multiple orders and mixed messages, processed the sale of the remaining one hundred shares of Mexico Tramways at 135. The timing for this trade could not have been worse. The shares began to rise quickly, and by November they were trading at 280 francs.[54]

Proust had finally rid himself of the troublesome stocks, but now he decided he wanted them back. He was convinced the bank had sold them by mistake and asked Hauser to help him dispute the transaction. His friend agreed that the bank had erred and advised Proust to write a letter requesting a redeposit of the one hundred shares of Mexico Tramways into his account, especially given that "Mexican shares have been very strong in the past days."[55] The bank, however, refused to acknowledge its mistake or to redeposit the shares. Hauser suggested finding an impartial mediator, and Proust asked Walter Berry, an American who worked at the embassy, to contact the bank. Berry enlisted the Romanian princess Helene Soutzo to help him. By the end of the year, Hauser, Berry, Proust, and the princess were all pleading with the bank to restitute the Mexican shares.[56]

As the dispute dragged on, the war came to an end, and Proust jumped at the opportunity to resume his speculative investments. He turned his eye toward Mexico once more and told Hauser he was interested in buying shares of Petróleos de México, [57] the largest oil company in the country.[58] Hauser was at his wit's end, and he wrote his friend an exasperated letter.

Mon cher Marcel, Te représentes-tu la tête que ferait un médecin qui, ayant pendant des semaines et des mois, lutté comme un forcené pour arracher à la mort un malade atteint de fièvre typhoïde, surprendrait celui-ci le jour où il entre en convalescence en train de déguster un plat de choucroute? Eh bien, c'est un peu l'impression que m'a produit[e] la lecture de ta lettre d'hier.[59]

(My dear Marcel, imagine the expression on a doctor's face if he had spent weeks and months, fighting like a madman, to save the life of a patient suffering from typhoid fever, and, when on the very day the said patient begins his convalescence, he surprises him in the act of devouring a plate of *choucroute*. Well, this is approximately the impression your letter from yesterday produced on me.)

Berry and Princess Soutzo continued to pressure the London bank to redeposit the Tramway shares, to no avail. Hauser extricated himself from the dispute, but thanked Proust for introducing him to Berry, who turned out to be a most useful contact. "The least you and I could do," Hauser wrote Proust, "would be to pay a visit to President Carranza to thank him for having deteriorated the network of Mexican Tramways, since without him I would have never had the pleasure of making the acquaintance of your friend [Walter Berry]." [60]

In early 1919, Proust received catastrophic news that made him forget his dispute with the London bank. The building on Boulevard Haussmann where he had lived for the past thirteen years had just been sold, and he would have to vacate his apartment in the coming months. He was feeling weaker than ever and feared he would not survive the move. At one point, Proust imagined moving into the luxurious villa owned by his friend Francis de Croisset, who had recently hosted Woodrow Wilson—who was in Paris to attend the negotiation of the peace treaties—at one of his soirées. After all his musings on Wilson, Mexican-American relations, and their effect on his investments, Proust came close to meeting the president at his friend's home and discussing the fate of his Mexico Tramways.[61]

By March 1919, Proust was speculating again. This time he considered transferring all his money to a Romanian bank to take advantage of higher interest rates. (Hauser told him this was pure folly.)[62] And in December, he asked a lawyer friend for advice on a Mexican oil company, Compañía Mexicana de Petróleos El Águila.[63]

Hauser was dismayed to see his efforts to sanitize his friend's finances come to naught, and on March 30, 1920, he wrote him a long, affectionate letter telling him, "I have completed my mission," and breaking up their professional relationship. He would no longer handle Marcel's investments, though "nothing will have changed between us, and I remain the friend I have always been for you."[64] This was one of the last communications exchanged between the two friends. Proust had only a year to live, and during his final months he managed to abstain from the reckless speculations that had decimated his fortune.

Proust's financial experiments found their way into his novel. In a passage near the end of *Albertine disparue,* the narrator admits to having suffered significant losses in the stock market as he tried to raise money to spoil Albertine.

> Depuis sa mort je ne m'étais plus occupé des spéculations que j'avais faites afin d'avoir plus d'argent pour elle. Or le temps avait passé; de grandes sagesses de l'époque précédente étaient démenties par celle-ci [. . .] et les titres dont M. de Norpois nous avait dit: "Leur revenu n'est pas très élevé sans doute mais du moins le capital ne sera jamais déprécié," étaient souvent ceux qui avaient le plus baissé. Rien que pour les consolidés anglais et les Raffineries Say, il me fallait payer aux coulissiers des différences si considérables, en même temps que des intérêts et des reports que sur un coup de tête je me décidai à tout vendre et me retrouvai tout d'un coup ne plus posséder que le cinquième à peine de ce que j'avais hérité de ma grand-mère et que j'avais encore du vivant d'Albertine.[65]

> (Since her death I was no longer engaged in the speculations that I had undertaken in order to have more money to spend on her. But time had passed; the received wisdom of the previous era was nullified by the present one [. . .] thus the shares of which M. de Norpois had said, "Doubtless their yield is hardly substantial, but at least their capital will never depreciate," were often those that had lost the most value. If only for the English Consols and the Say Refineries, I had to pay the brokers such considerable differentials, not to mention the interest and the sums carried forward, that I suddenly took it into my head to sell everything, and found myself forthwith the owner of barely one fifth of the wealth that I had inherited from my grandmother and still possessed while Albertine was alive.)[66]

This passage is one example of how Proust transformed his life experience into novelistic material. Through unnamed, the Mexican Revolution—and its impact on the financial markets—lingers in the background, as if it were the novel's political unconscious.

Unlike Proust, who bought risky shares against Hauser's objections, the narrator follows M. de Norpois's advice and makes conservative investments, though the goal was always to make money to buy lavish presents for a loved one: a Rolls Royce for Albertine in the novel and an airplane for Alfred Agostinelli, Proust's chauffeur and platonic crush, in real life. The period 1913-1914, the years of Proust's most intense speculation with Mexico Tramways stock, coincided with the most dramatic moments of his infatuation with the driver.[67] The novelist hired the chauffeur as a full-time assistant in 1913, but the young man, who dreamed of becoming a pilot,[68] lasted only a few months before quitting to enroll in a flying school in the south of France. Proust did all he could to lure Agostinelli back to Paris. He dispatched a friend to plead with him; he offered him money; he even asked Hauser to sell stock so he could buy him an airplane. None of these tricks worked, and Proust never got to give him the lavish present, as Agostinelli died in a plane crash off the coast of Nice on May 30, 1914. Proust was devastated and eventually transposed his grief into the story of Albertine's death in the novel.

Proust had a particular attraction to chauffeurs, muscular young men strong enough to turn cranks, change tires, and perform the many other arduous mechanical tasks involved in operating early automobiles. At one point he had two full-time drivers working for him. It is no coincidence that in the hopes of making money to spoil Agostinelli, Proust invested in Mexico Tramways—a company devoted to another form of mechanized transport that was also operated by strong, uniformed young men. The imaginary vision of these rough drivers maneuvering colossal tramways through the hustle and bustle of Mexico City must have whetted Proust's appetite for this company's stock. Proust was not the only chauffeur-loving gay man of his time. In the same years, Salvador Novo, a gay poet who once described himself as "a Mexican Proust," developed a crush on Mexico City's bus and tramway drivers and joined the staff of *El Chafirete*, a newspaper for chauffeurs, so he could publish erotic poems and other suggestive texts about automotive adventures.[69]

Proust's fondness for pain is well known,[70] and the novel includes many scenes of masochism, like Charlus's visit to Jupien's brothel. Perhaps his unfortunate trades in Mexican stocks should be seen as an unusual expression of this perverse disposition, since—as he explained to Hauser—"investments are like old mistresses, and one loves them precisely because of the problems they cause us."[71] Proust did not invest to gain but to lose, so he could indulge in the pain occasioned by his trading disasters, a form of financial masochism.

Proust's sexual and financial affairs were intertwined. The novelist satisfied his sexual needs by frequenting a male brothel run by Albert Le Cuziat—an establishment that served as the model for Jupien's hotel in À la recherche—located at 11, rue de l'Arcade, a street that runs from the Place de la Madeleine to the Saint Lazare railway station. A few doors down, at number 26, a stately building housed Lionel Hauser 's brokerage firm.[72] Proust could thus satisfy both his sexual and financial needs with a single visit to this block (though in practice he visited the brothel more often than Hauser's office—he could manage his investments by letter, while his business at Le Cuziat's hotel, for obvious reasons, could only be handled in person). Proust's sexual and financial fantasies converged in Mexico Tramways. Investing in this stock allowed the novelist to imagine a far-away capital he would never visit in real life and also to fantasize about the tropical Agostinellis he would never meet.

Proust sold his last shares in Mexico Tramways in 1918, thus concluding an unfortunate financial adventure begun in 1910. In 1920, the Mexican Revolution came to an end, and Mexico City's tramways resumed their operation. The Mexico Tramways Company prospered, and over the next two decades it expanded its network as the capital grew exponentially. Mexican writers and artists had a particular interest in tramways as symbols of the new, mechanized urban culture ushered in by the modern era. Manuel Gutiérrez Nájera had been one of the first to celebrate these ubiquitous wagons in his "Novela del tranvía"(1888). Salvador Novo spent his late teens and early twenties riding every form of motorized transport and chronicling his exploits in a series of 1923 articles for El Chafirete. In 1925, an eighteen-year-old Frida Kahlo was gravely injured in a tramway collision, an accident that prompted a life-long obsession with pain, damaged bodies, and the traumatic consequences of Mexican modernity. In 1954, at a moment when the capital's tramway culture was declining,[73] Luis Buñuel released Illusion Travels by Streetcar, a film about a heroic conductor who attempts to save his favorite tramway from being condemned to the junkyard.[74]

Much has been written on À la recherche as a war novel; it includes many

Figure P1.3. How many meters of railways in Mexico City were financed by Proust's investment? From Mexico Tramways promotional materials, ca. 1910.

passages—most notably in *Finding Time Again*—reflecting on World War I and its effect on Parisian life. Proust's letters to Lionel Hauser offer a chronicle of a different war that unfolded on the opposite end of the globe: the Mexican Revolution. Despite the cultural and geographical distance, Proust followed this armed struggle in great detail and wrote about the intrigues, political assassinations, and economic troubles that riddled the country. Of all the historical events that unfolded in Latin America during Proust's lifetime— the Spanish-American War, the Panama affair, the American invasion of Veracruz—the Mexican Revolution was the one he knew best and the one that had the most direct effect on his life. For almost a decade, his fortunes became entangled with those of Mexico. Proust's catastrophic financial situation in the last years of his life—he considered himself "ruined"—were among the least known collateral damages of the Mexican conflict.

It would be tempting to give this episode a political reading. Proust, a wealthy European, linked his fortune to one of the most traumatic events in Mexican history. Was this an instance of economic exploitation, an early example of global capital contributing to the political instability of a poor country? But Proust did not exploit Mexico. He did not make any money from his investment, and in the end Mexico Tramways turned out to be an important lessons on Latin American history. Proust's finances suffered from this deal—he lost the equivalent of $800,000 in 2013 dollars in these stocks[75]—but Mexico benefited from the deal. The novelist's investment contributed—even if modestly—to the construction of Mexico City's tramway network and to the birth of an early twentieth-century urban culture that was later celebrated by modernist artists and writers. The last tram rolled down the streets of Mexico City many decades ago, but visitors can still see, half-buried under the pavement, the tracks on which the wagons circulated (fig. P1.3). Which section of these tracks, one wonders, was paid for by Proust's investment in Mexico Tramways?

2 Gabriel de Yturri

An Argentinian in Paris

Not all of Proust's Latin American friends were as rich, successful, and integrated into French culture as Reynaldo Hahn. Gabriel de Yturri (figs. 2.1 and 2.2) came from a modest family, spoke French with a thick accent, and stood out as a foreigner in the salons. He was born in 1860 in the village of Yerba Buena, near Tucumán, in northern Argentina, and he did not move to Europe until he was twenty, after a family friend—the British priest Kenelm Vaughan—arranged a scholarship at the English College in Lisbon.[1] Gabriel remained in Portugal only a few months before making his way to Paris, where he found a job selling ties at Le Carnaval de Venise, a fashionable store near the Louvre. In 1885, when he was twenty-five, he met Count Robert de Montesquiou, who offered him a position as his personal secretary and took him in as a lover.[2]

Montesquiou—often cited as the main model for the Baron de Charlus in Proust's novel—was a thirty-year-old poet and socialite who lived in his family's mansion on the Quai d'Orsay, where he had created an apartment (fig. 2.3) that was so lavishly—and eccentrically—decorated that it became the model for des Esseintes's home in J. K. Huysman's *Against the Grain*.

Yturri came to share the count's passion for collecting and acquiring memorabilia and became an expert at scouting for paintings, sculptures, and antiques to furnish their numerous residences. One of his most celebrated finds was a monolithic marble basin that had once belonged to Madame de Pompadour, Louis XV's mistress. Yturri successfully negotiated to buy this vast tub—it was more than eighteen feet wide and weighed over a ton—and then arranged for it to be excavated, transported on a horse-drawn cart across town, and installed at Montesquiou's villa in Neuilly in 1900 (figs. 2.4 and 2.5). The Montesquiou papers at the Bibliothèque Nationale contain two photos showing a triumphant Yturri, riding

Figure 2.1. Photo of Gabriel de Yturri, ca. 1885–1890. Département de Manuscrits, NaFr 15146, f. 18, Bibliothèque Nationale de France, Paris.

Figure 2.2. Robert de Montesquiou, *Sketch of Gabriel de Yturri*. Département de Manuscrits, NaFr 15146, f.14, Bibliothèque Nationale de France, Paris.

Figure 2.3. Photo of Robert de Montesquiou's apartment, Quai d'Orsay, 1880s. Département de Manuscrits, NaFr 15037, f. 126, Bibliothèque Nationale de France.

atop the marble basin, beaming with pride like a hunter with his trophy. "Yturri loved this basin so much," Montesquiou later explained, "that he wanted to add to its past pedigree a more contemporary contribution,"[3] so the couple asked their poet friends to compose verses to the tub. Anna de Noailles and Jean Lorrain accepted the invitation, and the count capped the literary homage with a sonnet praising the object's illustrious past.

> Les larmes des objets sont dans ce bloc de Rance,
> Vasque de Montespan, miroir de Pompadour,
> Piscine qui mesure un incroyable tour,
> Et, du faste des dieux, symbolise l'outrance
>
> Les filons azurés, les veines de garance,
> Du bleu sang de nos rois, du sang vif de l'amour,
> Dans ce marbre immortel mêlent, encore un jour,
> Le souverain Éros aux monarques de France.

Des lignes de batiste ont traîné sur ces bords;
Les uns glissant au long de voluptueux corps,
Les autres ablués aux doigts de mains pieuses.

Car l'*Hermitage*, qui fut temple à Cupido,
Devient chapelle; et des candeurs religieuses,
Frôlant l'impur bassin, le changement d'âme et d'eau.[4]

(Objects' tears within the marbled block from Rance
Montespan's basin, Pompadour's looking glass
Pool of girth beyond belief
That all the pomp of gods exceeds.

In azured skeins and veins of madder
Blue blood of kings and scarlet blood of love
Shall mingle still in this immortal marble
Sovereign Eros with the Royalty of France.

White batiste pleats have brushed along this rim;
Some over a voluptuous body sliding,
Others by pious fingers softly rinsed.

Just as the *Hermitage,* that once was Cupid's temple,
Is now a shrine, so blessed whiteness th'impure basin
Cleansed, for soul and water both to be refreshed.)

Proust did not participate in this poetic mania, but he proposed to pay homage to the tub in person. "Allow me, one day," he wrote the count in 1901, "to come and see you by the basin that bathes its marbled flesh in the waters that yesteryear caressed the less voluptuous body of Madame de Pompadour."[5]

Montesquiou and Yturri became inseparable (see plate 5), and after some time they began to look alike. The two were tall, slender, smart dressers, and they often wore what seem like identical versions of the same outfit. They photographed themselves incessantly, looking like doubles, as we can see in the series of photos taken by Otto in 1886 (fig. 2.6). The humorist Sem (the pseudonym of Georges Goursat, 1863-1934) drew several cartoons of Montesquiou and Yturri, playing on their physical and sartorial similarities. Ilán de Casa Fuerte, a good friend of Proust's who also knew the couple well, wrote that "Yturri had become Montesquiou's shadow, his twin soul."[6]

Figure 2.4. Photo of Gabriel de Yturri atop the marble basin that once belonged to Madame de Pompadour, Neuilly, Pavillon des Muses, 1900. Département de Manuscrits, NaFr 15049, f. 8, Bibliothèque Nationale de France, Paris.

Figure 2.5. Photo of the marble basin that once belonged to Madame de Pompadour being transported on a horse-drawn cart, Neuilly, Pavillon des Muses, 1900. Département de Manuscrits, NaFr, f. 142, Bibliothèque Nationale de France, Paris.

Figure 2.6. Otto Wegener, Paris, *Robert de Montesquiou and Gabriel de Yturri in Conversation at the Apartment at 41, quai d'Orsay, ca. 1886–1888.* Albumen print, 9 x 6 cm. Robert de Montesquiou, *Ego imago: Mes photographies,* album II, folio 33. Private collection. *Robert de Montesquiou ou L'art de paraître* (Paris: Réunion des Musées Nationaux, 2000), 63.

Marcel met the couple in 1893, when he was a twenty-two-year old aspiring writer who had only published a handful of articles. He was starstruck by Montesquiou, who was aristocratic—he came from one of the oldest families in France and traced his lineage back to the Merovingians—rich, and, at thirty-eight, already a celebrity who had inspired literary portraits by Huysmans, Lorrain, and other novelists.[7] Yturri was younger—thirty-three —more down to earth, and easier to pin down: Marcel often wrote to Gabriel asking him for help in obtaining a rendezvous with the count.[8] In his letters, Marcel seems more comfortable writing to Yturri; he addressed Montesquiou as "Monsieur" but used a more familiar tone with Gabriel and called him "poet, colleague, and friend."[9] He developed a genuine affection for the Argentine, whose wit, intelligence, and literary talent he praised in his correspondence.[10]

After Marcel met Reynaldo, the two couples began to go out on double dates to dinners, recitals, poetry readings, and other society gatherings. When Marcel and Reynaldo performed their *Portraits de peintres*—their first collaboration—at La Bodinière in 1897, the count and his Argentine friend were among the guests.[11] Marcel lived with his parents, but this did not stop him from inviting Reynaldo, Montesquiou, and Yturri to dinner at his apartment.[12] Montesquiou, who had always been fond of doubles, probably saw Marcel and Reynaldo as a younger version of himself and Yturri. Like his own friend, Reynaldo was a Latin American—albeit from a very different background. Both Marcel and the count would have been struck by the differences between their southern companions. Reynaldo had assimilated to the point that few people recognized him as a foreigner, while Gabriel spoke French with a thick Spanish accent and never fully mastered the intricate social codes of Parisian life. Yturri was a conspicuous outsider, and many of the count's friends mocked his pronunciation.[13] Watching him, Proust learned much about class and cultural differences—observations he would later transpose into one of his early texts, a chronicle of a soirée at Montesquiou's to be discussed later in this chapter.

The four friends moved in the same circles, frequented the same salons, and even performed together on several occasions. Reynaldo would play the piano, and Montesquiou would recite poems dramatically while Gabriel, from the audience, applauded and extolled his friend's literary genius, as we can see in figure 2.7 and other caricatures of the period. The young Marcel saw Montesquiou as the type of literary figure he aspired to become: elegant, famous, and integrated into the aristocratic society he would later immortalize in *À la recherche du temps perdu*.

Marcel and Gabriel began exchanging letters in 1894 and maintained a regular correspondence until the Argentine's death in 1905. In these missives, they plan their upcoming social engagements, review the most recent soirées, discuss literature, and comment on each other's work. Most people knew Gabriel as Montesquiou's secretary and sidekick; few realized he was a talented writer with a special gift for narrative and the author of hundreds of travel chronicles, essays, and stories—mostly written in letters to the count. Occasionally, he would share a text with a few close friends, including Marcel, who read his poems and stories and praised the "grace and erudition" of his prose.[14] Proust, too, sent his work to Gabriel, including a copy of his first book, *Les plaisirs et les jours* (1896), with a gracious dedication stressing their kinship as budding writers.[15] Gabriel never published, and Montesquiou destroyed all of his correspondence and papers after his

LE COMTE ROBERT DE MONTESQUIOU A NEW-YORK

Figure 2.7. Sem [pseudonym of Georges Goursat], caricature of Robert de Montes-quiou lecturing in New York. Gabriel de Yturri, in the audience, exclaims "Prodi-gieux." *Le Gaulois,* January 18, 1903. Département de Manuscrits, NaFr 15063, f. 159-60, Bibliothèque Nationale de France, Paris.

death, though he reproduced some excerpts and letters in *Le chancelier de fleurs.*

Gabriel returned to Argentina only once, when he was thirty years old. In 1890 he spent six months in Tucumán and Buenos Aires. Just before boarding the ship that would take him back to Europe, civil strife broke out in the capital—a repeat of the political upheaval he had witnessed as a student, just before moving to Europe. In a letter to his mother, he marveled at the unhappy coincidence of having lived through two revolutions—1880 and 1890—during the brief time he spent in Buenos Aires.[16]

Yturri as Foreigner

Yturri's accent and his passionate temper made him stand out in the aris-tocratic salons of the Faubourg Saint-Germain, where he was considered an exotic presence and an inscrutable stranger. Many in Proust's circle were intrigued by his origins and wrote literary portraits of him. One of the most telling is by Léon Daudet, another friend of Proust's whose father, Alphonse, hosted one of the most celebrated literary salons of the nineteenth century, frequented by Marcel, Reynaldo, Montesquiou, and Yturri. In his memoirs, the famously harsh—and later anti-Semitic and monarchist—Léon mocks Montesquiou as a pretentious exhibitionist, but he presents an extremely empathetic portrait of Yturri. "Gabriel de Yturri," he wrote, "was, to my mind, far superior, in intelligence and sensibility, to his superconquentious master." [17] Léon became especially fond of the Argentine after he opened up to him.

> Comme [Yturri] avait tout de suite démêlé que je me fichais profondément du "pavillon des muses", de la baignoire de la Montespan, des pendules de Boule et des mobiliers de Riesener, en même temps que des hortensias bleus, verts, ou noirs, et que la poésie du maître de céans ne m'amusait guère, il ouvrait le compartiment moral et me racontait rapidement, à la dérobée, comme un gosse chapardeur qui mange un fruit, de savoureuses histoires sur les invités et les belles dames. Ce Tallemant des Réaux à l'accent espagnol avait le don de saisir les mouvements des âmes sous le masque mondain et de typifier la sottise ambiante. Il y avait en lui l'étoffe d'un puissant satirique. Son œil passait de la douceur mélancolique à la colère avec une promptitude ensoleillée et, s'il était perplexe devant un beau cas, il tripotait d'une main nerveuse un grain de beauté qu'il avait au visage. D'où venait-il, qui était-il, je l'ignore. Il semblait détaché de tout, bien qu'attaché en apparence à mille futilités. Il avait le cœur chaud, le geste frénétique, le sens du lyrisme et il voyait presque tout en noir, tel qu'une flamme promenée sur le néant.[18]

(Since [Yturri] instantly perceived that I did not care a fig for the "Pavilion of Muses," Montespan's bathtub, the Boule clocks or the Reisener furniture, any more than I did for hydrangeas be they blue, green or black, and that I was not taken with the poetry of mine host, he opened the moral compartment and began to regale me, as fast and furtively as a naughty boy gobbling down a fruit, with racy stories about the guests and their lovely ladies. This Tallemant des Réaux with a Spanish accent had a gift for discerning the movements of the soul beneath the worldly mask, and typifying the current silliness. He had the makings of a powerful satirist. His gaze would vary from melancholy mildness to anger with genial speed, and, when flummoxed by some especially fine case, he would nervously pluck at the beauty spot on his cheek. Where did he come from, who was he? I do not know. He seemed detached from everything, despite his apparent attachment to innumerable trifles. His heart was warm and his manner frantic, he was sensitive to lyricism and saw almost everything in black, like a flame flickering over the void.)

Daudet's portrait suggests Yturri was playing a role when he was around Montesquiou—he was, as Proust would later show in his short piece "Fête chez Montesquiou," a master *pasticheur,* imitating the count's style, gestures, and obsessions. Léon's lack of interest in the count's world—full of antiques and extravagant collectibles—led Yturri to let down his mask and show his real self.

Yturri's impersonations of the count's guests and their wives demonstrate a special gift for satire and for seeing through appearances—"a gift for discerning the movements of the soul beneath the worldly mask, and typifying the current silliness"—that captivated Léon, who was himself a great satirist and penned some of the most scathing chronicles of the belle époque. Daudet called Yturri "a Tallemant des Réaux with a Spanish accent," referring to the seventeenth-century author of *Historiettes,* a juicy collection of behind-the-scenes tales of courtly life that included portraits of kings Henri IV and Louis XIII, as well as sketches of La Fontaine, Pierre Corneille, Blaise Pascal, and Marie de Sevigné. Daudet assimilates Yturri into the French literary tradition and suggests that despite his exotic appearance, his wit and psychological intelligence placed him in the company of classical French writers.

Daudet is intrigued by the contrast between Yturri's public persona and his real self, between the *pasticheur* of Montesquiou's style and the master parodist, between the seemingly frivolous *mondain* and the clear-minded observer of the world. But Daudet is even more intrigued by the contrast between the world Yturri inhabits and his native land. "Where he came from, who he was, I do not know," he admits, before exclaiming, "This unique young man has remained for me a living riddle."[19]

Paul Verlaine—a Montesquiou protégé whose texts inspired a series of Reynaldo's *chansons*—left a very different portrait of the count's secretary. Yturri had met the poet around 1890, when Montesquiou began to help this starving artist and poète maudit. Verlaine often sent Yturri—on scraps of paper written in the hospital—desperate pleas for money to be transmitted to the count. "A loan of some hundred francs for essential expenses";[20] "lend me a fifty-franc note that would tide me over till the first days of March";[21] "I'd be most obliged if you would advance me an immediate sum by post to

no 39 (not 37) rue Descartes."[22] Verlaine even made one request in pidgin
English: "If it were possible to you," he pleaded, "how much thank-full for
an immediate money! *Par le facteur ou mieux par vous même* (By way of the
postman or better by your own hand.)"[23] But the funds never arrived quickly
enough, and the poet lamented: "The people who give me money are slow,
so slow! I must finally appeal to all kind hearts!"[24]

Like Léon Daudet, Verlaine was intrigued by Yturri's foreign origins, and
a sonnet he composed for him in 1893—to thank him for his help in securing
the count's financial assistance—zeroes in on his exotic background.

Yturry [*sic*]! C'est un nom terrible,
Évocation de Pyrénées
Prises, reprises, rançonnées
Par un chef au visage horrible.

Œil de feu sous le sombrero
Il se moque un peu du bourreau,
Tel le torero du taureau,
Balles pleuvent comme d'un crible,

Femmes se sauvant, dépeignées,
Par quels bras affreux empoignées,
Tout voyageur est une cible . . .

Fi! c'est le Cavalier exquis
Tout à l'ami qu'il a conquis
Parmi quelques Amaéguis.[25]

(Yturry [*sic*]! Terrifying name,
That brings to mind the Pyrenees
Seized, retaken, held to ransom
By some chief of horrid mien.

The fierce sombrero-shaded eye
Mocks the executioner somewhat
As toreros mock the *toro*. Bullets
Raining as through a sieve,

Women fleeing, all disheveled,
Dragged away in uncouth arms
Any traveler is at risk . . .

But no! This is Sir Exquisite
Fawning on the friend he conquered
Amidst a few Amaëguis.)

The sonnet plays on Yturri's status as a foreigner and on his passionate character. "Yturri is a te*rr*ible name," he writes, playing on the double *r,* so common in Spanish but unpronounceable in French, that marked
his friend's accent. Verlaine's free associations lead him to evoke Spain—
"Terrifying name/That brings to mind the Pyrenees"—and the myriad conflicts and civil wars that had plagued that country ("seized, retaken, held to
ransom.") As Proust would later do in his pastiche, Verlaine associates Yturri
with Spain, but in this case it is the Spain of Bizet's *Carmen* and Reynaldo's
Conchita Ciboulero: a stereotypical land full of "bulls," "bullfighters," and
"sombreros."

The last stanza interrupts the scenes of carnage and revolution with a
dramatic "Fi!" All fighting ends, and Yturri emerges from the debris, an "exquisite knight," who is "everything to the friend he has conquered." The
only conquest in the poem is thus a romantic and not a military one; Yturri
conquers his friend "amidst a few Amaëguis." The Marquise of Amaëgui
was a stock character in nineteenth-century French literature, a beautiful—
and exotic—Spanish woman, a Carmen-like seductress.[26] The last stanzas
allude to Yturri and Montesquiou's relationship. Yturri is "everything" to the
"friend he conquered amidst a few Amaéguis." Verlaine suggests the Argentine could have chosen among myriad Spanish seductresses, but he elected,
instead, to live with a French aristocrat.

Verlaine's portrait is more impressionistic than Daudet's. He paints Yturri
as a fiery southerner, at the mercy of his passions, who came from a region
torn apart by revolutions and civil wars. Interestingly, the poem focuses on
the Argentine's origins and it does not say much about the world he inhabited with Montesquiou. Like Léon Daudet, Verlaine seems more intrigued
by his foreign past than by his life with the count.

Most of the count's friends were not as subtle when it came to judging Yturri. The aristocrats in his circle never accepted him, and many of
them considered it a disgrace that Montesquiou had chosen a foreigner as
a companion. The Comtesse Greffulhe—who became a model for Proust's
descriptions of the elegant aristocratic woman—once called him "a South
American of questionable background" who became "Montesquiou's soi-
disant secretary, companion, and adored and adoring slave for many years."

She accused him of being a thief, blaming him for not returning the chin-chilla cape the count borrowed to pose for the famous Whistler portrait, now at the Frick Collection. But, above all, she considered the count's attachment to Yturri a treason to his class: "The very last thing he did [. . .] none of us could understand. It shocked us very much that he chose to be buried at Versailles next to that thief Yturri instead of in the Merovingian cemetery with his own family."[27] The countess's harsh words are a good indication of the violence with which the Faubourg Saint-Germain rejected those who did not belong. And Yturri had a triple reason to be excluded—he was a commoner, a foreigner, and a homosexual.

Ilán de Casa Fuerte recalls that "a good number of people refused to re-ceive Yturri,"[28] and Philippe Jullian, Montesquiou's biographer, adds that the count's father was one of them. Whenever the couple traveled together to the family château, Count Thierry would utter a series of insults "of which *rasta* was the least offensive."[29] Many of the count's friend called Yturri a "rasta"—short for *rastaquouère*—behind his back.[30]

As we saw in the introduction, the figure of the *rastaquouère*—a rich, gaudy, and extravagant Latin American—was a stock character of nine-teenth-century French literature from Balzac to Feydeau. It seems surpris-ing that Yturri would be considered a *rasta*: unlike Offenbach's Brazilian or Feydeau's General Irrigua, Yturri did not arrive in Paris with millions to spend. On the contrary, he was penniless, and even if he later shared Mon-tesquiou's apartments and lifestyle, he never amassed a personal fortune. In contrast to the *rastaquouère*, famous for displaying the worst possible taste in clothes, Yturri let the count set the fashion standards—which Proust and others admired as the *nec plus ultra* of elegance—and followed them to the letter.

The meaning of *rastaquouère* had evolved through the nineteenth cen-tury, and by the time Proust met Yturri, this slur had acquired new connota-tions. The Nicaraguan poet Rubén Darío, who lived in Paris during the first years of the twentieth century and wrote an insightful article called "The Evolution of *Rastacuerism*," argued that *rastaquouère* designated individuals lacking culture and good taste and that even though the French capital was full of foreigners of all nationalities who fit this description, the term contin-ued to be directed primarily at Latin Americans, owing to "the apparent in-justice Parisians display against Spanish Americans, when there are so many Wallachians, Greeks, and Levantines who deserve this famous epithet."[31] Darío noted that in the French imagination the *rastaquouère* "loves wearing precious stones," yet "no one would dare to call Robert de Montesquiou a *rastaquouère*."[32]

Darío did not know Yturri, but if he had, he would have noticed that though the count and his friend dressed, spoke, and acted alike to the point that they had become doubles, it was only Yturri who was considered a *rasta*. In this case, the epithet had nothing to do with taste or riches; it was simply a pejorative marker of national origin. Incidentally, Darío almost attended a party given by Montesquiou in 1902 to which Reynaldo Hahn was also invited. Had he attended, he could have met two of Proust's Latin Americans at Montesquiou's Pavillon des Muses (and he might have concluded that Montesquiou, by association, was more *rasta* than he had thought.)[33]

The term had thus evolved from its earlier connotation of excessive riches—the sense Proust gives it in the novel[34]—to become a generic slur for Latin Americans. But not all Latin Americans were *rastas*. The insult was not used against travelers simply passing through but rather against those who had settled in Paris and had adopted a French lifestyle. And it does not appear to have been used against those who assimilated to the point of being indistinguishable from the French. Reynaldo Hahn, for instance, was never called a *rasta* (though, as we saw, he was called other names, including "exotique inconnu").[35] Darío writes that he once even heard someone referring to the poet José-Maria de Heredia—who wrote in French, hosted a celebrated salon, and was elected to the Académie française—as a "*rasta*."[36] Yturri was a *rastaquouère* not because he was an uncultured millionaire but because he was a Latin American who adopted French language and customs while maintaining markers of difference—a foreign accent and a fiery temper.

Ironically, Yturri came to be seen as an outsider in his own country as well. The Franco-Argentinean writer Paul Groussac (1849-1929), who taught Yturri when he was a schoolboy at Tucumán's Colegio Nacional and whose caustic prose is mentioned by Jorge Luis Borges in his essay "The Art of Injury"—later ran into him in Paris, at Edmond de Goncourt's house, and left a scathing portrait in his memoirs.

[. . .] de repente se abre la puerta para dar paso a la inefable Pélagie que anuncia: *"Monsieur Gabriel de Iturri, secrétaire du comte de Montesquiou."* Y hace su entrada un joven acicalado, afeitado, amaricado, luciendo un lunar velloso en la pintada mejilla, y exhibiendo en su vestir el nauseoso rebuscamiento de una chaqueta de negro terciopelo, chaleco blanco y ancha corbata punzó prendida con sortija de brillante. El fantoche se acerca, esparciendo un olor de patchouli y, con una estereotipada sonrisa de bailarina, que enseña la más deslumbrante dentadura, tiende la mano a Goncourt, que le deja tocar la suya tras una imperceptible vacilación (pero ¡el secretario de un conde auténtico!) [. . .] esboza hacia mí un movimiento que contengo con la mano abierta.[37]

(. . . suddenly the door opened to admit the ineffable Pélagie, who announced: *"Monsieur Gabriel de Iturri, secrétaire du comte de Montesquiou."* In stepped a soigné, shaven, foppish youth with a hairy mole on his painted cheek, whose nauseatingly affected garb included a black velvet jacket, white gilet and broad red cravat traversed by a diamond pin. The popinjay advanced in a cloud of patchouli, and with a stereotyped dancer's smile, designed to expose his dazzling teeth, extended a hand to Goncourt, who allowed his own to be touched only after a smothered struggle (after all, it's the secretary of an authentic count!) [. . .] then started toward me in a movement which I checked with upraised hand.)

Groussac continues with a two-page harangue against Yturri. He calls him "desgraciado," laments his "career of vice and shame," recalls a cross-dressing performance he once did as a schoolboy, and closes with a jab against Montesquiou, "that degenerate scion of an old and illustrious military family."[38]

No doubt there was an element of jealousy in Groussac's outburst. Even though he was French, no one had heard of Groussac in Paris, while Yturri, as Montesquiou's secretary, was a fixture of salons, poetry readings, and literary soirées. Of the two, Gabriel was the more Parisian, while the expatriated Frenchman embodied all the provincial prejudices, intolerance, and small-mindedness that Gabriel had left behind in Tucumán. Yturri and Groussac seem to have traded places: Groussac, born in France, acts like a macho Tucumanian writer, while Yturri performs the role of the French androgynous dandy. Groussac also displays a textbook example of the reaction queer theorists have termed "homosexual panic." The sight of a joyful, perfumed Yturri, attired in velvet, sends the sartorially conservative writer into a rage. And he refuses to shake his hand, lest he be contaminated by "the popinjay"—as if Parisian dandyism were a communicable disease.

More recently, Argentinean writers from Juan José Hernández to Carlos Paez de la Torre have sought to reclaim Yturri as one of their own. In 1983, Hugo Foguet (1923-1985) published *Pretérito perfecto,* a novel in which one of the characters visits Yturri's grave. "Imagine," he writes, "a count with a secretary born in Yerba Buena [. . .] he attained a fragment of immortality in the pages of a great novel."[39] Juan José Hernández (1931-2007), Tucumán's most famous writer, spent the last years of his life writing a novel about Yturri's odyssey from provincial lad to metropolitan dandy,[40] and he also composed a playful poem rectifying Groussac's snub that ends with the following stanzas:

> No te hiere el severo y acaso candoroso
> rechazo de Groussac porque comprendes
> que en la ciudad festiva donde el azar
> los ha reunido, a pesar de su origen
> el extranjero es él.
>   Risueño y atildado,
> olvidas de inmediato el incidente fútil
> para volver a tus tareas de secretario
> de Montesquiou, el arbitrario conde un tanto cursi
> cuya tiránica arrogancia has conseguido dominar.
>
> Afuera, deslumbrante y efímera,
> *La belle époque fourmille de monstres innocents.*[41]

> (You are not hurt by Groussac's harsh and
> perhaps naive recoil, because you know
> that in this festive city where you meet again
> by chance, the foreigner—despite his origins—
> is him.
>   Laughing and spruce,
> you forget about the feeble slight at once,
> returning to your secretarial tasks with Montesquiou,
> the peremptory, somewhat tasteless count
> whose despotism you have overcome.

> Outside, dazzling and short-lived,

> La belle époque fourmille de monstres innocents.
> (*the Belle Epoque swarms with innocent monsters.*))

This wave of interest culminated with the publication of *El Argentino de oro*, the most complete Yturri biography to date, written by Carlos Páez de la Torre, a journalist from Tucumán. Though Argentinians are now fascinated by Yturri and his proximity to Proust, during his lifetime his countrymen were less open, and at times it seems that he was treated as a foreigner both in France and in his native land. Like Proust's narrator, Yturri belonged without truly belonging anywhere—except, perhaps, at the side of Robert de Montesquiou.

Fête Chez Montesquiou à Neuilly

In 1904 Proust wrote a literary portrait of Yturri in one of his pastiches, "Fête chez Montesquiou à Neuilly. Extrait des Mémoires du duc de Saint-Simon," a playful text that imagines Montesquiou and Yturri in the eighteenth-century courtly world chronicled by Saint-Simon in his *Mémoires*. Engaging in one of his favorite literary exercises, Marcel imitates the duke's language, tone, style, and even literary tics as he describes the inseparable couple.

> [Robert de Montesquiou] had often at his side a Spaniard, by name Yturri, whom I had met during my embassy at Madrid, as it has been written. In an age when none aspires to more than the profitable advertisement of his own worth, this fellow possessed the rarest of virtues, consistent in the employment of his every merit solely for the enhancement of the Count's, by assisting in his researches and dealings with librarians, and even with the laying of his table, for no task found he wearisome provided it spare the count the least inconvenience; his duty being merely to hear Montesquiou's utterances and spread them far and wide, like the disciples by whom the ancient Sophists were perpetually surrounded, as is evident in the writings of Aristotle and the dialogues of Plato. This Yturri had retained the excitable temper of his countrymen, who whip up a storm at every little thing, and for this Montesquiou would chide him often and most wittily, to the merriment of the company and above all of Yturri himself, who laughingly deplored the hot-headedness of his kind while taking every care to persevere in it, since obviously it pleased. He was knowledgeable about antiquities and this led many to seek his opinion, even as far as the retreat which our two hermits had found in the village of Neuilly, as I have said, not far from the house of His Grace the Duke of Orléans.[42]

Proust published a first version of this pastiche in *Le Figaro* in 1904, using the pseudonym "Horatio" for fear of offending Montesquiou.[43] The count found the portrait flattering and had the text reprinted in a *plaquette* he distributed among his friends. Eventually, Marcel acknowledged his authorship of the piece, and in 1909 he wrote Montesquiou to ask him for a copy—he had lost the original—so he could revise and expand it for inclusion in the collection that would be published in 1919 as *Pastiches et mélanges*, a volume that also included imitations of Gustave Flaubert, Henri de Régnier, the Goncourt brothers, Jules Michelet, Émile Faguet, and Ernest Renan. Montesquiou obliged and responded, "Enclosed: the pastiche whose paternity you have (finally!) decided to accept."[44]

The portrait of Montesquiou and Yturri is the longest and most elaborate of the texts included in *Pastiches et mélanges*; it grew from eight to twenty-eight pages when Proust revised it for inclusion in the volume. The longer version incorporates the earlier portrait of the couple into a story inspired, like the rest of the pastiches in the book, by the Lemoine Affair. A minor scandal had unfolded between 1904 and 1909, when an engineer named Henri Lemoine announced he had found a new procedure for manufacturing diamonds and convinced important financiers—including an officer of De Beers—to fund his researches. Eventually, he was exposed, tried for fraud, and sentenced to six years in prison. Proust seized on this *fait divers,* chronicled in *Le Figaro* and other major newspapers, as a pretext for imitating the style of major French writers.

In his pastiche of Saint-Simon, a text in which Saint-Simon himself appears as narrator, Proust imagines that Lemoine (identified as Le Moine, to keep with eighteenth-century spelling) has gained the confidence of the Duke of Orléans during the Regency following Louis XIV's death. Saint-Simon warns the gullible duke against Le Moine's duplicity and advises him to have him arrested. "Arrested?" retorts the regent. "And if his invention happened to be true?"[45] Proust's Saint-Simon then launches into a passionate tirade against tricksters like Le Moine who seek to occupy a social position beyond their rank—a diatribe that seems lifted verbatim from the original *Mémoires*: "On sait où conduisent ces sourdes et profondes menées de princerie quand elles ne sont pas étouffées dans l'œuf" (We know where these muffled, abyssal princely pretentions lead when they are not smothered in ovo). In the midst of this intrigue, the regent arranges a reception for the king of England at Saint-Cloud—a fictional banquet that allows Proust to introduce Montesquiou, Yturri, and other friends as imaginary guests at the royal reception.

By inserting Montesquiou and Yturri into a pastiche of Saint-Simon's memoirs, Proust offers an incisive commentary on the couple's place in French society. In his voluminous *Mémoires*—one of the crucial literary influences on Proust's novel—the Duke of Saint-Simon (1675-1755) composed a detailed chronicle of everyday life in the courts of Louis XIV and his successor, the Duke of Orléans, who ruled as regent until Louis XV was of age to assume the throne. Saint-Simon had a sharp eye for detail and a gift for irony, and he was especially fond of narrating the minor scandals that plagued the palace: the breaches of protocol, the usurpation of titles and privileges, and the caustic repartee overheard at dinners and receptions. This world was a perfect setting for Montesquiou, a famous snob, who often reminded those around him that he came from one of the oldest families in France. (In the text Proust hyperbolically describes his lineage as "one thousand years old.")[46] By projecting the count into Saint-Simon's text—through an operation Jean Milly has described as "temporal dissonance"[47]—Proust pokes fun at his pretentions and presents him like a living anachronism. Montesquiou lived in the Third Republic, more than a hundred years after the French Revolution abolished aristocratic privileges, but he acted—like Charlus in *À la recherche*—as if nothing had changed since the reign of Louis XIV.

In addition to Montesquiou, Proust inserts several of his aristocratic friends and acquaintances—Elisabeth de Clermont-Tonnerre, the Comtesse Greffulhe, Anna de Noailles, the Duc de Guiche—into his text. The first version of the pastiche—as Jean Milly showed—"included only persons whose ancestors were named in the *Mémoires*," with one notable exception: Gabriel de Yturri (and Le Moine, who appears not only as a con artist but also as a social climber).[48] Yturri is the odd one out in the text; he is a commoner, the only character who cannot trace his lineage to the reign of Louis XIV. How are we to read this insertion of Yturri into a world in which he does not belong? Is Proust, like many of the count's least sympathetic friends, criticizing Yturri for being an outsider, an intruder into the Faubourg Saint-Germain? The contrast between this Argentine and a group of French nobles would seem to suggest so, as would the fact that the only other plebeian happens to be Le Moine, a confidence man.

But if we read the text carefully, we discover that Yturri is not the lone plebeian in this otherwise regal world. The pastiche features another individual who does not come from a noble family, who does not have illustrious ancestors named in Saint-Simon's *Mémoires,* and who could also be described as a parvenu in the Faubourg Saint-Germain: Marcel Proust, who did not include himself as a character. As a bourgeois who was also half Jewish, he could have been as out of place in the royal receptions chronicled by Saint-Simon as the Argentine secretary. "Fête chez Montesquiou" thus suggests a kinship between Yturri and Proust, two commoners who made their way to the Faubourg Saint-Germain and who, despite gaining varying levels of acceptance, never fully belonged in this aristocratic world.

At first glance, the pastiche seems to present a rather superficial portrait of Montesquiou and Yturri. As in many of the texts published during his most social years, before he retreated from the world to compose À la recherche, Proust indulges in flattery; he extols the virtues of an elegant host in order to secure an invitation to a dinner or a party. Proust had already written a number of articles on Montesquiou, including "Une fête littéraire à Versailles" (1894)[49] and "De la simplicité de Robert de Montesquiou," unpublished during his lifetime.[50] The pastiche of Saint-Simon continues the laudatory intent, evoking Montesquiou's illustrious ancestry (the Montesquious, the narrator recounts, tongue-in-cheek, pretended they descended from Farmund, a legendary 4th century king of the Franks, "as if their antiquity were not great or acknowledged enough in order for them not to have the need to fabricate fables")[51] and singing his praises as a gentleman and a host. Yturri, too, is presented in the most admiring of terms. Despite his hot temper (he "had retained the excitable temper of his countrymen, who whip up a storm at every little thing"), he possesses "the rarest of virtues" (faithfulness), is "knowledgeable about antiquities," and is also a connoisseur of books.[52]

Proust's portrait of Yturri is more complex and intriguing than the one he offers of Montesquiou, and it raises a number of questions about the novelist's perception of his friend. Yturri, for instance, is introduced as "a Spaniard," even though Proust had always known he was an Argentine[53] and would have been aware of the cultural differences between Argentina and Spain. Why, then, would Proust turn his Argentine into a Spaniard?

An obvious reason would be to fit Yturri into the world of the Mémoires. Saint-Simon never wrote about Argentina, but he did write a fair amount about Spain, where he served as the regent's ambassador from 1721 to 1722. Proust plays on this historical reference by having the narrator state that he met Yturri "during my embassy at Madrid, as it has been written,"[54] and the author also uses the pastiche to project himself, writing in the first person, into Spain, a country he never visited. Proust was fond of using literature to travel to countries he would never visit—as we saw in the earlier discussion of his taste for reading train schedules in bed—and in this case it was Yturri who served as a pretext for an imaginary cosmopolitan experience.

Interestingly, Proust's—and Saint-Simon's—Spain is entirely different from the stereotypical land of gypsies and toreros most of Proust's contemporaries would have known from French art, music, and literature. Unlike the Spain of Bizet's Carmen or Verlaine's poetry, Saint-Simon's Spain was not a land marked by cultural alterity. On the contrary, during his ambassadorship in Spain, the duke worked on the delicate mission of arranging a marriage between the future Louis XV and the Spanish infanta, an alliance that would have effectively united France and Spain under a single crown. While the project ultimately failed, it still managed to spread anxiety among France's rivals. Saint-Simon considered Spain a sister kingdom, one that could naturally be united with France, and regarded Spaniards as members of an extended family.

By turning Yturri into an eighteenth-century Spaniard, Proust dissolves the aura of exoticism that enveloped his friend. Montesquiou once described Yturri as a "*jeune sauvage*, a young savage and a [. . .] southerner from America";[55] Proust, in contrast, imagined him as a fellow European. As an Argentine in the Faubourg Saint-Germain, Yturri stood out as a foreigner; as a Spaniard in the France of Saint-Simon, he would have fit in as a distant relative. As we saw in chapter 1, Proust also imagined Reynaldo Hahn as a Spaniard in one of his poems—"Where then did I read, Holy Virgin!/In the *Imparcial* or in the *Heraldo*/[. . .] That Spanish was Reynaldo"[56]—even though he had known from the beginning his friend was a Venezuelan. Marcel followed a similar strategy in both his letters to Reynaldo and "Fête chez Montesquiou"; he used pastiches to project his friends into the realm of European high culture. He imagined Reynaldo sculpted into a French cathedral, and he made Gabriel a character in Saint-Simon's *Mémoires,* linking these friends to two monuments—one architectural, the other literary—of French history and tradition. Reynaldo and Gabriel were foreigners who reinvented themselves as guardians of French culture. One championed the tradition of French music; the other developed an expertise in French books, antiquities, and artworks.

But perhaps Proust's most radical commentary on Yturri, and on the question of belonging, can be found in his approach to the pastiche as a genre. In *Palimpsests,* Gérard Genette offers a concise, useful definition of pastiche: both parody and pastiche, he writes, proceed by imitation, but parody mocks the original while pastiche "is an imitation in playful mode whose primary function is pure entertainment."[57] In the case of Proust, we might add that pastiche also renders homage to its model.

If we retain the definition of pastiche as a playful imitation designed as homage, we see that "Fête chez Montesquiou" stages several different forms of pastiche. By inserting Montesquiou and Yturri into a pastiche, Proust plays on a trait many of the couple's friends noticed and discussed.

Figure 2.8. Sem [pseudonym of Georges Goursat], caricature of Robert de Montesquiou and Gabriel de Yturri dining at the Ritz, no date. Département de Manuscrits, NaFr 15067, f. 68, Bibliothèque Nationale de France, Paris.

The Argentine admired the count so much that he not only devoted his life to assisting him with his intellectual and worldly projects—he employed "his every merit solely for the enhancement of the Count's" as we read in the text—but he also ended up speaking, acting, and dressing like Montesquiou. The artist Sem drew several caricatures of Yturri and Montesquiou; one of the most widely published (see plate 6) shows the two dressed in identical tuxedos, fur collars, and top hats. Usually Montesquiou pontificated while Yturri listened, but here the Argentine has adopted one of the count's famous expressions. Back straight, hand raised, finger pointed to the sky, he is delivering a speech with great authority. Yturri had become a *pasticheur* of Montesquiou.

But the admiration that characterizes pastiche went both ways. At times Montesquiou seemed to imitate Yturri imitating him, and at times it became difficult to discern who was imitating whom. Another of Sem's cartoons shows the two friends dining at the Ritz (fig. 2.8). Their postures, dress, and gestures are identical; this time both point upward with their fingers. The many photographs of the couple—including the portrait discussed earlier in this chapter—reveal a perfect mirroring, less a matter of imitation than of doubling. Yturri was a *pasticheur* of Montesquiou, and Montesquiou at times acted like a *pasticheur* of Yturri's pastiche, making it difficult to decide who was imitating whom. And it was this constant game of playful imitations and specular homages that turned them into one of the most original couples of

Figure 2.9. Gabriel de Yturri dressed for a costume party at the Pavillon de Muses. Département de Manuscrits, NaFr 15146, f. 34, Bibliothèque Nationale de France, Paris.

the belle époque, a couple in which there was no original, only imitations of imitations and pastiches in the second and third degree.

Pastiche, along with its fundamental mechanism of imitation, was one of the key elements of the type of dandyism practiced by Montesquiou and Yturri. One of their favorite pastimes was to dress up in period costumes. One photo (fig. 2.9) shows Yturri at the Pavillon des Muses in Neuilly, attired like an Indian maharajah in a silk robe, strings of beads, and a turban crowned by a feather—a living pastiche of Indian garb. On other occasions, the count and his friend imitated the dress of biblical figures, Buddhist monks, Arabic princes, and even Catholic monks.[58] During their years at Versailles, they even indulged in devising a pastiche of landscapes. They

Figure 2.10. Gabriel de Yturri lounging in Robert de Montesquiou's Japanese garden in Versailles, 1894-1897. Département de Manuscrits, NaFr 15146, f. 21, Bibliothèque Nationale de France, Paris.

created a Japanese garden at the Pavillon Montesquiou—tended by a Japanese gardener called Hata—and often donned Japanese-style dress as they lounged around its fountains and bridges (fig. 2.10). It was as if the two friends lived in a perpetual masked ball where there were no fixed identities, only playful imitations and constant pastiches. Gender became a performance, and so did religion, national origin, and all other markers of selfhood. Despite their seemingly conservative context—the aristocratic salons of the belle époque—this performative impulse anticipated by decades the deconstruction of identity proposed by queer theorists like Eve Kosofsky Sedgwick in the 1990s.[59]

Marcel Proust, too, participated in this game of imitations. In his youth he was an avid impersonator of the most colorful literary figures. One of his favorite models was Montesquiou, and he would often regale his friends with performances mimicking the count's voice, gestures, and gait. Montesquiou found out and confronted Marcel, who pleaded not guilty by arguing that pastiche is always an homage: "I have only allowed myself," he wrote in a contrite letter, "to communicate to others my admiration for you" and added that his most recent novella, "La mort de Baldassare Silvande," could

also be considered an imitation of the count's style.[60] The count—like contemporary readers—might have taken Marcel's excuse with a grain of salt,
but as this episode demonstrates, pastiche operates on a fine line between
homage and parody.

As *pasticheur,* Proust shared much with Yturri. Both were commoners in
a world of aristocrats, both proved expert at imitation, and both chose the
same aristocratic model for their performances. The only real differences
between Marcel and Gabriel as imitators of the count were the degree of
involvement—Yturri was closer to his subject and able to observe and emu-
late him more precisely—and cultural origin. Unlike Marcel, Yturri had to
learn the language, customs, and traditions of a new land. Like all foreigners, he proceeded by imitation. One can only learn a new language—and the
customs that go along with it—by mimicking the speech of native speakers,
copying their intonation, tone of voice, and colloquial expressions. Yturri
went a step further, becoming a *pasticheur* of the French language but also
a master *imitator* of the manners and habits of the Faubourg Saint-Germain.

"Fête chez Montesquiou à Neuilly" is thus the ultimate pastiche. Proust
inscribes a portrait of Yturri, *pasticheur* of Montesquiou, within his own
pastiche of the *Mémoires* of Saint-Simon. Pastiche is both the subject of
the text and its primary literary mechanism. Like a set of Chinese boxes,
the pastiche of Yturri is nestled within several others: a *mise-en-abîme* of the
practice of pastiche.

Despite the upbeat and playful tone of "Fête chez Montesquiou à
Neuilly," the text is framed by death. It was published in 1904, one year after
the death of Proust's father and only months before the deaths of Yturri and
Proust's mother in 1905. When Proust wrote this text, Yturri was already
quite ill, and those close to him knew he did not have long to live. But the
text neither mentions nor alludes to death: there are embassies, receptions,
and usurpations, but no one in this imaginary Saint-Simonian universe ever
considers the question of mortality.

Yturri's Malady

In his late thirties, Gabriel was diagnosed with diabetes, and his health
began a slow and painful decline. Friends noticed that he smelled of rotten
apples—a telltale symptom of the disease and a humiliating development
for a dandy.[61] When Marcel got word of his plight, he felt closer than ever
to his Argentine friend.[62] Marcel had always been frail and sickly—and a bit
of a hypochondriac—and by his early thirties, he spent most of the spring

and summer months in bed, paralyzed by hay fever, allergies, and asthma attacks. He felt that only those who suffered from grave illnesses could understand him. In one letter he addressed Yturri as a "colleague in malady,"[63] and in another he told Montesquiou, "I know that Yturri's condition is serious. I know it better than anyone."[64]

At one point Marcel arranged for Gabriel to have a consultation with his father, Dr. Adrien Proust, an eminent physician who had published a treatise on diabetes that Montesquiou acquired for his library.[65] Dr. Proust recommended that Yturri spend time in dry climates,[66] and though he followed the recommendation—he spent long periods away from Paris in Italy, Greece, and Algeria—the malady had run its course. Montesquiou attributed the illness to the violent change in climate between Tucumán and Paris and blamed the "expatriation and the transplantation into an environment that is so different from that of his race."[67] Gabriel died in 1905, at age forty-five, at the Pavillon des Muses.

Montesquiou buried his friend at the Gonards cemetery in Versailles, in a simple, unadorned tomb crowned by one of Yturri's latest acquisitions, a seventeenth-century lead statue of an angel holding a finger to his lips and crushing a serpent underfoot: "the angel of silence," as the two friends called it (see fig. 2.11). Montesquiou inaugurated the funerary monument in November before a small group of friends.[68] In a radical gesture, Montesquiou asked to be buried not at the family château—in the company of several generations of his ancestors—but in the same tomb as Yturri.[69]

Marcel sent the count a long letter of condolence. "I cannot console myself of the thought that I did not see him again," he lamented. Their last meeting had been a month earlier, when the count gave a reading of his new book, *Professionnelles beautés*, at Marcel's apartment. "My friendship for him [Yturri] increased on that last evening when I saw him at my apartment, on the day of your reading, thanks to the sweetness of his temper and his affection for you. Age and suffering had instilled in him an almost maternal quality [. . .] When, soon after, I learned that he was once more unwell, I felt this invalid to be still dearer to me than before, even though I had always been fond of him, always appreciated his extraordinary intelligence, and always felt grateful for everything he represented and did for you. And I never saw him again!" Proust closed his letter by expressing his desire to tell the world about Yturri: "It will give me great joy to speak of him and make his name better known."[70] He kept his promise. The expanded version of his pastiche of Saint-Simon, published in 1919, is one of the few contemporary portraits

Figure 2.11. The Angel of Silence, Tomb of Montesquiou and Yturri, Gonards Cemetery, Versailles, 1905. Robert de Montesquiou, *Le chancelier de fleurs,* 290.

of Yturri and one of the rare testimonies about his life and personality written by a sympathetic friend.

Montesquiou was moved. "What touched me in your words," he wrote Proust, "is that you speak about him and not about me, as most do, who speak about him in relation to me, rather than speaking about me in relation to him—and this, I repeat, moves me a hundred times more."[71] The count, who was fond of mediums and séances, even fancied a supernatural link between Marcel and his departed friend: "I like to imagine mysterious exchanges between the two of you. The ingenuity of his devotion from beyond the grave seeks, no doubt successfully, to enter into the minds and hearts of others, disposing them to understand me better and to love me more." [72]

After Gabriel's death, Montesquiou planned a literary tribute to his lover. He collected condolence letters and testimonies about Yturri's life from friends and acquaintances and incorporated them into *Le chancelier de fleurs*, a luxury book—bound in leather and distributed among a select few. Published in 1907, it was part biography of Yturri, part memoir of their years together, and part anthology of his friend's writings.[73] Over the years Montesquiou had accumulated hundreds of letters from Gabriel that included poems, travel writings, reflections on their relationship, and even stories about his native Argentina. The count quoted select excerpts and explained that he had complied with Gabriel's wish to have his papers destroyed after his death: "There are hundreds of these letters; I have to press them, to distill them in order to extract from them, before their extinction, the dark sap contained in their ink, the velvet of feeling, the flavor of genius."[74] The count burnt the letters along with his own responses, lest these fall in the hands of "busybodies [who] would merely pore in search of spelling errors and character defects." The count argued that correspondence "is fungible; it belongs to that most efficacious group of venerable things that perish by and after their usage."[75] "I shall keep the empty envelopes," he concluded, "empty cages from which are flown—and never to return—what the poet called 'the divine birds of the heart.'"[76]

Marcel was only thirty-one when Yturri died, but, already too ill to venture far away from his apartment, he missed the funeral ceremonies organized by the count. In a letter, he told Reynaldo he hoped to visit the tomb as soon as his health permitted.

> If I had had but one good day, I would visit—sooner than the palace or the Trianon—the Gonards cemetery, particularly since Monsieur de Montesquiou was not at Versailles, and could not go himself; I would have had the very tender sense of substituting for him, of coming to poor Yturri on his behalf, just as Yturri often came to me on behalf of Montesquiou. Besides, I know from you and from others that the tomb was a peerless work, full of emotion and beauty. And since I barely think of anything other than tombs, I would have liked to see what Montesquiou put there, and the form in which his good taste ennobled his pain.[77]

Reynaldo Hahn, who was traveling when Yturri died, visited the grave on his own and wrote Montesquiou a heartfelt letter.

> My dear Sir,
> I went to the cemetery and gazed at length upon the grave, steeped, as you told me, in the most arresting sense of mystery and silence. The color of the stone,

the form of the stele at once mystic and free, the somber nobility of the marble, and finally the expressiveness and beauty of that singular statue, induce a mood of reverent meditation while exuding a strange warmth. In this unusual ensemble we recognize the union of the artist's hand and the friend's heart. When the trees have grown their leaves and springtime lightens this funereal spot with its majestic aura, *your work* will acquire even more significance and profundity.

I am glad to have admired it, and, at one with your soul's sentiments, I feel certain that *the deceased* could not have wished for a more affectionate and magnificent sepulcher.

Your devoted

Reynaldo Hahn[78]

In the months that followed, Montesquiou took as many friends as he could, including Ilán de Casa Fuerte, to visit the tomb.[79]

Montesquiou heard about Proust's desire to visit Yturri's grave and offered to take him. "Perhaps we could agree on a day this Holy Week, to go and pay a visit together to our Friend, if your health permits" the count proposed on March 23, 1907. A few days later he reminded Proust about their "project for a funerary pilgrimage," and then some weeks later he wrote again to announce that "some friends have taken the opportunity of coming here to see *the Mausoleum* and to accompany me on that pilgrimage of memory. I wish you were among them; but I no longer dare hope." Despite his good intentions, it does not appear that Marcel ever made the trip to Yturri's grave.[80]

On June 27, 1908, Montesquiou hosted a memorial to Yturri at the Pavillon des Muses. He read excerpts from *Le Chancelier* and presented the book to his friends. Proust was not among the guests—he had refused too many invitations and the count had given up on him—but when he found out about the soirée he sent the count an emotional letter: "How unkind of you not to have invited me to the commemorative reading of which I've been told and which, as you know well, mine would have been the intelligence and the heart most capable of entirely appreciating." Marcel conceded that he rarely left his bed but he would "have tried to do so for that reading, which must have been sublime." He continued, "Had I been forewarned of the ceremony by you, even if I had been unable to attend, I should have felt a stronger bond between us, one of those bonds that bring the faithful together and that used to inaugurate cults."[81] This last image is striking: Marcel imagines himself and the count members of a sect devoted to honoring the

Plate 1. Draner [pseudonym of Jules Jean Georges Renard (1833-1926)], drawing of the actor Jules Brasseur (1862-1932) playing the Brazilian in Jacques Offenbach's *La vie parisienne*. Théâtre du Palais Royal, 1866. Bibliothèque Nationale de France, Paris.

Plate 2. Draner [pseudonym of Jules Jean Georges Renard (1833–1926)], drawing of the actor Jules Brasseur (1862–1932) playing the Brazilian in Jacques Offenbach's *La vie parisienne,* Théâtre du Palais Royal, 1866. Bibliothèque Nationale de France, Paris.

Plate 3. Léon Bakst, costume sketch for Reynaldo Hahn's *Le dieu bleu* (1912). Watercolor, gouache, and gold on paper. Private collection. Photo: Erich Lessing / Art Resource, New York.

Plate 4. Mexico Tramways Company Stock Certificate, 1933. Image courtesy of the author.

Plate 5. *Robert de Montesquiou and Gabriel de Yturri,* ca. 1880s. Whistler Papers, PH1 / 162, University of Glasgow Library, Department of Special Collections.

Plate 6. Sem [pseudonym of Georges Goursat], caricature of Robert de Montesquiou and Gabriel de Yturri. Colored lithograph. Département de Manuscrits, NaFr 15146, f. 50, Bibliothèque Nationale de France, Paris.

Plate 7. Claudius Popelin, *José-Maria de Heredia as Pedro de Heredia,* 1868. Enamel painting. Bibliothèque Nationale de France, Paris, Dist. RMN-Grand Palais / image Bnf 12–589528.

Plate 8. Antonio La Gandara, *Gabriel de Yturri*, 1886. Oil on wood. RMN-Grand Palais (Musée d'Orsay) / Hervé Lewandowski.

memory of Yturri. In his imagination, he sacralizes Gabriel, just as earlier he had sacralized Reynaldo in his sketches of Mâle.

To make amends for neglecting to invite him, Montesquiou proposed to visit Proust's apartment for a private reading of *Le chancelier*. Proust was horrified—he found the count exhausting and tried to postpone the visit—but Montesquiou insisted, arriving at two in the morning to accommodate Marcel's nocturnal schedule. In a July 1908 letter to Reynaldo, Proust described the visit, recounting how Montesquiou compared himself and Yturri to other famous couples in Western culture, from Orestes and Pylades to Flaubert and Bouilhet.

> Sachez qu'hier soir, après maintes lettres échangées, sur un ton pontifical mais pressant, le fatal Comte est venu me lire puis me donner le livre sur Yturri [. . .] J'aurais voulu que vous l'entendissiez sur le coup de deux heures du matin, sans pitié des Gagey, s'écrier en frappant les talons, "Et maintenant, Scipion et Lelius, Oreste et Pylade, Horn et Posa, Saint Marc et de Thou, Edmond et Jules de Goncourt, Flaubert et Bouilhet, Aristobule et Pythias, accueillez-moi, j'en suis digne, dans votre groupe suréminent."

> (I must tell you that last night, after the exchange of innumerable letters in a pontifical but pressing tone, the fatal Count came to read to me and then present me with the book about Yturri [. . .] I should have loved you to hear him at two o'clock in the morning, without a thought for the poor Gageys, stamping his heels on the floor while declaiming: "And now, Scipio and Laelius, Orestes and Pylades, Horn and Posa, Saint Mark and de Thou, Edmond and Jules de Goncourt, Flaubert and Bouilhet, Aristobulus and Pythias, welcome me, for I am worthy, into your pre-eminent company.")[82]

Montesquiou gave Proust a copy of *Le chancelier* but warned him to exercise extra care. "Let me remind you that this is a sacred book," he wrote. "Do not lend it, or only seldom, and then, not lightly: I mean, neither to those incapable of appreciating it, nor to those who, on the contrary, are capable of appreciating it so much that they would not give it back." The book, he concluded, should be "read with emotion stemming from both mind and heart."[83]

Proust was genuinely moved by Montesquiou's homage, and after reading it he penned an emotional letter in which he abandoned the strict protocol he had observed for over two decades and addressed the count, for the first time, as "Cher ami" instead of the habitual "Monsieur": "I reread the book with great pleasure, with, if I may say, the emotion of feeling the counterpart of all these things in my past, in my recollection, and in my heart." Marcel was surprised to find his condolence letters—as well as his "Fête chez Montesquiou à Neuilly"[84]—included in the volume. "I am happy and tenderly moved that you write of me in these pages," he told the count. "You did well to publish this book."[85]

Some days later, Proust sent the count another letter and shared some more thoughts sparked by *Le chancelier*. "You have given me a great book," he wrote, "a portrait that will endure, and in which future readers will find the involuntary portrait of the painter no less than the intended portrait of the model. Yturri by Montesquiou seeks only to be the portrait of Yturri, but its objectivity renders it a subjective portrait of Montesquiou. One only gives oneself away when one forgets oneself. It is in speaking of another that you have revealed your finest secrets."[86]

As Proust well noticed, the play with doubles continued after Yturri's death. Montesquiou could no longer photograph himself next to Yturri or wear the same clothes, but he could write a book about Yturri that was in reality a work about himself. In Yturri he found a reflection of his own life, and to write about himself, he began by writing about his friend. The process of doubling had moved from the visual to the textual field.

Yturri in À la recherche du temps perdu

Many of Montesquiou's friends—especially those, like the Comtesse Greffulhe, who were blinded by class prejudices—did not realize they were witnesses to one of the greatest love stories of the belle époque. Against social convention, Montesquiou and Yturri moved in together; became lovers, conspirators, and intellectual collaborators; and built a life of shared passions and interests. At a time when most homosexuals would never show their lovers in public—as Proust demonstrated in his novel—they flaunted their friendship as they hosted dinners, attended parties and receptions, and even traveled to New York together. They had the kind of life most gay couples could not even dream of until well into the twentieth century.

The two lived a beautiful love story that also had all the complications and ups and downs of any relationship. In his memoirs, Montesquiou only remembered the good days spent next to "my dear Yturri, who shared my life for twenty years, whom I miss even now, and whose memory I will forever bless."[87] But friends of the couple recall many tempestuous moments. Ilán de Casa Fuerte evokes one particularly dramatic quarrel.

Lucien me rapporta à ce propos que se trouvant, une autre fois, entre Montesquiou et Yturri dans un sapin qui les conduisait au "Pavillon des Muses" en traver-
sant le Bois, les deux amis avaient commencé à se disputer et s'étaient mis à hurler
de telle manière que lui, n'y tenant plus, pris entre ces deux organes déchaînés,
avait ouvert la portière et sauté du fiacre sans que les deux hurleurs s'en fussent
aperçus.[88]

(Lucien reported that he once found himself seated between Montesquiou and
Yturri in a carriage bound for the "Pavillon des Muses." While traversing the Bois
de Boulogne, the two began to fight and to scream so loudly that Lucien, caught
between these two unbridled fiends, could not stand it any longer: he opened
the door and jumped off the coach. The two howlers did not even take notice.)

Montesquiou was famous for his sharp tongue and arrogant behavior. Yturri
was a hot-blooded South American displaying "the excitable temper of his
countrymen," as Proust put it. It is not surprising that these two strong
personalities would sometimes clash . . . or explode in an emotional
display.

Proust was a keen observer, and he incorporated elements from the
couple's dynamic into his novel. Many critics—from George D. Painter to
Jean-Yves Tadié—have shown the degree to which Montesquiou served as a
model for the Baron de Charlus, but no one so far has discussed how Yturri
also left his mark in *À la recherche* or how his character traits were spread
among several figures.

Proust, for instance, gave Yturri's diabetic symptoms—including the
pungent smell—to the dying Swann. Painter recalls that friends could still
remember Yturri's "dreadful smell of rotten apples."[89] The narrator describes
the dying Swann in similar terms.

[Swann] était arrivé à ce degré de fatigue où le corps d'un malade n'est plus qu'une
cornue où s'observent des réactions chimiques. Sa figure se marquait de petits
points bleu de Prusse, qui avaient l'air de ne pas appartenir au monde vivant, et
dégageait ce genre d'odeur qui, au lycée, après les "experiences," rend si désagré-
able de rester dans une clase de "Sciences."[90]

([Swann] had arrived at that degree of fatigue in which the body of a sick man is
no more than a retort in which chemical reactions are to be observed. His face
was marked with small specks of Prussian blue, which appeared not to belong
to the world of the living, and gave off that kind of smell which, at school, after
"experiments," makes it so unpleasant to remain in a "Science" classroom).[91]

More significantly, Proust incorporated the stormier aspects of Montesquiou and Yturri's relationship into the novel. In one of the notebooks he
used to jot down ideas, he pointed to the Argentinean as a model for Charlus's lover.

> Je ne sais pour qui, ni si ce sera dans ce chapitre (je préférerais pour l'amant de
> Charlus dont je ferais aussi une sorte d'Yturri cru seulement aimé mais aimant
> d'autres, parce que les choses sont plus compliquées qu'on ne croit, la complexité
> autant que la symétrie qui l'organise étant un élément de beauté).[92]

> (I don't know for whom, or even if it will be in this chapter (I would prefer to use
> it for Charlus's lover, whom I will make a sort of Yturri, thought to be only loved,
> but also loving others, because things are more complicated than one thinks—
> complexity, as much as symmetry in its organization, is an element of beauty).

Yturri was not only a "faithful friend" and devoted lover. He also flirted with
other men and had adventures and affairs. And it was the complexity and
beauty of this double status—loved one and lover—that most interested
Proust.

Jean-Yves Tadié once wrote that "Yturri is a bit Morel, a bit Jupien,"[93] and
we certainly find traces of him in both of these young men. Jupien works as
a tailor, which recalls Yturri's past as a tie salesman, as does Morel's status as
the younger lover from a different social class. But Morel is not Yturri's mirror image: Morel is a working-class Frenchman, the son of a servant who
becomes a respected musician. Yturri, in contrast, was a lower middle-class
foreigner lacking a traditional profession. Morel breaks with Charlus after a
brief flirtation, while Yturri spent his life with Montesquiou and, despite the
occasional lover's quarrel, never quit his side. The narrator and the other
characters make much of Morel's unpatriotic behavior during World War I;
Yturri died more than a decade before the war, and even if he had lived he
could not have enlisted because of his status as a foreigner. In the end Morel
is not a very likeable character—he is cowardly, insensitive, and a treacherous friend—while Yturri, as we have seen, was extremely charismatic and
conquered even the curmudgeonly Léon Daudet.

But despite these differences, we find many traces of Yturri in Morel. First
of all, the age difference between Charlus and Morel mirrors that between
Montesquiou and Yturri. They come from different classes, and the narrator's comment on the odd couple formed by the baron and the musician
—"La disproportion sociale à quoi je n'avais pas pensé d'abord était trop

immense"[94] ("The social disproportion, which I had not at first considered, was too vast")[95]—could also be applied to Montesquiou and his friend. As the count did with Yturri, Charlus plans to turn the younger man into a companion and collaborator (though his plan fails): "Voilà quelqu'un par qui j'aimerais être accompagné dans mes voyages et aidé dans mes affaires. Comme il simplifierait ma vie!"[96] ("Here is someone I'd like to be accompanied by on my travels and helped by in my business affairs. How he would simplify my life!")[97] To the criticism that his liaison with a poor musician could affect his social status, Charlus responds that his position is so solid that his friendship will elevate Morel without debasing him: "Le seul fait que je m'intéresse à lui et étende sur lui ma protection a quelque chose de suréminent et *abolit le passé.*"[98] ("The mere fact that I take an interest in him and extend my protection over him has something supereminent about it and abolishes the past.")[99] It's a phrase that could easily have been pronounced by Montesquiou.

Morel begins to imitate Charlus and to adopt his mannerisms and aristocratic prejudices, just like Yturri did with Montesquiou: "Dans les plus petites choses, Morel qui se croyait devenu un M. de Charlus mille fois plus important, avait compris de travers en les prenant à la lettre, les orgueilleux enseignements du baron quant à l'aristocratie."[100] ("In the smallest things, Morel, who saw himself as having become an infinitely more important M. de Charlus, had understood amiss, by taking them literally, the Baron's arrogant teachings concerning the aristocracy.)[101] He even apes the baron's arrogance and considers snubbing minor nobles, going as far as to ignore the Cambremers' invitation to dinner: "Morel avait recueilli pieusement cette leçon d'histoire, peut-être un peu sommaire; il jugeait les choses comme s'il était lui-même un Guermantes et souhaitait une occasion de se trouver avec les faux La Tour d'Auvergne pour leur faire sentir par une poignée de main dédaigneuse, qu'il ne les prenait guère au sérieux."[102] ("Morel had piously taken in this perhaps somewhat cursory history lesson; he judged things as if he were himself a Guermantes and hoped for an opportunity of finding himself with the false La Tour d'Auvergnes so that he could let them see, by a contemptuous shake of the hand, that he hardly took them seriously.")[103]

Both Proust and Casa Fuerte remember Yturri as having a hot temper. Morel, likewise, is prone to "grandes colères" and "injustifiables accès de mauvaise humeur"[104] ("his greatest rages, his gloomiest and least justifiable outbursts of bad temper.")[105] The narrator diagnoses him as a "neurasthenic"[106] and describes how, on occasions, he could even explode at Charlus in front

of guests: "Parfois même à quelque mot que lui disait le baron, éclatait de
la part de Morel, sur un ton dur, une réplique insolente dont tout le monde
était choqué."[107] ("At times even, at some remark made to him by the Baron,
there would burst from Morel, in a harsh voice, an insolent riposte by which
everyone was shocked.")[108] The dynamic between the hot-blooded younger
man and the conceited aristocrat was more complicated than one might
imagine, since at times it was Morel who had the upper hand.

> Pour M de Charlus [. . .] il avait beau appartenir à une famille plus ancienne que
> les Capétiens, être riche, être vainement recherché par une société élégante, et
> Morel n'être rien, il aurait beau dire à Morel, comme il m'avait dit à moi-même:
> "Je suis prince, je veux votre bien," encore était-ce Morel qui avait le dessus s'il ne
> voulait pas se rendre.

> (It did not matter that [Charlus] belonged to a family older than the Capets, that
> he was rich, that he was sought after in vain by a smart society while Morel was
> nobody, it would have been no use saying to Morel, as he said to me: "I am a
> prince, I have your interests at heart," Morel still had the upper hand so long as
> he did not want to surrender.)[109]

One could easily apply this description to Montesquiou and Yturri, and
imagine how, at times, it was the Argentine, with his hot temper and strong
personality, who had the upper hand in the relationship.

Morel resembles Yturri in other minor details as well. He is described as
"very dark complexioned" ("excessivement noir"),[110] and once, while playing
cards at the Verdurins', Cottard puts on a *rastaquouère* accent to address the
musician, a gesture that only makes sense if we imagine the doctor speaking to an Argentine.[111] Finally, the inscription on the books Charlus gives
Morel—*non mortale quod opto*—is the same Latin phrase Montesquiou had
carved on his and Yturri's grave.[112]

Above all, Proust considered Yturri a multifaceted figure, and it was this
complexity and its beauty that he sought to incorporate into Morel's character. The narrator describes the musician as "full of contradictions"[113] and
compares him to his *paperolles*.

> [. . .] sa nature était vraiment comme un papier sur lequel on a fait tant de plis
> dans tous les sens qu'il est impossible de s'y retrouver. Il semblait avoir des prin-
> cipes assez élevés, et avec une magnifique écriture, déparée par les plus gros-
> sières fautes d'orthographe [. . .][114]

([. . .] his nature was really like a sheet of paper in which so many folds have been made in every direction that it is impossible to know where you are. He seemed to have quite lofty principles, and in a magnificent handwriting, marred by the crudest spelling mistakes [. . .])[115]

Elsewhere, he likens Morel to a medieval book: "Il ressemblait à un vieux livre du Moyen Âge, plein d'erreurs, de traditions absurdes, d'obscénités, il était extraordinairement composite."[116] ("[He] resembled an old book of the Middle Ages, full of errors, of absurd traditions, of obscenities, he was extraordinarily composite.")[117]

But the aspect of Yturri's life that most interested Proust—the fact that he had a talent for writing but never published—is, surprisingly, not given to Morel but to the Baron de Charlus. At the end of the novel, the narrator wonders why Charlus—with his immense culture and his natural eloquence—never managed to write.

j'ai toujours regretté, dis-je, et je regrette encore que M de Charlus n'ait jamais écrit [. . .] Je le lui dis souvent, il ne voulut jamais s'y essayer, peut-être simplement par paresse, ou temps accaparé par des fêtes brillantes et des divertissements sordides, ou besoin Guermantes de prolonger indéfiniment des bavardages.[118]

(I have always regretted and still regret that M. de Charlus never wrote anything [. . .] All the same I believe that if M. de Charlus has tried his hand at prose, beginning with the artistic subjects on which he was so knowledgeable, he would have struck a spark, the lightning would have flashed out, and the man of fashion would have become a master of the pen. I often said this to him, but he would never try, perhaps simply from laziness, or being constantly busy with brilliant parties and sordid amusements, or the Guermantes family need for endless chat.)[119]

Unlike Charlus, Montesquiou did write; some of his contemporaries even quipped that he wrote too much. It was Yturri who never published, despite having written many chronicles, stories, and reflections in his letters to the count. Proust admired what little he read, and he must have always wondered why Yturri never put his thoughts in print. The same questions the narrator asks of Charlus could be directed at Yturri: Did he not publish because he was lazy? Because his time was completely taken up by socializing? Or was it because he was afraid of competing with Montesquiou, of detracting attention from the count's writings? Yturri was a much better storyteller than the count, as we can see from the fragments of his writing included in *Le chancelier de fleurs*. Montesquiou would often get lost in genealogies and family histories, while Yturri had a natural talent for painting a scene and sketching a character in a few phrases.[120]

Yturri's death must have shaken Marcel. Until then, both of them had been aspiring writers. Proust had published a few articles and a collection of short pieces, but he was lagging behind most of his peers. Like Yturri, he thought there would always be time in the future to publish a great work, an important book. Seeing Yturri die without realizing his goal must have reminded Marcel that life is finite and that many of his friends would die without ever fulfilling their literary ambitions.

In his early years, Proust looked up to Montesquiou as the type of writer he hoped to become one day: elegant, respected in society, surrounded by riches, beauty, and glamour. As he matured, he became more interested in Yturri and grew closer to the dying friend than to the glamorous dandy. Yturri became Marcel's "colleague in malady" and taught him much about illness and death. Marcel had always liked his Argentinian friend, but it was only after he fell ill that a truly special bond developed between the two. Most of Proust's writings on Yturri—the letters to Montesquiou and other friends; the use of his character traits in *À la recherche*—came after his friend's death, and these are more complex than the light pastiche published during Yturri's life. Marcel identified with the sick Yturri but even more with the dead Yturri.

Watching Yturri die unpublished made Marcel fear for his own destiny: Would he also die without publishing a major work? What if he, too, disappeared without leaving a trace? The figure of the cultured man who could have written but never did haunted Marcel, and it made its way into the novel, where the narrator repeatedly laments that some of the most brilliant characters, including Swann and Charlus, never bring themselves to publishing a book. Yturri was one of the first to teach him about this missed opportunity, which would become one of the fundamental tropes of *À la recherche*.

Proust incorporated into his novel the verse from Ovid's *Metamorphoses* that Montesquiou chose for Yturri's grave: *non est mortale quod opto*. This line, which can be roughly translated as "your destiny is that of a mortal; you ambition that of an immortal," echoes one of the main themes in Proust's novel. Only literature allows us to transcend our mortal condition, only through writing can one achieve immortality. It is significant that Montesquiou inscribed this phrase on a tomb, while Proust placed it in a novel that is the literary equivalent of a tomb, a repository of lost time.

Montesquiou wrote but did not achieve immortality; his poems, he himself confessed, were no more than *bibelots*. Yturri did not achieve immortality either, mainly because he never published. Proust, in contrast, avoided the fate of Swann, Charlus, and Yturri. He achieved his share of immortality, and he did so, in part, by observing Yturri's tragic end and turning his reflections into literature. Perhaps it would not be an exaggeration to conclude that Yturri's death jolted Marcel into action and allowed him to write the book he had always planned but had been unable to write. After 1905, in order to avoid the destiny that befell his Argentine friend, he retired from the world, locked himself in his cork-lined room, and wrote until he died. By then his name had been inscribed, for eternity, in the pantheon of literary history.

Paperolle No. 2

Proust's Peruvians

Among the hundreds of characters in *À la recherche du temps perdu,* the only bona fide Latin American is an anonymous Peruvian who attends Charlie Morel's recital, organized by Charlus at Madame Verdurin's home, and finds himself enmeshed in a socialite's intrigues, as Madame de Mortemart, one Charlus's cousins, schemes to organize a soirée to which only a select few will be invited. As she whispers her invitations, her cunning gaze falls on those around him, including the Peruvian.

Ce regard fut même si fort qu'après avoir frappé Mme de Valcourt, le secret évident et l'intention de cachotterie qu'il contenait rebondirent sur un jeune Péruvien que Mme de Mortemart comptait au contraire inviter. Mais soupçonneux, voyant jusqu'à l'évidence les mystères qu'on faisait sans prendre garde qu'ils n'étaient pas pour lui, il éprouva aussitôt à l'endroit de Mme de Mortemart une haine atroce et se jura de lui faire mille mauvaises farces, comme de faire envoyer cinquante cafés glacés chez elle le jour où elle ne recevrait pas, de faire insérer, celui où elle recevrait, une note dans les journaux disant que la fête était remise, et de publier des comptes rendus mensongers des suivantes, dans lesquels figureraient les noms, connus de tous, de personnes que, pour des raisons variées, on ne tient pas à recevoir, même pas à se laisser présenter.[1]

(Indeed the gaze was so powerful that after striking Mme de Valcourt, the unmistakable secretive intention that it conveyed bounced off and hit a young Peruvian whom Mme de Mortemart was in fact intending to invite. But he, filled with suspicion, seeing so plainly the smokescreen that was being set up without realizing it was not meant for him, promptly experienced a violent hatred for Mme de Mortemart and swore to play countless cruel jokes on her: to have fifty iced coffees sent to her on a day when she had no guests, for example, or, when she did have a party, to put a note in the papers saying it was postponed, and to write lying accounts of subsequent parties which would include the well-known names of people whom, for various reasons, no one would wish to invite, or even be willing to meet.)[2]

Despite his fleeting appearance in Proust's novel—we never hear about him or Mortemart again, and we have no idea if he manages to carry out his revenge—this minor character sparked a lively debate among Peruvian intellectuals. Luis Loayza, an important literary critic (and a friend of Mario Vargas Llosa, who dedicated his *Conversation in the Cathedral* [1969] to him), devoted an article to Proust's anonymous Peruvian in 1962. "Why a Peruvian?" he asks, "And what is the meaning of this literary ghost?" Loayza believes that "in the first place, [this] character exists because [he] is a Peruvian, that is to say, an exotic figure in France," who belongs to the class of "rich travelers, the children of wealthy families who only expected one thing from their native country: their rents paid on time." The Peruvian has succeeded in Paris: he is invited to Madame Verdurin's soirée and spends his time "visiting the salons and has enough money to spend it in pranks of poor taste." Loayza questions the young man's allegiance to his country: "Would he ever think of going back? He is very comfortable where he is [. . .] in Lima there are no Verdurins—at least not yet. Why return?" Loayza closes his reflection by speculating on whether this Peruvian could have been based on one of Proust's Latin American acquaintances: "At the turn of the century there were many Latin Americans in the elegant circles of Paris. It is likely that Proust thought about one of them and that, as he often did to hide his tracks, he called him a Peruvian to hide the portrait, or that this was the first exoticism that came to his pen."[3]

Loayza's inquiry was later developed by Fernando Iwasaki, another critic from Lima, who proposed to crack the mystery of the "conceited and capricious Peruvian" by searching for a model among Proust's acquaintances. He found a likely candidate mentioned by both George D. Painter and Ghislain de Diesbach—a Latin American "who had been born in Lima around 1864" and whom the two biographers identify as none other than Gabriel de Yturri! Based on this biographical error, which Painter introduced and Diesbach and others repeated, Iwasaki concludes that the Peruvian at Madame Verdurin's was a stand-in for Yturri: "I wouldn't be surprised if Gabriel Yturri—decorator of Polar bedrooms, trickster of Versaillesque nuns [a reference to the story of the marble basin] and escort of Parisian aristocrats—had once sent fifty iced coffees to those salons he knew so well. Proust perhaps remembered [this episode] when he wrote *In Search of Lost Time*."[4] The Argentine Manuel Mujica Láinez believes the error in Yturri's nationality was started by Montesquiou, who might have "considered Peru more chic than Argentina."[5]

Despite this error, Iwasaki is right in proposing a connection between the Peruvian and Yturri. One of the imagined pranks—"inserting a notice in the papers to the effect that the party was postponed"—corresponds to an actual episode in Montesquiou's life. On June 12, 1912, the count was to give a lavish party at the Palais Rose, his new home in the Parisian suburb of Le Vésinet. On that morning, a note appeared in *Le Figaro* announcing the reception had been cancelled. Montesquiou called his guests to reassure them that there had been no change of plans, but in the end only a handful of friends appeared at the soirée and the scant attendees were outnumbered by the dozens of valets, waiters, and servants.[6] Yturri had been dead for seven years, but the prank made such an impression on Proust that in his novel he attributes it to a mischievous Latin American, thus suggesting this was something the Argentinean might have done. There are several similarities between the fictional character and Yturri: the Peruvian has a hot temper, and it takes very little (in this case an awkward gaze) to send him into a rage. His sudden, "violent hatred" for Madame de Mortemart recalls how Montesquiou, Proust, Casa Fuerte, and others painted Yturri as a passionate South American prone to fits and emotional outbursts. Proust seems to have transposed some of Yturri's character traits to his Peruvian.

But leaving aside the question of possible models, the presence of the anonymous Peruvian at the Verdurin home raises a number of questions about the role of Latin Americans in Proust's circle. Although this Peruvian seems wealthy and has been admitted into the salons of the Faubourg Saint-Germain, his social success seems to be limited. Madame Verdurin is one of the most vulgar and unsophisticated hostesses, and being invited to her home places him at the bottom of the Parisian social hierarchy.

Or perhaps not. On that evening, the recital has been organized by Charlus, who has invited only his most aristocratic relatives and friends. In an effort to help Morel, the baron composes the most exclusive guest list and brings to Verdurin's home scores of elegant Parisians who would never deign to talk to her (and who—the narrator observes—refuse to greet her or even acknowledge her in her own home, a slight that will later prove fatal for Charlus). Was the Peruvian invited by Verdurin or by Charlus? The reading of this character hinges on this crucial question; he could be either a *rastaquouère* (if he is Verdurin's guest) or a Latin American admitted into

the bosom of Parisian aristocracy (if he happens to be Charlus's friend). Or
perhaps he could be both.

At first sight, the Peruvian fits in better as a guest of the Verdurins. It
is hard to imagine the snobbish Charlus—obsessed with genealogies and
family histories—befriending a Peruvian, but the Verdurins are newly rich
and social omnivores. The presence of a Peruvian *rastaquouère* in their salon
could be another detail used by the narrator to highlight their vulgarity.

But the text suggests the Peruvian might be more sophisticated than it
first appears. Madame de Mortemart plans to include him in her select soirée (designed, in part, to please Charlus), so the Peruvian must be known
to Charlus's family. The Mortemarts are related to Charlus and to the Guermantes, and Proust named Madame de Mortemart, who only appears in this
brief scene, after a prominent family in Saint-Simon's *Mémoires*. At several
points in the novel, Proust mentions the "Mortemart wit," and in his correspondence he confesses to a friend that it was the Mortemarts who inspired
him to create his Guermantes.

> [. . .] ce qui m'avait poussé à écrire comme un pensum tant de répliques de la
> Duchesse de Guermantes, et à rendre cohérent, toujours identique "l'esprit des
> Guermantes," c'était la déception que j'avais eue, en voyant Saint-Simon nous
> parler toujours de "l'esprit des Mortemart," du "tour si particulier" [. . .] de ne pas
> trouver un seul mot, la plus légère indication, qui permît de saisir en quoi con-
> sistait cette singularité de langage propre aux Mortemart. Ne pouvant recon-
> stituer dans le passé "l'Esprit des Mortemart," je fis la gageure d'inventer "l'esprit
> des Guermantes." Hélas je n'ai pas le génie de Saint-Simon. Mais du moins ceux
> qui me liront, sauront ce qu'est l'esprit des Guermantes.[7]

> (what pushed me to write, like a school assignment, so many phrases uttered by
> the Duchesse de Guermantes, and to render "the Guermantes spirit" so coherent
> and always identical, was the deception upon reading Saint-Simon's mentions
> of "the Mortemart spirit" and of "its very special turn" without finding a single
> word, or even the least indication, that would allow me to grasp the singularity of
> this language used by the Mortemarts. Since I could not recreate in the past the
> "Mortemart spirit," I challenged myself to invent "the Guermantes spirit." Alas,
> I lack Saint-Simon's genius. But at least those who will read me will understand
> the "Guermantes spirit.")

In his *Mémoires*, Saint-Simon notes that the Mortemarts produced many
illustrious figures, including Madame de Montespan, Louis XIV's mistress.

Like the Guermantes, the Mortemarts stand for history, tradition, sophisti-
cation, culture, and wit. They are, in brief, the opposite of the Verdurins. By
entering Madame de Mortemart's circle, the Peruvian has achieved a social
coup that is as spectacular as the narrator's acceptance into the Guermantes' salon.

There is one more textual clue that might explain how the Peruvian
landed in Madame de Verdurin's home. As we saw in the introduction,
Proust's drafts included another Peruvian who did not make it into the
novel—the bankrupt guest at the Hôtel de Balbec. This character has lost all
his money—probably at the casino—and spends the night wandering through
the hallways, hoping to run into a rich guest like Nissim Bernard, who might
pay him for keeping him company.[8] Could it be this same Peruvian who reappears at the Verdurin salon? If so, he seems to have found a way out of his
financial predicaments, since he plans to spend lots of money—ordering
fifty iced coffees—to get his revenge on Madame de Mortemart.

If this is indeed the same Peruvian, we can easily imagine how he got
from Balbec to the Morel recital. When he was penniless, he became a gig-
olo for hotel guests. His possible clients would include the rich older men
who offer money to handsome youths in the novel. Could it be Charlus—
the most notable of these sugar daddies—who got the Peruvian out of his
financial straits in exchange for his erotic services? If Charlus was satisfied
with the services rendered, he might have invited the Peruvian to Morel's
recital at the Verdurins', a move that would also explain why Madame de
Mortemart—who seeks to ingratiate herself with her cousin—plans to include the young man in her soirée.

The Peruvian would thus belong to the class of young men in the novel—
Jupien, Morel, the elevator boy at Balbec, the tomato brothers—who make
themselves available for hire. He would be the only one among them, along
with Morel, who gets invited to the salons and enjoys a degree of social mobility. Could Proust have been thinking once again of Yturri, who went from
tie salesman to lover of one of the richest and most aristocratic dandies in
Paris?

Proust could have also been thinking of a Peruvian acquaintance who
belonged to the circle of Latin American diplomats in Paris: the writer Ventura García Calderón (1886-1959), who was born in Paris, worked at the Peruvian consulate in Paris between 1906 and 1910, and then served as consul
in Le Havre from 1916 to 1921.[9] In several letters from 1920, Proust mentions
this Peruvian writer-diplomat, who published a selection of the novelist's

texts in *América Latina*, the journal he edited.[10] Ventura Calderón was very interested in Proust: he not only published him but also requested so many photographs that at one point the novelist warned his editor "do not send him any photographs, since he has quite a few."[11] Like Enrique Gómez Carrillo and Lucio V. Mansilla—his Latin American colleagues in the diplomatic corps—García Calderón was a diplomat, dandy, and frequent guest at the Parisian salons. But it would be hard to imagine a consul engaging in the kind of adolescent behavior Proust attributes to the mischievous guest, lest he provoke a diplomatic incident between Peru and France.

Peru came into Proust's life only once. In a letter from 1917, Lionel Hauser explained to Proust that his financial outlook seemed brighter and added that even if "your situation is evidently not comparable to that of Peru before its conquest by the Spaniards, it is already a great improvement."[12] Hauser was playing on an old French expression, "C'est n'est pas le Pérou avant la conquête des Espagnols" (It is not Peru before the conquest) used to denote the absence of riches. (Incidentally, Mozart played on this phrase in *Così fan tutte,* where two characters exclaim "Ah, questo medico vale un Peru" [this doctor is worth all the gold in Peru].)[13] Financially, Proust was in worse shape than Peru before the conquest but better off than the bankrupt Peruvian in his novel. Hauser's comment does not elucidate the identity of Verdurin's guest, but it does show that in Proust's world a Peruvian is always in the eye of the beholder.

3 José-Maria de Heredia
A Cuban Conquistador

As a young man seeking to enter the literary world, Proust looked up to two figures as models for the type of writer he hoped to become. The first was Robert de Montesquiou. The second was José-Maria de Heredia (1842-1905), a Cuban-born poet who became the first Latin American to enter the Académie française (figs 3.1-3.3). If Montesquiou was the prototype of the literary dandy, Heredia was a more sober type: a wealthy, elegant poet who hosted a weekly salon frequented by poets, novelists, and artists. He was born on a coffee plantation near Santiago de Cuba in 1842 to a French mother and a Cuban father who traced his ancestry to the first Spanish settlers of the Americas. He was named after an illustrious cousin on his father's side, the poet José María Heredia y Heredia (1803-1839), the author of one of the masterpieces of Cuban literature, the "Ode to Niagara." José-Maria de Heredia (who always spelled his name the French way, using a hyphen between his first and middle name and dropping the accent in "María") grew up bilingual, and at age nine he was sent to boarding school in France. At seventeen he returned to Cuba, but he had trouble adapting to life there and moved back to Paris in 1861, never to return to his native country.

In Paris, Heredia settled into a comfortable, carefree life, supported by a considerable fortune and the income produced by the family's coffee plantations. Soon after his arrival, he met Charles Leconte de Lisle (1818-1894), a poet who would become an important friend and mentor. Heredia became associated with the Parnassian movement and published his poems in *Le Parnasse contemporain* alongside works by Leconte de Lisle, François Coppée, and Théodore de Banville. The Parnassians rebelled against the legacy of Romanticism, arguing that poetry should focus on great historical episodes and not on the poet's emotions, which they dismissed as frivolous.

Figure 3.1. Nadar, portrait of José-Maria de Heredia (1842–1905), Cuban-born French poet. Inv.: ND189678906a. / Ministère de la Culture/Médiathèque du Patrimoine, Dist. RMN/Art Resource, New York.

They preferred the past over the present, heroic deeds over tales of love, and an epic register over the intimate tone favored by their predecessors. In his 1894 acceptance speech to the Académie française, Heredia criticized "cette voie toute personnelle où on a entraîné la poésie; cette façon familière de mettre son cœur à nu devant le public" (that entirely personal path down which poetry has been led; that familiar way of baring one's soul to the public) and added that "ces confessions publiques, menteuses ou sincères, révoltent en nous une pudeur profonde" (these public confessions, whether mendacious or sincere, offend against our profound sense of decorum). He believed that "la vraie poésie est dans la nature et dans l'humanité éternelles et non dans le cœur de l'homme d'un jour, quelque grand qu'il

Figure 3.2. Portrait of José-Maria de Heredia as a young man. Bibliothèque de l'Arsenal, Ms. 14362, f.5, Bibliothèque Nationale de France, Paris.

soit [. . .] Le poète est d'autant plus vraiment et largement humain qu'il est plus impersonnel. D'ailleurs, le moi, ce moi haïssable, est-il plus nécessaire au drame intérieur qu'à la publique tragédie?" (True poetry lies in the eternity of nature and humanity, not in the heart of the man of a single day, no matter how great . . . The more impersonal a poet, the more truly and widely human he is. And why should the self, the hateful self, be any more necessary to dramas of interiority than to public tragedies?)[1]

True to his Parnassian beliefs, Heredia devoted his poetry to singing the heroic deeds of the past. He spent most of his life writing the hundred or so sonnets he published in 1893 under the title *Les trophées*. It was a book Proust read, admired, and often quoted, and it consecrated Heredia as one of the most important poets of the nineteenth century. A year after its pub-

Figure 3.3. Portrait of José-Maria de Heredia as an old man. Bibliothèque de l'Arsenal, Ms. 14362, f.6, Bibliothèque Nationale de France, Paris.

lication, he was elected to the Académie française, an honor that increased his stature as an intellectual and extended his fame around the globe. Writers from Cuba to Argentina marveled at the curious fate of this fellow Latin American who had been received with open arms into the bastion of French literature.

Heredia strengthened his ties to Latin America in the last years of his life. In 1901 he became a correspondent for *El País,* a Buenos Aires newspaper, and in 1903 he accepted an invitation from the mayor of Santiago de Cuba to write a poem for the centenary of his cousin—the other José María Heredia, who dropped the aristocratic-sounding particle "de" from his last name as a republican gesture. Our Heredia died in Paris in October 1905, a few months after Gabriel de Yturri.

Figure 3.4. Portrait of Marie de Heredia. Bibliothèque de l'Arsenal, 17(1)-NB-B-171571,
Bibliothèque Nationale de France, Paris.

Proust was in his twenties when he first met Heredia, who was nearly
thirty years older, at the salon of Princess Mathilde. Heredia was at the
height of his fame; *Les trophées* had just been published and was a great
critical and commercial success. Although he was not an aristocrat, Heredia
had formed around him an aristocracy of letters, including the poets of the
Parnassian movement. Dazzled by this elegant dandy, Proust went out of
his way to befriend him and his three daughters, Hélène, Marie, and Louise.
On several occasions during the 1890s, Proust invited the Heredia family to
dinner at his parent's apartment.

Proust became especially close to Marie (figs. 3.4 and 3.5), who was four
years younger than he and the liveliest and smartest of the three sisters. Together they formed the "Académie des Canaques," a playful version of the

Figure 3.5. Portrait of Marie de Heredia. Bibliothèque de l'Arsenal, 506MS-15380 (754), Bibliothèque Nationale de France, Paris.

venerable French institution that had just elected Heredia to its ranks. The Canaquadémie, as the institution was also known, counted Pierre Louÿs, Léon Blum, and Henri de Régnier as members.[2] Proust was named perpetual secretary, and Marie was given the title "Queen of the Canaques." The two exchanged many playful letters mimicking the solemn tone of the official communications of the Académie française. In one, Marie told Marcel, "Je vous fais des canaques adieux; la Reine est très triste de se séparer de ses sujets et en particulier du premier Canaque de France."[3] (I bid you my *canaque* adieux; the queen is saddened to separate herself from her subjects and especially from the first Canaque of France.) Robert Proust noted that "Marcel persista toute sa vie à commencer ses lettres à celle qui fut la souveraine des Canaques jusqu'à dix-neuf ans par les mots protocolaires: Ma Reine."[4] (For the rest of his life, Marcel persisted in starting his letters to Marie, who had been the sovereign of the Canaques until her nineteenth birthday, with the solemn greeting: My Queen.)

Early in their acquaintance, during the summer of 1895, Proust wrote Marie to tell her he had just written a collection of poems, "Portraits of Painters and Musicians," in collaboration with Reynaldo and that he wanted to dedicate them to her father. A few months earlier, he had declaimed these verses, accompanied by Reynaldo at the piano, at Madeleine Lemaire's salon. Proust had some doubts about the poems and asked Marie—perhaps half in jest—if she would be willing to correct them.[5] Later, Marie married Henri de Régnier—a writer who once fought a duel against Montesquiou— became an established writer (under the pen name Gérard d'Houville), and started an affair with Pierre Louÿs, her brother-in-law and one of the great erotic writers of the twentieth century. Proust remained friendly with her until the end of his life. A few months before his death, on May 27, 1922, he sent her a copy of *Sodome et Gomorrhe II* with a dedication to "sa Majesté la Reine des Canaques."[6]

Marie's father was an important figure for Proust during his early years as a writer. When he published his first poems in *Les plaisirs et les jours,* critics rejected them as being too influenced by Heredia's Parnassian poetics.[7] Heredia represented the young novelist's early ideal of a worldly poet who was equally at home in the salons and at the Académie française, and Proust mentioned him frequently in the articles he wrote during the 1890s and early 1900s. He first wrote about him in "Une fête littéraire à Versailles," an article about the elaborate reception given by Robert de Montesquiou in May 1894. A twenty-three-year-old Proust was awed by the parade of elegant aristocrats and artists in attendance: there were various countesses and marquises, as well as the Heredia sisters, attired in pink muslin dresses. Their father was there, too, as a special guest. At one point in the evening, the actress Julia Bartet, dressed in "a white lace skirt and blue muslin corset," recited Heredia's "Le récif de corail" and a poem by his daughter.[8]

Heredia and Montesquiou had much in common as poets who adored and were adored in society, and they frequented many of the same salons. Proust noticed the resemblance and wrote that the count resembled "those conquistadors immortalized by Monsieur de Heredia."[9] The two poets were good friends and exchanged many letters, and in 1895 Heredia prefaced Montesquiou's *Parcours du rêve au souvenir.*[10] In 1897, Marie de Heredia insulted Montesquiou, joking that he had used his cane to make his way out of the fire at the Bazar de la Charité—a tragic accident that killed more than one hundred people, most of them aristocrats. The count was so outraged that he fought a duel with Marie's husband and ceased his dealings with the Heredia family for some time.[11]

Proust was fascinated by Heredia's social success. In a 1903 piece he wrote for *Le Figaro* about the salon of Princess Mathilde, he described admiringly how the poet could use his grace and charm to flatter the hostess even while contradicting her. The princess had turned against her old friend Hippolyte Taine after he had criticized her family in his *Napoléon Bonaparte*. Heredia was present when the princess lashed out against Taine, but he "prit la défense de Taine avec une chaleur qui déplut à la princesse et elle le lui témoigna avec une certaine vivacité. 'Votre altesse a bien tort,' dit Heredia. 'Elle devrait, au contraire, en me voyant prendre, même contre elle, le parti d'un ami absent, comprendre qu'on peut, que surtout elle peut, compter sur ma fidélité'" (Heredia "sprang to Taine's defense with a warmth that displeased the princess, and she tartly let him know it. 'Your Highness is misguided,' was Heredia's response. 'Upon hearing me speak up on behalf of an absent friend, albeit against herself, she ought on the contrary to understand that one can—that she can, above all—rely on my fidelity.'")[12] Proust admired Heredia's deft use of rhetoric and elegant tropes to extricate himself from a difficult social situation, and the scene evokes the brilliant repartee the novelist would later attribute to Swann and Charlus in *À la recherche du temps perdu*.

While Proust admired Heredia's literary and social success, he—like several critics—questioned whether Heredia's poetry lived up to its fame. In an early short story, "Un dîner en ville," written around 1893, Proust reproduced the frivolous literary conversations overheard in the salons. One of the dinner guests shocks the company after "ayant osé avec l'imprudence de la jeunesse d'insinuer que dans l'œuvre de Heredia il y avait peut-être plus de pensée qu'on ne le disait généralement"[13] (having dared, with the imprudence of youth, to insinuate that Heredia's work contained more ideas than was generally acknowledged). Here Proust's character suggests that Heredia's poems—like many of the Parnassians' compositions—were beautiful and well crafted but lacked intellectual content.

Proust also mentions Heredia in *Jean Santeuil*. In one passage, the narrator alludes to writers who like to shock their audience with pronouncements like "That is the end of the French language" or "Heredia has taken up free verse."[14] This last affirmation would have caused a stir, since Heredia was a master of the sonnet and wrote almost exclusively in this form. Like most schoolchildren of his generation, Proust memorized several of Heredia's best-known sonnets. He quoted, sometimes approximately, the poet's verses in his correspondence, including, on several occasions, the famous closing verses of "Les conquérants," which he was especially fond of repeating to his banker Lionel Hauser: "Ils regardaient monter en un ciel ignoré/Du fond de l'Océan des étoiles nouvelles."[15] Proust continued to quote Heredia's poems until late in life, and in a 1920 letter to Henri de Régnier, Proust praised "le grand génie que reste pour moi et que restera toujours aussi longtemps que la langue française José Maria de Heredia"[16] (the great genius that remains for me and that will endure, as long as the French language, José Maria de Heredia).

In *À la recherche du temps perdu,* Proust mentions Heredia only once, as an example of a salon intellectual. In *À l'ombre de jeunes filles en fleurs,* the narrator describes how Bloch's father disapproved of his son's interest in "bohemian" writers like Heredia but would have approved of his new acquaintance with the Marquis de Saint-Loup.

> Car Bloch était mal à l'aise chez lui et sentait que son père le traitait de dévoyé parce qu'il vivait dans l'admiration de Leconte de Lisle, Heredia et autres "bohèmes." Mais des relations avec Saint-Loup-en-Bray dont le père avait été président du Canal de Suez! (ah! bougre!), c'était un résultat "indiscutable."[17]

> (Within the family, he lived usually in a state of some unease, feeling that his father believed he had gone to the dogs with his admiration of poets like Leconte de Lisle, Heredia and other such "Bohemians." But to be friendly with Saint-Loup-en-Bray, whose father had been the president of the Suez Canal Company (Egad!), was an "incontrovertible" advantage.)[18]

Heredia is mentioned as an example of a "bohemian," a term that Bloch's father uses as an antonym of the rich world embodied by Robert de Saint-Loup. This judgment was not too far from the truth; compared to aristocrats like Montesquiou, who inherited vast family fortunes, Heredia was a man of modest means. When he settled in Paris in 1861, his finances looked bright. The family's coffee plantations produced a handsome revenue that allowed him to live comfortably in a good neighborhood. But by the end of the century, most of the family's Cuban properties had been destroyed during the island's many uprisings and revolts—most significantly the 1898 Cuban-Spanish-American War—and Heredia, who had a passion for gambling, lost his entire fortune not once but twice.[19] By the time he died in 1905, he was penniless and in debt.

Proust's Heredia

Like many of his contemporaries, Proust associated Heredia primarily with his most famous poem, "Les conquérants," a sonnet from *Les trophées* celebrating the adventurous spirit of the first Spaniards who sailed to the new world.

Comme un vol de gerfauts hors du charnier natal,
Fatigués de porter leurs misères hautaines,
De Palos de Moguer, routiers et capitaines
Partaient, ivres d'un rêve héroïque et brutal.

Ils allaient conquérir le fabuleux métal
Que Cipango mûrit dans ses mines lointaines,
Et les vents alizés inclinaient leurs antennes
Aux bords mystérieux du monde Occidental.

Chaque soir, espérant des lendemains épiques,
L'azur phosphorescent de la mer des Tropiques
Enchantait leur sommeil d'un mirage doré;

Ou penchés à l'avant des blanches caravelles,
Ils regardaient monter en un ciel ignoré
Du fond de l'Océan des étoiles nouvelles.[20]

(As gerfalcons who leave their native prey,
Captains and men from Palos of Moguer,
Weary of bearing their proud misery,
Set Forth, drunk with heroic, brutal dreams.
They go to conquest of the fabled gold
Cipango ripens in its far-off mines;
The trade-winds strain the sloping yards; they sail
To shores of wonder in the western world.
  An epic morrow is each evening's hope.
  The tropics' phosphorescent sea of blue
  Enskies their dreams with a mirage of gold;
  Or from the bow of the white caravel
  They watch and see from out the ocean depths
  New stars come up and glow in unknown skies.)[21]

This sonnet, along with the other poems Heredia grouped under the title "Les conquérants," helped shape Proust's and his contemporaries' views on Latin American history. Heredia's portrayal of the conquest as a heroic deed and the conquistadors as courageous explorers might surprise twenty-first-century readers, seasoned by several decades of postcolonial critiques of the event now refereed to as "the Encounter." Heredia's idealization of the conquerors, his exaltation of Spanish culture, and the near absence of Indians, make the poem a one-dimensional depiction of a historical episode that was fraught with violence and destruction. But "Les conquérants" offers a more complex portrait of the conquistadors than we might first suspect. The poem opens by comparing Columbus's men—identified by the reference to Palos de Moguer, the port from where the caravels first sailed—to "gerfalcons," birds of prey. At the outset there is nothing heroic about them: they joined the expedition to "flee" from a life of "misery" and appear "drunken" with a "dream" that while "heroic" is also "brutal." Their main motivation seems to be economic, as they plan to "conquer" not a new land but the "fabled metal." The sonnet stresses that their goal is to reach "Cipango," as Japan was known in fifteenth-century Europe.

But once the winds have pushed their ship to "the mysterious confines of the Western world," the men undergo a transformation. They begin to long for "lendemains épiques" (an epic future), are mesmerized by the phosphorescent blue of the ocean, and spend their time dreaming. Earlier they sought gold, but now they are satisfied with the "golden mirage" imprinted on their dreams. They no longer aspire to material riches but are content with the immaterial "gold" hues adorning the ocean views. By the last tercet, the Spaniards have become enthralled by the seascape and spend their time leaning on the bow, marveling at the "new stars" rising over an "unknown sky"—a reference to the new constellations the explorers discovered when they first crossed into the southern hemisphere.[22] Although these first conquistadors start out as vulgar gold seekers, motivated only by hopes of financial gain, the voyage transforms them into Romantic figures devoted to contemplating the colors of the sea and gazing at the night sky. The transatlantic journey has turned materialists into dreamers, gold seekers into nature lovers, and vultures (or gerfalcons) into doves. The conquistadors start out as adventurers but end as poets devoted—like Heredia—to singing the beauties of nature.

The poem also redefines the sense of adventure. These men set out in search of gold and yearn for adventures ("lendemains épiques"), but by the end of the poem they have made no real exploits—they have fought no battles, they have not encountered new civilizations, they have not discovered new lands. Their only adventure is the inner voyage sparked by the contemplation of the oceanscape and the night sky. These visions lead them to retreat into an interiority—an inner experience marked by reflection and meditation—that the reader would not have attributed to the rude adventurers presented in the poem's first verses. The poem ends in suspense, and we never see the conquistadors reach the Americas. In the end, they do not conquer anything; rather, they are conquered, the poem suggests, by the forces of nature.

In addition to "Les conquérants," the section devoted to the conquistadors in *Les trophées* includes seven other sonnets related to the conquest. "Jouvence" is an homage to Juan Ponce de León's quest for the fountain of youth (the poem closes with the verse "La gloire t'a donné la jeunesse immortelle"). "Le tombeau du conquérant" is an elegy to Hernando de Soto's tomb. "Carolo Quinto Imperante" celebrates Charles V, the Spanish king who ruled over the conquest ("Castille a triomphé par cet homme, et ses flottes/Ont sous lui complété l'empire sans pareil/Pour lequel ne pouvait se coucher le soleil" (This man assured the triumph of Castile, whose fleets/At his command the peerless empire won,/O'er which there never hung a setting sun). "L'ancêtre," dedicated to the artist and poet Claudius Popelin (1825-1892), celebrates the poet's ancestor, Pedro de Heredia, "l'aïeul fier et mélancolique," who founded Cartagena de Indias in Colombia and was one of the settlers of the Dominican Republic and Panama. In 1886, Popelin completed an enamel portrait of José-Maria de Heredia dressed as Pedro de Heredia, in which he appears under the coat of arms of Cartagena (see plate 7); the hand-painted text identifies him as "an Hidalgo and one of the *conquistadors*" and recalls that "after defeating the Indians, against whom he fought several battles, he founded Cartagena de Indias in the year 1533." *Les trophées* includes three poems to this illustrious ancestor: "A un fondateur de ville," "Une Carthage neuve au pays de la Fable," and "Au meme." There is also a poem, "A une ville morte," lamenting the ransacking of Cartagena by English pirates in the 16th and 17th centuries.[23]

Les trophées includes one more section devoted to a Latin American topic: "Les conquérants de l'or," a fragment of an unfinished epic about the conquest of Peru. First published as "La détresse d'Atahuallpa" in 1869,[24] it is the longest poem in the collection. It narrates Francisco Pizarro's journey from Panama to the Inca Empire in Peru, a voyage that leads the Spaniards through endless obstacles—dangerous reptiles and a treacherous, exuberant nature—before they reach the Andes. The poem ends abruptly, just before the Spaniards confront the natives, and does not describe either the encounter or the fierce battles that followed.

Heredia's poetry omits the violent episodes we have come to associate with the Conquest. There are no violent clashes, no murders, no tortures, no hostage taking, nor any of the other cruel activities chronicled in history books; Heredia seems to whitewash the unsavory events in this contentious historical episode. As Miodrag Ibrovac has written, "De cette aventure 'héroïque et brutale,' Héredia n'a voulu chanter que le mirage épique" (Of this heroic, brutal adventure, Heredia elected to sing only of the epic mirage).[25] Heredia's embellished vision contrasts sharply with other historical accounts of the Conquest. Compare, for instance, Heredia's homage to Pedro de Heredia to a more recent account by the Colombian historian Jorge Orlando Melo. The conquistador, Melo writes, "ordered his men to burn villages and fields, to capture young men and women, and to capture those who did not submit to his orders. A bearer of European morals, he had all those who practiced cannibalism or sodomy condemned to death and sent to the gallows."[26] Another historian adds that "in the 1530s Pedro de Heredia and his companions explored and raided the Sinú country between Cartagena and Darién, ransacking the tombs of the Sinú peoples for mortuary regalia."[27]

Heredia, in his effort to pay tribute to an era he associated with chivalry and epic deeds, turned a blind eye to atrocity. And while it is true that the darkest side of the Conquest would not be fully explored until the twentieth century, the poet had at his disposal plenty of documents—including Bartolomé de las Casas's sixteenth-century texts—that directly contradicted the poet's vision of the conquistadors as epic heroes.

Another striking feature in Heredia's poems about the Conquest is the complete absence of Indians. "Au même" mentions several Indian civilizations vanquished by the conquistadores—Aztec, Inca, and Yaqui—and "Les conquérants de l'or" includes the sighting of an Inca campground, but the natives never appear as characters. Heredia gives a much more detailed account of American flora and fauna than he does of the native inhabitants. The reader gets the impression that the Incas are always around the corner, about to confront the advancing Spaniards, but the poem ends without ever introducing Atahualpa or his subjects.

Heredia and Latin America

Of the four Latin Americans studied in this book, Heredia was the one who kept the strongest ties to his native country. He was in contact with Latin American writers living in Paris—including the Cubans Emilio Bobadilla, Armand Godoy, Augusto de Armas, and José Barnet—and with many others who passed by. (Rubén Darío almost came to visit him, but changed his mind at the last minute.)[28] Unlike Reynaldo Hahn or Gabriel de Yturri, Heredia was an important reference for Latin American intellectuals of his period. Many admired him as a fellow poet who had attained the dream of being admitted into the bastion of French letters. Rubén Darío wrote articles on Heredia, as did the Mexican Amado Nervo, the Guatemalan Enrique Gómez Carrillo, and the Dominican Pedro Henríquez Ureña.[29] The Spanish critic Enrique Díez Canedo wrote eloquently about the fascination Heredia exerted on Latin American poets. His sonnets were translated into Spanish by illustrious contemporary intellectuals, including Antonio de Zayas, Max Henríquez Ureña, Justo Sierra, and Miguel Antonio Caro. "I have counted," writes Díez Canedo, "at least fifteen different translations of the single sonnet 'Les conquérants.'"[30]

Not all Latin Americans praised Heredia. Some accused him of abandoning his homeland and his native language. Manuel Sanguily, a Cuban critic, published an article called "José María de Heredia is not a Cuban poet," arguing that the poet "gave up his country of birth, made France his only homeland, his only residence, his only *nation,* and transformed himself, for good, into a Frenchman."[31] The Cuban critic summarizes Heredia's life as follows: "Son of a French mother, educated in France, alumnus of the École des Chartes, friend and follower of Leconte de Lisle, Parnassian, pessimist, objectivist: What is—what could ever—be *Cuban* about a poet who has written such magnificent French verses without devoting a single one of them to Cuba, to its past, present, or future?"[32]

In contrast with these ultranationalist critics, Heredia had complex ideas about his own cultural identity. When he was elected to the Académie française in 1894, he used his acceptance speech to reflect on his position as a Latin American living in France and writing in French. "En m'accueillant dans votre Compagnie, vous avez consacré mon adoption par la France," he told the other academicians. Heredia went on to explain his multicultural experience.

La France me fut toujours chère. Elle était la patrie de mon intelligence et de mon cœur. Je l'ai aimée dès le berceau. Sa langue est la première qui m'ait charmé par la voix maternelle. C'est à l'amour de ce noble langage, le plus beau qui, depuis Homère, soit né sur des lèvres humaines, que je dois de siéger parmi vous. Grâce à vous, Messieurs, et je ne vous en saurais trop remercier, je suis deux fois Français. Et ce n'est pas le poète seul qu'honore votre choix; l'honneur en rejaillit sur notre sœur latine l'Espagne et, plus loin encore, jusqu'à ce Nouveau Monde que se sont disputé nos communs ancêtres, par-delà l'Océan qui baigne l'île éclatante et lointaine où je suis né.[33]

(By welcoming me into your Company, you have set the seal on my adoption by France. France has always been dear to me. She was ever the motherland of my intelligence and my heart. I loved her from the very cradle. Her language was the first to charm me, through my mother's voice. My seat among you here is owed to my love for that noble language, the most beautiful, since Homer's day, ever to be uttered by human lips. Thanks to you, gentlemen—and for this I can never thank you enough—I am a Frenchman twice over. And it is not the poet alone who has been honored by your choice; the honor rebounds upon our Latin sister, Spain, and reaches further still to the New World disputed by our common ancestors, across the Ocean that bathes the distant, dazzling island of my birth.)

Heredia considers France as his "patrie," his motherland, and identifies himself as doubly French (by naturalization and by election to the Académie française). The poet does not identify with the land where he was born but with the language and culture that informed his literature. For him, identity has less to do with soil or blood than with language. Since Roman times, citizenship had been conferred either by birth in a country's territory (*jus solis*) or by being directly related by blood to a citizen (*jus sanguis*). Heredia rejects these two means of transmission in favor of language, which he proclaims to be the most important element for citizenship, a form of *jus linguae*.

But Heredia also stresses his Latin American identity. The "aura" of the Académie, he tells his colleagues, will extend to Spain—until 1898 Cuba was a Spanish colony and Heredia a Spanish subject—and to "the faraway island" where he was born. The mention of "nos communs ancêtres" evokes the historical rivalry between Spain and France for control of the Americas and suggests a connection between Heredia's conquistador forebears and the French explorers. His associations move from his ancestors to the history of the Caribbean and back to France. This section of the speech opens with

"La France" and ends with "l'île éclatante et lointaine où je suis né," as if Heredia were traveling backward in time, retracing the crossing of the Atlantic he undertook in 1861. Was this a homecoming of sorts?

Proust, Heredia, and the Eclipse

One wonders what Proust would have thought of Heredia's portrayal of the Spanish conquistadors. Would the novelist have shared this epic vision? Would he have considered poems like "Les conquérants" and "Les conquérants de l'or" too idealistic? So far, no critics have written on Proust's views on the Conquest—an omission that might seem justified, since this episode, unlike other moments of European history from the Dreyfus Affair to the Great War, does not feature prominently in either *À la recherche du temps perdu* or the correspondence. But Proust did write one early text about the Conquest when he was fifteen years old: "L'éclipse"(1886), a story about Columbus in the Caribbean (included in the Pléiade edition of *Contre Sainte-Beuve* but not in the English edition of this work).

Proust set his story in 1502. Christopher Columbus has just been released from prison, and he sets out to make a fourth—and last—voyage to the New World. The young Marcel paints a sympathetic portrait of the explorer: "C'était toujours aussi le savant admirable qui par l'étendue et la profondeur de ses connaissances, par la précision et l'élévation de ses recherches, était parvenu à faire la merveilleuse découverte qui devait l'illustrer et qui, à cette époque, tenait du miracle et du prodige." (He was still, too, that admirable scholar whose breadth and depth of knowledge, along with the accuracy and far-sightedness of his research, enabled him to make the wondrous discovery which immortalized his name and which, for that era, verged on the miraculous and the prodigious.)[34]

Like Heredia in "Les conquérants," Proust narrates the voyage across the Atlantic and describes Columbus "se réglant toujours sur les mouvements des astres qu'il connaissait avec une exactitude merveilleuse" (always setting his course by the movement of the stars, which he knew with wonderful exactitude). As the Spaniards approach Cuba, they hit a violent tropical storm that badly damages the ship and forces them to crash-land in Jamaica, an island Columbus "had discovered in 1494 and which belonged to Spain since then." At first the Spaniards are well received by "les indigènes," but after a few days the natives rebel against them and threaten to cut off their supplies. Columbus is in a quandary. He has sent a good number of his men to the nearby island of Santo Domingo in search of another vessel, and he has fewer than fifty sailors with him. At one point, 100,000 natives surround them. The Spaniards want to flee, "mais comment franchir ce rempart de corps et de lames qui les environne" (but how to pass through this wall of bodies and blades surrounding them)?[35]

Columbus urges his men to remain calm and confronts the Indians with a most unusual threat. "'Hommes Caraïbes,' he told them, 'vous vous révoltez contre votre seigneur et maître, le roi d'Espagne; mais la colère divine s'appesantira sur vous et dans quelques heures la lune qui maintenant brille si claire au ciel, se voilera et Dieu vous plongera dans l'obscurité la plus profonde.'" ("Caribs," he told them, "you have risen in revolt against your lord and master, the king of Spain; but now divine wrath will descend upon you, and in a very few hours the moon that shines so brightly in the sky will be obscured, and God will plunge you into complete darkness.") Through astronomical calculations, he determines that a lunar eclipse is imminent, and he decides to use this to his advantage. The moon shines on the tropical landscape, and the young Marcel—who already seems to have an eye for homoerotic imagery—paints a dazzling portrait of the scene: "tous ces corps nus et cuivrés, armés de lames brillantes, ce vieillard à la longue barbe blanche qui regardait le ciel, cette végétation luxuriante et extraordinaire de la Jamaïque" (all those naked copper bodies, armed with glinting blades; that old man with a long white beard, gazing up at the sky; that wild luxuriance of Jamaica).[36]

As Columbus has predicted, the sky goes dark, and the moon disappears. "Les Peaux-Rouges alors sont saisis de terreur; éperdus, ils se précipitent aux genoux de Colomb en le suppliant de leur pardonner." (At this the redskins were seized with terror; frantically they groveled at Columbus's feet, begging for forgiveness.) Proust dwells on this moment, stressing how "c'était un spectacle touchant que celui de ces pauvres sauvages terrifiés et fous d'angoisse, conjurant Colomb de leur laisser revoir l'astre bien-aimé." (The poor savages were an affecting sight indeed, gibbering with fear, imploring Columbus to let them see their beloved moon again.) In the end, he relents, "Colomb leur pardonne aisément et l'espace résonna longtemps des joyeux trépignements des Caraïbes, anxieux encore, cependant, car la lune était toujours voilée." (Columbus pardoned them with no more ado, and the ground long reverberated with the joyful capering of the Caribs, who nevertheless were anxious while the moon's face remained veiled.) Eventually, the eclipse ends, and the moon shines again. Proust closes with "une scène splendide et symbolique, où les sauvages apaisés, toujours à genoux devant

Colomb, semblaient une image vivante de la barbarie adorant et divinisant la civilisation" (a splendid, symbolic scene, in which the pacified savages, still kneeling before Columbus, offered the very picture of barbarism adoring civilization as though it were a god).[37]

Proust adapted this story from a well-known episode in the histories of Columbus's travels. Although Columbus did not include this incident in the diary of his fourth voyage, it is mentioned by Diego Méndez de Segura, a friend who settled in Santo Domingo and represented him in a trial against the Spanish crown.[38] Later historians brought the scene to life by exploiting its dramatic potential, as we can see, for instance, in Washington Irving's *Life and Voyages of Christopher Columbus.*

> The horrors of famine began to threaten the terrified crew, when a fortunate idea presented itself to Columbus. From his knowledge of astronomy, he ascertained that within three days there would be a total eclipse of the moon, in the early part of the night. He summoned, therefore, the principal caciques to a grand confer-ence, appointing it for the day of the eclipse. When all were assembled, he told them by his interpreter, that he and his followers were worshippers of a Deity who lived in the skies, and held them under his protection; that this great Deity was incensed against the Indians, who had refused or neglected to furnish his faithful worshippers with provisions, and intended to chastise them with famine and pestilence. Lest they should disbelieve this warning, a signal would be given that very night in the heavens. They would behold the moon change its colour, and gradually lose its light; a token of the fearful punishment which awaited them.
>
> Many of the Indians were alarmed at the solemnity of this prediction, others treated it with derision; all, however, awaited with solicitude the coming of the night. When they beheld a black shadow stealing over the moon, and a mysteri-ous gloom gradually covering the whole face of nature, they were seized with the utmost consternation. Hurrying with provisions to the ships, and throwing them-selves at the feet of Columbus, they implored him to intercede with his God to withhold the threatened calamities, assuring him that thenceforth they could bring him whatever he required.[39]

Irving's biography of Columbus was published in French in 1864, and it is likely that Proust read the tale of the eclipse in this source or in an excerpt reproduced in one of his schoolbooks.[40]

Proust could have taken the facts from any history of Columbus's voy-ages, but the portrayal of Columbus as a hero and an emissary of civilization clearly owes much to Heredia's "Les conquérants." Although *Les trophées* was not published until 1893, "Les conquérants" was first included in Heredia's *Sonnets et eaux-fortes* (1869), and it quickly became one of the period's most popular poems. It was reprinted in the 1874 and 1875 editions of *Le livre des sonnets*, in Catulle Mendès's *La légende du Parnasse contemporain* (1884), and in an 1885 issue of *La Revue Bleue*. By the time Proust wrote "L'éclipse" in 1886, "Les conquérants" had become one of the most famous Parnassian poems, often recited in salons and poetry readings.

Like Heredia's conquerors, Proust's Columbus is strong, determined, and valorous: his attributes include terms like "hardiesse," "fermeté," "précision," and "élévation." He presents Columbus, who was only fifty-one at the time of his fourth voyage, as an "illustre vieillard" sporting a white beard, a feature that makes him more recognizable as a tragic hero. But it is Proust's descriptions of the tropical skies and verdant nature that most recall Heredia's poem. A line like "La lune brillante et claire au milieu d'un ciel pur et constellé d'étoiles épandait sur les plaines fertiles de l'île des larges bandes de lumière pâle et mystérieuse" (The clear, bright moon in the middle of a cloudless sky scintillating with stars cast wide beams of pale, mysterious light over the fertile island plains) brings to mind "Les conquérants," with its verdant seascapes and final verse on the rise of "les étoiles nouvelles." Proust's "vegetation luxuriante et extraordinaire" also rhymes with Heredia's American landscapes in "Les conquérants de l'or" and other poems.[41]

The influence of the Parnassians can also be seen in the choice of subject. Heredia believed poetry should only look to history—and to the heroic episodes of the past—for inspiration. This brief story was Proust's only incursion into the genre of historical fiction. Never again would he write about events that occurred on another continent, centuries before his birth.

Marcel closes his text with the Indians kneeling before Columbus, "a true image of barbarism adoring and exalting civilization." Marie Miguet-Ollagnier, one of the few critics who has written about this early story, argues that it reflects the values and political views of late nineteenth-century France: "This piece provides documentary testimony of the reception of the navigator's behavior by a bourgeois schoolboy. In the politically stable world of the Third Republic, taking its values for granted, the young man elevates a father-figure, a sage, a leader, to heroic status. [. . .] Imbued with humanist culture, the *lycée* student sees Christopher Columbus as a new Aeneas mastering the storm, a Ulysses trumping brute force with cunning and eloquence. The need to look up to an authority grounded in reason is patent in 'The Eclipse.'"[42]

For the twenty-first-century reader, the most disconcerting element of the story is its forceful colonialist message. Marcel does not seem to doubt, even for an instance, that Columbus represents the virtues of "civilization" and that the Indians embody the forces of "barbarism." But as Miguet-Ollaguiner observes, this message has to do less with Proust's individual vision than with the canonical view of history that bourgeois children of his generation learned both at home and at school. "The Eclipse" is a school assignment designed to promote a particular vision of European history— along with a set of corresponding values—among French schoolboys.

All French schools in the Third Republic taught this Manichean view of history, which became an important part of the French "civilizing mission." This view reached its peak in the same years that Marcel entered the *lycée*, and, as Alice L. Conklin demonstrates, it "rested upon certain fundamental assumptions about the superiority of French culture and the perfectibility of humankind. It implied that France's colonial subjects were too primitive to rule themselves but were capable of being uplifted. It intimated that the French were particularly suited, by temperament and by virtue of both their revolutionary past and their current industrial strength, to carry out this task. Last but not least, it assumed that the Third Republic had a duty and a right to remake 'primitive' cultures along lines inspired by the cultural, political, and economic development of France."[43]

As Marcel was writing "The Eclipse," the French government was hard at work propagating this "civilizing mission" around the globe. The last decades of the nineteenth century witnessed the largest colonial expansion in French history. After the ill-fated Mexican campaign (1861-1867) and Napoleon III's imperial projects in Cambodia, China, and Cochinchina, the Third Republic established colonies in Tunisia (1881), Vietnam (1884-1885), Indochina (1887), Laos (1893), China (1898), and in vast areas of Africa. Marcel learned his first lessons about French colonialism not only from his schoolteachers but also from Heredia's poems, which provided a literary justification for the "civilizing mission" and reinforced the ideology of European cultural superiority that had begun with the Conquest of the Americas.

Heredia and French Colonialism

Despite the abundance of publications on Heredia—most written during the late nineteenth and early twentieth century—we know little about his political views. This is not surprising, given that the entire edifice of Parnassian poetry was built on the notion of separating poetry from the author's experience, a realm that included affects as well as politics. Even so, it is astonishing to think that Heredia lived through such violent and traumatic episodes as the Franco-Prussian War of 1870, French colonial expansion under the Second Empire and the Third Republic, the Dreyfus Affair, and the Spanish-American War without commenting, in print or in his private correspondence, on any of these events. Critics have wondered how Heredia managed to remain tight-lipped even as his native Cuba broke free from Spain in 1898.[44]

Despite his ideal of living a life insulated from the ugly world of politics, Heredia was sometimes forced by circumstances to take a stand on important debates. After joining the Académie française, he often sided with his fellow members in political matters. In 1898, when the Dreyfus Affair polarized French society, members of the Académie joined a conservative group called the Ligue de la patrie française (League of the French Fatherland). On December 31, 1898, the league published an open letter calling for national unity and extolling the virtues of the "ideas, customs, and traditions of the French nation." Heredia signed the letter, along with his fellow academicians François Coppée and Albert Sorel; other signatories included Edgar Degas, Auguste Renoir, Frédéric Mistral, Pierre Louÿs (Heredia's son-in-law), and Charles Maurras.[45]

Heredia joined the league out of solidarity with his colleagues from the Académie, and he was among the moderate members.[46] Even so, it is surprising to think that a poet who had been born in Cuba, who had been a French citizen for only a few years, and who was once described by Coppée as "un beau créole de la Havanne" (a handsome Creole from Havana),[47] would join an anti-Dreyfus group with a nationalist agenda.[48] To his credit, Heredia was a member of the league for less than one year; on January 20, 1899, the poet sent a letter to Jules Lemaître, one of the founders, announcing his resignation.[49]

Even more striking is Heredia's silence on French colonial ambitions in Latin America. In 1861, while he was a student at the École des Chartes, Napoleon III launched a "Mexican expedition" designed to bring Mexico under French control while the United States was embroiled in the Civil War. In 1864, Maximilian von Hapsburg, the eccentric younger brother of the Austro-Hungarian emperor Franz Josef, was proclaimed Mexican emperor with the support of a small faction of Mexican conservative royalists and an army of forty thousand French soldiers.

When the Civil War ended, the United States made it clear that it would not tolerate a European incursion at its doorstep and extended its support to Maximilian's opponents, led by former president Benito Juárez. As tensions with Prussia escalated and war loomed, Napoleon III recalled his troops and left Maximilian to fend for himself. Without French military support, the Mexican Empire was doomed. Maximilian's advisers encouraged him to return to Europe, but he insisted on fighting until the end. In 1867, he was captured, tried for treason, and executed by the firing squad, sealing the failure of the French intervention in Mexico. His execution sent shock waves around Europe and was later painted by Édouard Manet.[50] Maximilian was also a conquistador—though a failed one—and it is striking that the news of his execution did not elicit even a minor comment from the Cuban poet.

A few years after the failed Mexican expedition, there was another episode that pitted France against the Americas. In the 1870s and 1880s, as Heredia was at work on his unfinished epic "Les conquérants de l'or," France launched one its most ambitious international projects, the construction of the interoceanic canal in Panama, then a province of Colombia. The plan followed on the heels of the successful completion of the Suez Canal in Egypt by a team led by Ferdinand de Lesseps. Inaugurated in 1869, the Suez was financed in part with bonds sold to small investors, and hundreds of thousands of middle-class Frenchmen saw their savings multiplied thanks to the Suez bonds. There was "scarcely a small tradesman or peasant who has not his share in the Suez Canal," as de Lesseps wrote in his memoirs.[51]

Buoyed by his success in Egypt, de Lesseps launched another ambitious project in the 1870s: a passageway across Central America to connect the Atlantic and Pacific oceans—an idea that had been under discussion since the early years of the nineteenth century. Goethe had mentioned the possibility of a canal in the 1820s, and the United States had also considered the option of building an American-controlled waterway.[52] Technically, the Panama Canal was a much more complicated endeavor than Suez; de Lesseps imagined a causeway without locks and projected cutting through the Culebra mountains, which ran through the middle of the proposed canal path.[53]

De Lesseps enlisted the help of Baron Jacques de Reinach, an ingenious financier who brought in Gustave Eiffel, the builder of the famous tower, as a technical consultant. Reinach raised funds by selling stock in the Universal Panama Interoceanic Canal Company, which went public in 1880. The company had no problems raising cash. Most French investors considered

Figure 3.6. Louis-Oscar Roty (1846–1911), medal commemorating the launching of the Panama Canal Works, 1880. The legend reads "Excavation of the Isthmus of Panama." RMN-Grand Palais (Musée d'Orsay)/Tony Querrec. Figure 3.7. Louis-Oscar Roty (1846–1911), medal commemorating the launching of the Panama Canal Works, 1880. "Panama Canal/Universal Company of the Interoceanic Canal. 7 and 8 December 1880. To its investors, the Parisian Bank." RMN-Grand Palais (Musée d'Orsay) / Tony Querrec.

it a second Suez and jumped at the opportunity to invest in what promised to be a lucrative venture. In 1880, the company offered freshly minted silver medals to its subscribers (see figs. 3.6 and 3.7).

Workers began excavating the canal in 1882, but the company soon ran into major problems. Digging through the Culebra Mountains generated vast amounts of rubble that had to be cleared away at enormous expense. The costs rose exponentially, and in its first six years de Lessep's company had to raise additional capital by launching four bond sales. An article published in *Harper's Weekly* chronicles the plight of the canal's laborers. "Negroes," the author wrote, "are the only laborers who can work in such pestilential climates without imminent risk of being stricken down by malarial disease. The fevers cut off other workmen in hundreds. White laborers disappear like snow before a July sun."[54] The author doubted that the project would be completed in a reasonable time frame: "With time, with men, with money in fabulous sums, *M. de Lesseps* can complete the canal; and if it is done in 1898 he will have executed wonders. After four years' work, and the expenditure of over $90,000,000 gold, but a twentieth is done, admitting the accuracy and fullness of the company's figures."[55]

Reinach and de Lesseps tried to raise additional capital through a fifth bond sale but were unsuccessful. The company suspended payments in 1888 and went bankrupt a year later. It was discovered that Reinach had concealed the company's financial straits and even bribed government officials to secure preferential treatment for his project. An investigation was launched, and in 1892 the courts pressed charges against de Lesseps and several of his associates, including Eiffel. Many elected officials were mired in the scandal, including Antonin Proust (no relation to Marcel), a deputy from the department of Deux-Sèvres who was also France's first fine arts minister and a supporter of many artists, including Rodin, Pisarro, Monet, and Manet, a lifelong friend who painted his portrait in 1880. Reinach—a nineteenth-century Bernard Madoff of sorts—was accused of having run a vast Ponzi scheme in which thousands of investors lost their life savings. Before the sentence was handed down, he was found dead at his home in 1892 after what was widely believed to have been a suicide. Conservative groups, trumpeting Reinach's Jewish origins, fanned anti-Semitic sentiment, which had been running high since Dreyfus's indictment.[56]

The French government sold what remained of the company—along with all the equipment, real estate, and infrastructure in Panama—to the United States for $40 million, a fraction of its real value. President Theodore Roosevelt signed the Isthmian Canal Bill in 1902, giving his country control of the canal. Colombia protested, since the contract with France included a clause stating that the rights to the canal could not be transferred to a third country. To overcome this obstacle, the United States backed a group that declared Panamanian independence in 1903 and installed a government favorable to American interests. The actual delivery of the canal works took place in the isthmus on May 5, 1904, at the headquarters of the New Panama Canal Company.[57] The original plans were altered to allow for locks, and the canal was finally completed in 1914, more than three decades after de Lesseps had launched the project.

Although now largely forgotten outside of France, the Panama Affair was, along with the Dreyfus Affair, one of the great French scandals of the day. For several years after the collapse of de Lesseps's company, Panama was the talk of the town and the subject of endless newspaper and magazine articles. Those mired in the scandal became known as "Panamistes," and millions of ordinary French citizens were affected by the fallout. On August 15, 1900, Marcel Proust's mother wrote her son a letter from Evian, telling him that she and her husband had just run into Adolphe Salles, an engineer who was distraught over the news that his father-in-law, Gustave Eiffel, had been implicated in the scandal. The older Prousts invited him for dinner, "pour le consoler et de l'absence de sa femme et des affaires de son beau-père" (to console him for his wife's absence and for his father-in-law's affairs).[58]

In an early draft of his novel, Proust recounts how the maid Françoise lost the small inheritance from Aunt Léonie after she invested in Panama bonds: "Ayant perdu presque tout ce qu'elle avait dans le Panama, ses yeux se mouillaient d'attendrissement en disant qu'elle ne pouvait pas en vouloir à M. de Lesseps qui avait <fait> quelque chose de si beau que le Canal de Suez, qui évitait tant de [peine] à nos pauvres vaisseaux."[59] (Though she had lost almost everything in Panama, her eyes would grow moist with tender feeling as she explained that she could never find it in herself to blame M. de Lesseps—not after he had built something as wonderful as the Suez Canal, that spared our poor ships such a tremendous amount of trouble.)[60] Proust also alluded to the Panama affair in *Jean Santeuil*: "Le scandale Marie" presents a fictional account of the fall of Maurice Rouvier, an eminent politician who was forced to resign his post as finance minister when his ties to Reinach were made public in 1892.[61] Rouvier was shunned by former colleagues and friends but eventually made his way back to politics and became a leader of government in 1905. Proust refashioned this fallen and rehabilitated politician into the character of Charles Marie.

Heredia, too, would have been shaken by the scandal. Perhaps it was not entirely a coincidence that in 1869, the same year that the Suez Canal opened and de Lesseps began planning his Central American project, Heredia published "Les conquérants de l'or," a text that opens with a scene set in Panama and recounting the Spaniard's crossing of the isthmus.

Panama was called Castilla del Oro, or Golden Castille, by Vasco Núñez de Balboa, the first Spaniard to cross the isthmus in 1513 and to reach the Pacific Ocean, which he baptized "Mar del Sur" (Southern Sea). In a dramatic move, he claimed the entire ocean and all the islands contained therein for the Spanish crown. The city of Panama was founded on the shores of this "new" sea in 1519, and its port witnessed the launching of various expeditions in search of the mythical El Dorado, which the Spaniards believed was located somewhere in South America. In 1531, Pizarro sailed from Panama

with a crew of several hundred men and became the first of his countrymen
to reach the Inca Empire in Peru.

In "Les conquérants de l'or," Heredia presents an abridged version of
these events. His most important source was William H. Prescott's *History
of the Conquest of Peru*.[62] Heredia's poem opens with a description of Balboa
and his men struggling to cross the Isthmus of Panama.

> Après que Balboa, menant son bon cheval
> Par les bois non frayés, droit, d'amont en aval,
> Eut, sur l'autre versant des Cordillères hautes,
> Foulé le chaud limon des insalubres côtes
> De l'Isthme qui partage avec ses monts géants
> La glauque immensité des deux grands Océans.[63]

> (When once Balboa had spurred his goodly horse
> Through virgin woods along the river's course,
> And, beyond high Cordillera's farther slopes,
> Had trodden the hot silt of insalubrious coasts
> Where the Isthmus splits, with its high craggy chain,
> The murky reaches of the two great Ocean plains.)

Heredia presents Panama as a land of "uncleared forests" and "insalubri-
ous coasts," a description he took from the Spanish chroniclers. "Golden
Castille," Prescott writes, echoing the first accounts, "the most unhealthy
and unprofitable region of the Isthmus, held out a bright promise to the
unfortunate settler, who too frequently instead of gold found there only
his grave."[64] Heredia's poem highlights the same perils—relentless humidity,
pestilent swamps, swarms of mosquitoes—reported in the countless newspaper and magazine articles about the construction of the Panama Canal.

In Heredia's poem, the isthmus is merely an obstacle to be overcome in
Balboa's quest for El Dorado.

> Tous les aventuriers, dont l'esprit s'enflamma,
> Rêvaient, en arrivant au port de Panama,
> De retrouver, espoir cupide et magnifique,
> Aux rivages dorés de la mer Pacifique,
> El Dorado promis qui fuyait devant eux,
> Et, mêlant avec l'or des songes monstrueux,
> De forcer jusqu'au fond de ces torrides zones

L'âpre virginité des rudes Amazones
Que n'avait pu dompter la race des héros,
De renverser des dieux à têtes de taureaux
Et de vaincre, vrais fils de leur ancêtre Hercule,
Les peuples de l'Aurore et ceux du Crépuscule.[65]

(All these adventurers with souls aflame,
When to the port of Panama they came,
Dreamed with splendid, venal hope
Of finding near the molten Pacific coasts
The promised El Dorado that fled ever yonder,
And monstrous visions mixed with those of plunder
Of forcing, in the wilderness of torrid zones
The fierce virginity of uncouth Amazons
Whom the race of heroes had not brought to heel;
Of overthrowing gods with heads like bulls,
And crushing, with their father Hercules's might,
The peoples of the Dawn and those of Night.)

Echoing a theme presented earlier in "Les conquérants," the Spaniards long for gold—in this case for an entire golden city—but also for great adventures, imagining future battles against Amazons and encounters with exotic peoples (Les peuples de l'Aurore et ceux du Crépuscule) that seem taken out of a Greek epic or a book of chivalry.

But unlike the sailors in Heredia's earlier poem, Balboa's men didn't undergo a change of heart upon encountering the American landscape. In "Les conquérants de l'or" they never become contemplative poets, admire the colors of the seascape, or gaze up to look at the new stars. On the contrary, these "conquerors of gold" have a sadistic streak; they dream not of contemplating the skies but of raping Amazons and shattering idols. These "easy dupes of their own credulous fancies," as Prescott called them,[66] also hope to discover the fountain of youth, the golden temple of Doboya, the golden tombs of Zenu, and many other fantastical sites.[67] In any case, the Isthmus of Panama—initially celebrated as a new Golden Castille—becomes in the end a no-man's-land, a mere pit stop on the way to Peru and other more profitable destinations marked by more benign climates and easier passages.

Heredia published his verses on Panama in the same years that the interoceanic canal emerged as the Third Republic's most important political and economic project. During the 1870s and 1880s, as Heredia rose to fame as a Parnassian poet and his work was anthologized in books and journals, newspapers carried the latest news about the French engineering project in Panama. More than one reader must have made the connection between the Spaniards hailed in "Les conquérants" and these modern-day conquistadors, and they must have recognized that Heredia's Panama had much in common with de Lessep's.

One wonders what Heredia thought of the Panama affair. Did he see it— as Proust was taught in school—as a triumph of civilization over barbarism? Did he consider it a heroic deed, a modern form of cultural conquest? Did he champion de Lesseps as a latter-day conqueror? Did he invest, like so many of his fellow Parisians, in Panama bonds and lose part of his life savings? The Heredia Archive at the Bibliothèque de l'Arsenal does not include any documents that could shed light on these questions.

The Great Turn: 1900

Around 1900, Heredia published a number of articles in which he reaffirmed his identity as a Cuban and his affective ties to Latin America. These texts—various essays published in Argentinean and French newspapers, along with three Spanish sonnets composed to honor the memory of his cousin José María Heredia—also reveal a crucial shift in the aesthetic and intellectual positions the poet had held during most of his life.

Heredia had never written about Cuba's history or its political problems, even though his life coincided with some of the most important events in the island's history: the revolutionary struggles in the 1880s and 1890s, the Spanish American War in 1898, the American occupation, and the declaration of independence. The poet broke his silence in 1900, when he began writing for the Argentinean newspaper *El País* and devoted several articles to the Cuban condition. In one letter to the editor, Heredia stressed the importance he attributed to addressing, for the first time in his life, a Latin American audience.

Pour moi, né à Cuba, la dernière colonie d'Amérique qui lutta pour son indépendance, ce m'est un plaisir de saluer l'Argentine, la première qui poussa le cri de liberté.

En écrivant pour l'Amérique où je suis né il me semble accomplir un devoir naturel. Je suis le premier et le seul Américain qui ait eu l'honneur de siéger dans cette antique et illustre Compagnie qui est l'Académie française. Et si, comme j'ose le croire, sans outrecuidance, il revient à l'Amérique quelque chose de l'honneur que m'a fait la France, j'espère que vous, vos collaborateurs et vos lecteurs, vous voudrez me faire le bon accueil qui est dû au compatriote depuis longtemps absent et qui n'a pas démérité des lieux.[68]

(As a native of Cuba, the last American colony to fight for its independence, it is a pleasure for me to salute Argentina, the first to utter the shout of freedom.

To write for the America in which I was born seems only the fulfillment of a natural duty. I am the first and only American to have been honored with a seat in that ancient and illustrious company, the Académie française. And if, as I dare to believe without presumption, the Americas are in part beneficiaries of the honor awarded me by France, I hope that you, your contributors and your readers will accord me the welcome due to a compatriot who has been away for a long time, but who has not proved to be unworthy.)

This article marks a departure from Heredia's longtime position that poets and their craft were above political matters. For the first time in print, Heredia makes reference to the Cuban-American war of 1898 and to Cuban independence. When Heredia wrote these lines, Cuba had become a protectorate of the United States—the island would not obtain its independence until 1903—and his passionate language reveals his sympathy for the Cuban's "cry for freedom." He considers this first address to the Latin American public a "devoir naturel" and an ethical obligation, and he identifies himself, for the first time in his public life, as a Latin American intellectual (thus he calls Argentinians his "compatriots"). He describes himself as an "American" and stresses the kinship between Argentina and Cuba, the first and last nations to win their independence from Spain. With these words, he adds his voice to a long list of nineteenth-century intellectuals—Simon Bolívar was perhaps the most famous—who, writing from countries as diverse as Mexico, Cuba, Colombia, Argentina, and Uruguay, crafted a pan-American vision of a unified continent running from Mexico to Patagonia with a common culture based on shared Spanish heritage.[69]

An article Heredia published in 1901 in a French newspaper is, without a doubt, his most politically engaged text. The article was a version of the prologue to *Voyage en Patagonie* (1901), a travel book by Count Henry de La Vaulx, an aristocrat who traveled to Patagonia in 1895 and spent several months using questionable methods—inebriating the local *caciques* and tricking them into revealing the location of their burial grounds—to collect bones and other funerary objects that he later deposited at the Museum of Natural History in Paris.

Heredia found de La Vaulx's book—and the account of his interactions with the Indians—deeply disturbing. He had been invited to write a prologue, but instead he composed a critical text, which the author nonetheless included in his book. (Heredia's standing as an academician, it seems, trumped his critical stance.) Heredia opens with an anecdote from his youth about French colonialism in Argentina, recalling how, shortly after arriving in Paris from Cuba, he joined the staff of a literary journal. One day, as he was correcting proofs, he received a most unusual visitor, an eccentric man—"Olympian, fatalistic, and bearded"—who introduced himself as the King of Patagonia (his full title was Orllie-Antoine I, King of Araucania and Patagonia).[70]

The King of Patagonia was actually a lawyer from Périgord named Antoine Tounens—"a truffled Gascon," Heredia calls him—who traveled to Chile in the 1850s, wandered around the country, and convinced a band of Mapuche Indians to elect him their monarch. The Chilean government jailed and later expelled him, and Tounens returned to France, where he spent the rest of his life plotting, unsuccessfully, to regain his kingdom. On the day he visited the literary journal, he asked Heredia and his coworkers to help him fight the Chileans. In exchange, he offered to name the poet governor of Tierra del Fuego and his colleague president of the Great Council of Araucania. These visits, Heredia recalls, "lasted a few months. One day, the King stopped coming. We never saw him again. I suspect he died in exile, that is to say in France, where he was born."[71]

The King of Patagonia was one of the most colorful characters in nineteenth-century history, and he has been the subject of various books. Unlike others who saw him as a tragic figure or a romantic dreamer, Heredia denounced him, with an unusual passion, as a "precursor" to the French colonial expansion in the Americas.

Ce Tartarin de Périgord était, paraît-il, un précurseur. Vous l'avez vous-même constaté. Orllie-Antoine eut le sentiment, ou, pour dire mieux, le pressentiment, de notre politique actuelle d'expansion coloniale. On le crut fou. Il n'était que hanté par une idée fixe, comme tous les hommes de génie. La Fortune le trahit. A la plupart des aventuriers, pour ne paraître point ridicules ou insensés, il ne manque souvent que d'avoir été heureux jusqu'au bout: et le rêve de royauté patagone de l'ex-avoué de Périgueux n'est pas relativement plus extravagant que la tentative d'empire mexicain où fut alors même entraîné le chevaleresque et infortuné Maximilien de Hapsbourg.[72]

(This Tartarin of Périgord was, it would seem, a precursor. You have shown it [in your book]. Orllie-Antoine had the intuition, or rather the premonition, of our current policy of colonial expansion. He was considered mad. Yet he was only haunted by a fixed obsession, like all men of genius. Fortune betrayed him. Most adventurers only escape the appearance of ridicule or insanity by virtue of being lucky to the end: the fantasy of Patagonian royalty harbored by the former lawyer from Périgueux was scarcely more egregious than the bid for a Mexican empire in which the quixotic and luckless Maximilian of Habsburg lost his life around the same time.)

Heredia had previously refrained from expressing his political views in print, but reading de La Vaulx's book sparked an anti-colonialist passion that must have taken his readers by surprise. The poet drives himself into a fury as he denounces the instances of French colonialist arrogance he has witnessed during his life in Paris: Maximilian's empire, the King of Patagonia's delusions, and now, de La Vaulx's looting of Argentinean tombs.

> Aussi aventureux qu'Orllie-Antoine, vous avez été plus sensé. [. . .] Aussi n'avez-vous pas tenté de fonder un royaume. Vous vous êtes contenté d'aller chercher du nouveau, au bout du monde. Vous y avez goûté des sensations fortes, des plaisirs singuliers: entre autres, celui d'être impunément sacrilège et quelque peu cannibale. Et vous l'avouez ingénument sans honte et sans remords. La passion ethnographique excuse tous les forfaits. En ce siècle de lucre, il est beau de n'être criminel que par amour de la science et par désir de la gloire.[73]

(You shared Orllie-Antoine's passion for adventures but you were more careful. [. . .] You did not try to found a kingdom. You contented yourself with sailing, in search for novelty, to the other end of the world. There you enjoyed intense experiences and unusual pleasures: committing sacrileges with impunity and even becoming a cannibal of sorts. And you admit to all of it, naïvely, without shame or remorse. A passion for ethnography excuses all crimes. In this profiteering century, it is marvelous to become a criminal for mere love of science and yen for glory.)

Heredia compares de La Vaulx to the King of Patagonia and denounces him as one more colonial adventurer; he calls him "sacrilegious" for having violated indigenous tombs, "cannibal" for having eaten human flesh with Patagonian caciques, and "criminal" for having stolen objects that belonged to the Indians. But above all he debunks the count's pretentions. He did not contribute to the advancement of science, Heredia tells him, but simply continued the ransacking of Patagonia that had begun with Orllie-Antoine.

Heredia denounces the same deeds that de La Vaulx vaunts as ingenious and heroic. In his book, the count boasts about his ability to trick the Indians into disclosing the location of their tombs, presenting it as a victory of science over superstition, since the objects are to be taken back to a French museum. Heredia, however, portrays these activities as morally and ethically reprehensible: "You profane the land of the dead, you violate their tombs, without the least scruple for the terrorized Indians who consider you a sorcerer and even a bit of a vampire."[74]

Heredia's indignation reaches a climax when he discusses the most striking episode in *Voyage en Patagonie*. Near the end of his trip, de La Vaulx learns of a Patagonian "giant" who has recently died, and he becomes obsessed with finding his grave. Despite the relatives' pleas, the count locates the burial site and exhumes the body so he can add it to his collection.

"Of all your finds," Heredia writes, "the Patagonian giant was the most striking, the most terrifying, and the most serendipitous." In an inspired passage, the poet recounts how the adventurer located the giant's skeleton, unearthed it, and dismembered it.

Ses parents, désolés de sa mort récente, avaient inconsidérément vanté devant vous la force et la taille extraordinaires de cet homme exceptionnel. Vous vous faites aussitôt indiquer sa tombe. Aidé d'un indigène qu'a séduit l'attrait des liqueurs fortes, vous déblayez le sol, vous fouillez la terre, vous découvrez le linceul, un cuir de cheval bariolé, vous l'arrachez, vous vous efforcez de tirer hors de la fosse le corps putréfié. La puanteur est telle que l'Indien, épouvanté, s'enfuit. Ne pouvant, à vous seul, transporter ce cadavre gigantesque, vous le taillez avec un méchant couteau, vous le désarticulez, vous le disséquez. Des lambeaux de chair adhéraient encore aux os. Il fallut le feu, l'eau, et la marmite de campement pour en venir à bout. Je cite textuellement:—"Comme la marmite était bien petite, je ne pus faire cuire qu'un morceau à la fois."—Enfin, vous fîtes bouillir la tête.[75]

(His parents, distraught over his recent death, had thoughtlessly boasted before you the extraordinary strength and size of this exceptional man. At once you searched out his grave. With the help of a native softened by strong liquor, you cleared the ground and delved into the earth, you uncovered the shroud, a colorful horsehide, you tore it off and tried to pull the rotting body away from the soil. The stench was such that the Indian ran away in terror. Unable to carry the giant corpse by yourself, you hacked at it with a rusty knife, dismembered and dissected it. Scraps of flesh were still sticking to the bones. It required the use of fire, water, and the encampment cooking pot to get the better of it. And I quote your words: "Since the pot was rather small, I was only able to cook one piece at a time." Finally, you boiled the head.)

Heredia sets up an opposition between the Patagonians and de La Vaulx, between the giant's grieving parents, full of pride and love for their deceased son, and the deceitful French explorer who behaves like a cannibalistic sociopath (he does not eat the body but uses the encampment's cooking utensils to boil the bones). This contrast between empathy and apathy sets up an opposition between civilization and barbarism in which de La Vaulx emerges as the savage. "Today, my dear La Vaulx," Heredia writes after commenting on this sadistic episode, "you are enjoying, in peace, the result of so many crimes."[76]

Heredia visited the Natural History Museum where de La Vaulx's plunder was exhibited, and he describes the scene as follows: "One of the beautiful rooms of the Museum houses your zoological, entomological, paleontological, and anthropological collections. They are complemented and illustrated by maps, photographs, thousands of tools made of flint or other stones, and over one hundred Indian skulls, prehistoric or modern." As he surveys the collection, Heredia's gaze stops on the most impressive object: the Patagonian giant's skeleton.

Là, au centre de la grande vitrine, dépassant de tout ce qui fut sa tête ses neuf compagnons d'exil, se dresse, haut de deux mètres, le squelette du pauvre géant Patagon, impitoyablement arraché à la terre qui l'avait vu naître, vivre et mourir, et où son corps et son esprit sauvages auraient dû trouver, auprès des ancêtres, le repos éternel dont vous l'avez privé.[77]

(There, at the center of a large display case, two meters high, taller by the length of what once was his head than his nine companions in exile, stands the skeleton of the poor Patagonian giant, ruthlessly torn from the earth where he was born, lived, and died, and where his wild body and spirit should have found, amongst the ancestors, the eternal rest you robbed from him.)

De La Vaulx assumed that his readers would identify with him, the European explorer who sought to advance science. Heredia, in contrast, took the Patagonians' side and portrayed the count as a heartless colonizer who committed terrible crimes against a people that had been welcoming and hospitable and who treated Patagonians as objects that could be dismembered, packed, shipped, and exhibited in a French museum. Whereas de La Vaulx presented his adventures as a clash between civilization and barbarism, Heredia saw an encounter between two groups of human beings governed by different expectations and value systems. If there are any savages in this tale, Heredia suggests, they were de La Vaulx and his travel companions.

Why did Heredia feel so much sympathy for the Patagonians? Was it a question of human rights? Certainly, he depicts the Indians as human beings who have the same rights—to be respected, trusted, and listened to—as Europeans. But we can also detect Heredia's desire to identify with Argentina's indigenous population. Even though he had spent most of his life in France, wrote in French, and belonged to the Académie française, he took the side of the Patagonian giant and denounced the French explorer. His eloquent plea for empathy is a way of highlighting the historical and affective ties linking a Francophile Cuban poet and an illiterate Patagonian giant. By defending the Patagonians as his Latin American compatriots, Heredia expresses his belief in a cultural kinship that transcends geographical and political boundaries, a utopian ideal that is not far from Bolivar's pan-American project.

Heredia's article must have taken the public by surprise. Most of his readers would have expected the poet of *Les trophées* to praise de La Vaulx as a modern-day conquistador. Like Columbus's men, the French adventurer had crossed the ocean to explore new lands and encounter unsuspected adventures, and European readers would naturally see de La Vaulx as an epic hero. It was a view that Heredia might have espoused in his youth, but age and experience had transformed his vision of the world. After the collapse of the Mexican Empire, the Panama scandal, and the colonial campaigns in Africa and Asia, Heredia could no longer cling to the same romantic perspective on Europe's relationship to Latin America.

Heredia links de La Vaulx's voyage to French colonial episodes that demonstrated Europe's continued desire to dominate and subjugate Latin America. Given his outcry against these incursions, one wonders whether Heredia, at this late stage in life, began to have second thoughts about his idealized view of the Conquest. After all, Pedro de Heredia and the other conquistadors celebrated in his sonnets had much in common with Henry de La Vaulx. It would not be a stretch to read the poet's essay about *Voyage en Patagonie* as a radical rewriting of "Les conquérants" and even as a *mea culpa* (or perhaps, thinking of sixteenth-century Spanish adventurers, a *sua culpa*). After a lifetime of promoting Europe's encounter with the Americas as a heroic epic, the poet acknowledged the darker side of the Conquest.

Heredia's Spanish

The year 1903 brought one more radical change in Heredia's work: he wrote his first poem in Spanish, a gesture that makes him the only one of Proust's Latin Americans to have used Spanish in his professional life. Before writing these verses, Heredia had translated a number of Spanish classics into French. In 1885, he published a French translation of Fernán Caballero's *Juan Soldado,* which was followed, in 1887, by the first volume of Bernal Díaz del Castillo's *True History of the Conquest of New Spain* and in 1894 by *La monja alférez.* The Heredia papers at the Bibliothèque de l'Arsenal also include fragments of an unfinished translation of *Don Quixote,* as well as various French versions of his cousin José María Heredia's poems.[78]

Heredia had read Spanish and Latin American literature all his life, but he had never written in his native language—not even as a child. His first poems, written in Cuba before he ever set foot in France, were composed in French. But in 1903, the mayor of Santiago de Cuba, Emilio Bacardí y Moreau, asked Heredia to write a poem in Spanish to be read as part of the festivities planned to mark the centenary of his cousin Heredia's birth. The poet had always been extremely proud of his relative, and he accepted the invitation and composed three Spanish sonnets celebrating his cousin's life. They are written in hendecasyllables—the metric equivalent in Spanish poetry of French *alexandrins*—and pay homage not only to his relative but also to Cuba, Latin America, and the Spanish language. In many ways, these poems enact Heredia's homecoming.

I

Desde la Francia, madre bendecida
De la sublime Libertad que, bella,
Sobre los mundos de Colón destella
En onda ardiente de pujante vida;

A ti, soldado de coraza unida
Por la virtud que el combatir no mella,
A ti, creador de la radiante Estrella
De la Isla riente por el mar mecida.

A ti, de Cuba campeón glorioso
Que no pudiste ver tu venturoso
Sueño de amor y de esperanza cierto,
Con entusiasmo en mi cantar saludo
De pié, tocando tu vibrante escudo
Que es inmortal porque tu voz no ha muerto.

(From France, the blessed mother
Of Liberty sublime, that shines
Over the worlds Columbus found,
In waves ablaze with thrusting life;

To you, soldier, with breastplate welded
By virtues strenuous combat cannot mar;
To you, creator of the radiant Star
For an Isle rocked laughing in the ocean's cradle;

To you, O Cuba's glorious champion,
You that never lived to see
Your dream of love and hope achieved,
I joyfully sing, and on my feet salute you;
Your deathless shield beneath my touch vibrates
Because your voice has never died away.)

II

Desde la Francia madre generosa
De la Belleza y de su luz divina,
Cuya diadema de robusta encina
Tiene la gracia de viviente rosa;

A ti, pintor de la natura hermosa
De la esplendente América latina,
A ti, gran rey de la Oda, peregrina
Por tu gallarda fuerza melodiosa;

A ti, cantor del Niágara rugiente
Que diste en versos su tronar al mundo,
Y el cambiante color iridiscente
De su masa revuelta en lo profundo
Del hondo abismo que al mortal espanta
Grande Heredia, otro Heredia aquí te canta!

(From France, the generous mother
Of Beauty and its light divine
Whose diadem of oak entwined
Seems graceful as a budding rose;

To you, who painted nature's loveliness
In Latin America's splendorous abode,
To you, great master of the Ode
Made rare by gallant strong melodiousness;

To you, who sang the roaring Niagara
And gave in poetry its thunder to the world,
Its changing iridescent hues foretold,
Wild whirlpools in the chasms of the falls,
High sheer abyss that mortal men appals,
To great Heredia, another Heredia sings!)

III

Y abandonando el habla de la Francia
En que dije el valor de los mayores,
Al evocar los Conquistadores
En su viril, magnífica arrogancia;

Hoy recuerdo la lengua de mi infancia
Y sueño con sus ritmos y colores,
Para hacerte corona con sus flores
Y envolver tu sepulcro en su fragancia.

Oh! Sombra inmensa que la luz admira!
Yo que cogí de tu heredad la lira
Y que llevo tu sangre con tu nombre,
Perdón si balbuceo tu lenguaje,
Al rendir, en mi siglo, este homenage [sic]
Al Gran Poeta con que honraste al Hombre![79]

(Deserting now the lovely tongue of France
In which I told the deeds of men of yore
And brought to life the stern Conquistadors
In all their virile, splendid arrogance,

Today my childhood language I recall
Dreaming aloud of its rhythms and colors
To braid you a crown with its sonorous flowers
And envelop your tomb in their fragrant pall.

Oh! Immense shadow, awing the light!
I, who found this lyre amidst your bequest,
And with your blood along with your name am blest,
Forgive me for haltingly babbling your language
As I render, this century, a reverent homage
To the Great Poet whose life honoured Mankind!)

These verses express the intense emotions Heredia felt upon revisiting his native tongue and writing in Spanish for the first time. They also show us how a master of French verse—Heredia's sonnets in alexandrines flow as naturally as everyday speech, and his rhymes are so carefully chosen that they seem effortless—struggles with the musicality and rhythms of a language that has become as unwieldy for him as a foreign tongue. These poems lack the light, airy quality of his alexandrines, and the rhymes are often clumsy (a shortcoming Heredia acknowledges when he describes himself as "babbling" [balbucear] Spanish). But it is admirable that Heredia, at age sixty-one, sought the challenge of writing in a new form and a new language —one that happened to be his own.

These poems introduce another important change. Breaking with the Parnassian precepts, Heredia writes poetry with a political theme. The first sonnet celebrates his cousin, who devoted his life to fighting for his country's independence from Spain, as a "glorious champion" of Cuba. Heredia laments, "You did not live to see your fortunate/dream of love and hope achieved." Nowhere else had Heredia been so candid about his support for the island's revolutionary ideals. He presents the struggle for sovereignty as an ideal that Cuba developed based on French ideas. "Sublime" freedom, the poem reminds us, was an ideal conceived in "the blessed motherland" during the French Revolution and then embraced by intellectuals in "the lands of Columbus." If Les trophées, celebrated the historical ties between Europe and Latin America, the Spanish sonnets highlight the legacy of Enlightenment ideals—freedom and independence—in Cuban revolutionary circles.

In the second sonnet, Heredia salutes his relative as the "painter" of "Latin America's resplendent nature" in a verse that marks the poet's first use of the term *Latin America*. (Heredia was the only one of the figures examined in this book to use the term.) This verse alludes to the many works the other Heredia devoted to evoking American landscapes; his most famous poem, "Ode to Niagara," celebrates the roaring waterfall as a symbol of America's natural wonders. In keeping with his relative's Romantic ideals, Heredia places nature at the center of the Latin American ideal—countries from Mexico to Argentina share a common language, a cultural heritage, and also a dramatic landscape dominated by natural forces.

This second sonnet closes with an apostrophe to the dead cousin: "Grande Heredia, otro Heredia aquí te canta!" (Great Heredia, another Heredia sings you here!) As in his poems about Pedro de Heredia, he celebrates and identifies with an ancestor who lived in a nobler, more heroic time, except the hero is no longer a conquistador but his cousin José María, a freedom fighter who lived in a century of revolutions. Heredia no longer identifies with the conquistadors but with those who fought to reconquer their native countries.

But the most intriguing part of this poetic project is the third sonnet, a self-reflexive meditation on what it means for Heredia to return to Spanish after a lifetime of writing in French. By "abandoning the language of France," he is able to "remember the language of [his] childhood" and to "dream of its rhythms and colors." This return to Spanish is inextricably linked with a reflection on death and the passage of time; Heredia describes his sonnet as a funerary wreath made of Spanish "flowers" and designed to "envelop his tomb with its fragrance." The language of his childhood, which lay dormant for so many decades, has now blossomed again, and Heredia offers the garland made of these word-flowers to his Cuban cousin.

Heredia paints Spanish as a vibrant language, full of "rhythms," "colors," "flowers," and "fragances," which contrasts sharply with the funerary images that envelop his cousin's tomb. These last verses are structured by a double movement, a dialectical oscillation between life and death. Heredia lives, and he sings the praises of a dead relative. But the poet has reached the end of his life—he died two years after writing these sonnets—and, conscious of his own mortality, hails his cousin as an "eternal" poet, made immortal by literary fame. These verses play on the epithet—*les immortels*—applied to members of the Académie française. Since its founding in the seventeenth century, the venerable institution was conceived as a pantheon for living writers. In the sonnet, Heredia elevates his cousin to the rank of immortals while he—the *immortel*—steps down to the realm of mere mortals. The imagery of death is everywhere in these last verses. An "immense shadow"—a symbol of death—"admires the light" of the tropics. In the closing stanza, the author points to his own life as evidence that the other Heredia continues to live: "I carry your blood with your name," he tells his cousin, stressing the continuity across generations that links a nineteenth-century Cuban poet and a twentieth-century Franco-Cuban Académicien.

In a striking line, Heredia apologizes to his cousin for "babbling your language" (balbuceo tu lenguaje). In his old age, he has become a child again; he struggles to write fluently and rhythmically in a language that is at once familiar and strange. Like a babbling baby, Heredia plays at arranging words and composing phrases. Turning—or rather returning—to Spanish is a life-affirming gesture on the part of dying poet. Spanish has been a dormant tongue for Heredia, but it now comes alive again, a vital tongue, full of energy and light, one that evokes the brightest associations of a happy, tropical childhood.

In *Echolalias,* Daniel Heller-Roazen analyzes the forgetting of language as an important trope in Western literature; from Ovid to Hannah Arendt, the tradition is full of characters who have forgotten languages they once spoke.[80] Heredia's case is more complex. He never forgot his Spanish, but he had rarely written it since he arrived in France. His acceptance speech to the Académie française celebrated French as the language of literature; almost two decades later—in a kind of linguistic homecoming—he "abandons" French to celebrate Spanish as the language of life and light.

These Spanish sonnets pay tribute to a poet whose aesthetics and politics could not have been more different from his own. The earlier Heredia had been a Romantic poet, and his verses are full of the kind of individual affects the Parnassians loathed. More significantly, the earlier Heredia had been a politically engaged poet who devoted considerable time and energy to the cause of Cuban independence, a dream that he did not live to see and that was finally consummated in 1903, just as our Heredia was finishing his Spanish verses. In his tribute, Heredia seems to question the poetic values he upheld for most of his life, relaxing the strict separation between a poet's life and work, between politics and poetry.

As we have seen, José-Maria de Heredia's work has more ties to nineteenth-century history and politics than critics have generally acknowledged. He lived in Paris during the greatest colonial expansion in French history, and his life overlapped with the French campaigns in Mexico, Indochina, and North Africa. While the poet composed his sonnets about the conquest of America, his adoptive country engaged in various attempts to conquer the continent in which he was born. Heredia's readers would have recognized a connection between "Les conquérants" and the "civilizing mission" France took to the rest of the world.

Heredia's poems also served a didactic function. A young Marcel Proust learned his history—and his vision of the relations between Europe and the rest of the world—in part through reading "Les conquérants," a poem he learned by heart and quoted often in his correspondence. As we can see in "The Eclipse," Marcel was conditioned to see the clashes between Europe and the Americas as a struggle between civilization and barbarism. Like Heredia, the future novelist considered Spain's victory over pre-Columbian civilizations a triumph of culture and progress.

Much has been written about the epic vision of conquest in Heredia's work. It is true that sonnets like "Les conquérants" or "À un fondateur de ville" present an idealized vision of the Spaniards as heroes blessed with a poetic sensibility that allows them to marvel at the natural wonders of the New World. But "Les conquérants de l'or" presents a more nuanced view. In this poem, Heredia paints the dark side of the Spaniards, describing them as gold-obsessed adventurers who dream not of stars but of raping Amazons and smashing idols. His description of Panama's pestilent landscape foreshadowed the reports the Paris papers would publish years later about the canal project. Out of all of his poems, "Les conquérants de l'or" is the most directly related to the political context of nineteenth-century France. For years, Heredia affirmed the principles of the Parnassian movement, especially the idea that poetry should narrate the great episodes of history rather than express the poet's feelings or political views. But near the end of his life, he had a change of heart and wrote texts that voiced a passionate anti-colonialist stance. His late work engages the great political questions of his time in a more complex way than has been generally acknowledged.

Of the five figures studied in this book, Heredia is the only one who published in Spanish and translated from Spanish. He demonstrated the great-est interest in Latin American literature and had the most contact with Latin Americans in Paris. He was the only one who used the term *Latin America* in print and subscribed to the vision of a cultural, linguistic, and historical unity linking regions as diverse as Cuba and Patagonia. Heredia was, in brief, the most Latin American of Proust's Latin Americans.

Paperolle No. 3

Proust's Mexican Painter

One of the least studied figures in Proust's circle is the artist Antonio de La Gandara (1861-1917), born in Paris to a Mexican father and a Franco-English mother. La Gandara, who lived as a Mexican citizen in France until he naturalized at age thirty-four, studied at the École du Louvre, set up a studio in Montmartre (fig. P3.1), and gained success as a society painter. Like Jacques-Émile Blanche (1861-1942), he created portraits of some of the most celebrated figures of the belle époque, including many of Proust's friends and acquaintances: Anna de Noailles, Elisabeth de Caraman-Chimay, Louisa de Mornand, Sarah Bernhardt, and Paul Verlaine. But while Blanche has been the subject of important publications and exhibitions, La Gandara has slipped into relative oblivion. During Proust's time, however, he was a well-known artist, and his portraits hung in many of the salons Proust frequented during his socialite years.

La Gandara befriended Proust, painted Montesquiou and Yturri, knew Reynaldo Hahn and his family, and crossed paths with Heredia at countless receptions and dinners. He was acquainted with many Latin Americans living in Paris and painted portraits of Chilean ambassador Alberto del Solar, Argentinean ambassador Enrique Larreta's wife, and Leonor Achorena de Uriburu, a wealthy heiress from Buenos Aires (fig. P3.2).[1] In 1885, La Gandara met Robert de Montesquiou, who had already commissioned portraits by Whistler, Blanche, and Boldini. The narcissistic count became an important patron to La Gandara, commissioning at least four portraits of himself—an oil on ivory in 1885,[2] a charcoal sketch in 1891,[3] an undated pencil sketch, and an oil on canvas in 1892[4]—plus several more of Gabriel de Yturri, including an 1886 oil on wood (see plate 8), now in the collections of the Musée d'Orsay in Paris, which the painter inscribed "Al señor Yturri, su amigo Ant. De la Gandara."[5] Antonio was only a year older than Yturri, and the two

Figure P3.1. La Gandara's painting studio. From left to right: Manuel de La Gandara, Gabriel de Yturri, Marie Zwanzi, unknown, the Villon brothers, model, Bon. Image courtesy Xavier Mathieu.

bonded over their Latin American origins. Montesquiou credited Gabriel with launching the painter's career, and he regretted that La Gandara never completed his project of a more ambitious portrait of Gabriel. As he wrote in *Le chancelier de fleurs*:

> La réelle amitié qu'eut, pour lui [Yturri], Antonio de la Gandara, aurait dû avoir pour résultat un beau, un définitif portrait d'Yturri par cet artiste de mérite. J'ai le regret de devoir dire qu'il n'en est pas ainsi. Quand ce modèle rencontra ce peintre, ce dernier n'en était pas même à ses débuts dans la notoriété, que le premier favorisa de tout son pouvoir, qui était réel. Gandara fit alors quelques études peintes, pas très attachantes, de très jolis dessins à la mine de plomb, malheureusement emportés au pays, dont ils ne sont pas revenus. Plus tard, il y eut encore deux intéressants fusains; mais, je le répète, le grand, le beau, le vrai portrait qui était projeté, et sans doute allait s'accomplir, je le pleurerai toujours; et si mon compagnon revit dans ce Livre, l'avenir regrettera ce noble frontispice.[6]

(The true friendship Yturri had for Antonio de la Gandara should have resulted in a beautiful, definitive portrait of Yturri by this artist of merit. I am sorry to have to say that this is not the case. When this model met this painter, the latter

Figure P3.2. Antonio de La Gandara posing with the portrait of Leonor Anchorena de Uriburu and her son Emilio Uriburu Anchorena. Image courtesy Xavier Mathieu.

had not even begun to enjoy notoriety, which the former supported with all his power, which was real. Gandara produced several not very attractive painted studies and some very pretty graphite drawings, unfortunately taken by him to the country, from where they never returned. Later, there were also two very interesting charcoals; but, I repeat, the great, the beautiful, the true portrait that was planned, and which doubtless was to be accomplished, I will regret it forever; and if my companion comes back to life in this book, the future will miss that noble frontispiece.)

One of La Gandara's most expressive works is his 1891 sketch of Yturri reading a book (fig. P3.3).[7] Gabriel appears seated by a side table, elegantly dressed in a black jacket and wearing an ascot; his youthful face shines with

Figure P3.3. Antonio La Gandara, *Gabriel de Yturri Reading,* 1891. Chalk. Private collection, Paris. Image courtesy Xavier Mathieu.

wonder and illuminates the book that captures his entire attention, while
the rest of the composition dissolves into darkness. This work could have
been called *Portrait of the dandy reading.*

In 1896, La Gandara painted Reynaldo's sister, María,[8] who had married
the painter Raimundo de Madrazo (1841-1920), a relative of Mariano Fortuny, one of the most celebrated designers of the belle-époque. In 1916,
Marcel would write María asking her for specific details about the Fortuny
robes he planned to include in his novel. Earlier, María had put Proust in
touch with her cousin, Marie Nordlinger, who helped him translate Ruskin's
Sesame and the Lys and *The Bible of Amiens.*[9] During this time, La Gandara—
along with Reynaldo, his sister María, and Yturri—was a key presence in
Proust's circle of Latin American friends.

After Yturri's death in 1905, La Gandara sent Montesquiou a condolence
letter, telling him that Gabriel, from the grave "sees with joy how much
you love him, how very much you love him!" The count replied that "your
conduct during these past days, during these last hours, has proven to me
once more that you belong to those [select souls], and it will reaffirm our

friendship by adding sighs to our memories."[10] In *Le chancelier de fleurs*, Montesquiou hailed La Gandara—along with Paul Helleu, Maurice Lobre, Georges Hœntschell, Federico de Madrazo y Ochoa, and Proust—as one of Yturri's close friends.[11] The count quotes several letters in which Yturri had written about spending time with the painter and his family in Paris or in La Gandara's native city of Blois.

Proust met the La Gandaras while he was still in his twenties. He became close to Antonio and also befriended his brother Édouard, an actor who worked with Sarah Bernhardt and later became an antiquarian. In 1897, Marcel invited Antonio—along with Anatole France, Montesquiou, Yturri, Reynaldo, and several aristocrats—to one of the dinners he organized at his parent's apartments.[12] La Gandara and Proust were both socialites, and they crossed paths often at receptions and dinners. In "Une Fête littéraire à Versailles," Marcel's 1894 chronicle of one of Montesquiou's extravaganzas, he mentions the La Gandaras, along with Heredia, among the guests.[13] La Gandara also plays an important role in *Jean Santeuil,* where, in a fictional scene, he paints the portrait of the protagonist. The unfinished novel includes a long passage describing the imaginary painting.

> Cette année-là La Gandara exposa au Champ-de-Mars un portrait de Jean Santeuil. Ses anciens camarades d'Henri-IV n'auraient certainement pas reconnu l'écolier désordonné, toujours mal mis, dépeigné, couvert de taches, l'attitude fiévreuse ou abattue, le geste plus expressif que noble, le regard exalté s'il était seul, timide et honteux s'il était devant du monde, toujours pâle, les yeux tirés, cernés par l'agitation, l'insomnie ou la fièvre, le nez trop fort dans les joues creuses avec de grands yeux pensants qui versaient seuls quelque beauté, avec leur lumière et leur tourment, sur cette figure irrégulière et maladive, dans le brillant jeune homme qui semblait encore poser devant tout Paris, sans timidité comme sans bravade, le regardant de ses beaux yeux allongés et blancs comme une amande fraîche, des yeux plus capables de contenir une pensée qu'en ayant pour le moment aucune, comme un bassin profond mais vide, les joues pleines et d'un rose blanc qui rougissait à peine aux oreilles que venaient caresser les dernières boucles d'une chevelure noire et douce, brillante et coulante, s'échappant en ondes comme au sortir de l'eau. Une rose coupée au coin de son veston de cheviote vert, une cravate d'une légère étoffe indienne qui imitait les ocellures du paon, venaient témoigner à la vérité de sa mine lumineuse et fraiche comme un matin de printemps, de sa beauté, non pas pensante mais peut-être doucement pensive, de la délicatesse heureuse de sa vie.

Et pourtant M. et Mme Santeuil qui avaient d'abord encouragé Jean à aller dans le monde, qu'avait bientôt flattés la grande situation qu'il s'y était faite, étaient ennuyés de voir Jean ne plus travailler, ne plus lire, ne plus penser et n'en avoir même plus, au moins depuis quelques mois, de regrets ni de honte.[14]

(That year Le Gandare [sic] exhibited at the Champ-de-Mars a portrait of Jean Santeuil. His former companions at the Lycée Henri IV would certainly not have recognized the untidy schoolboy—always badly dressed, with tousled hair and stained clothes, his manner either feverishly excited or dejectedly limp, his gestures expressive rather than well-bred, with exaltation in his face when he was alone, though when with other people he was shy and abashed, always pale with tired eyes circled in dark shadow as a result of excitement, sleeplessness, or fever, his nose over-large, his cheeks hollow, and his great brooding eyes, brilliant and tormented, which alone gave a touch of beauty to the irregular and sickly countenance—in the radiant young man self-consciously posing before all Paris, with neither shyness nor bravado in his looks, gazing out from light-coloured elongated eyes, with an air about them of fresh almonds, eyes less expressive of actual thought than seemingly capable of thought, like deep but empty cisterns, with full round cheeks of a faint pink just flushing to red in the ears brushed by the curling ends of his black and silky hair, which showed, shining, undulating, loose, as though he had just emerged from water. A rose in the buttonhole of his green tweed jacket, a tie of some delicate Indian fabric patterned with peacock's eyes seemed to echo looks which were as fresh, as luminous, as a spring morning, beauty not perhaps thoughtful so much as pensive, the very visual sign of a delicate and happy life.

Yet Monsieur and Madame Santeuil, who had at first encouraged Jean to go out and about in Society where he revelled in the position he had made for himself, were irritated now when they saw that he was no longer either working, reading, or even thinking, and for the last few months at least had shown no sign of anything approaching regret or shame.)[15]

Jacques-Émile Blanche had painted Proust's portrait—now one of the most famous images of the novelist, reproduced on the covers of countless books and biographies—in 1892 and exhibited it at the Champ-de-Mars in 1893.[16] The description of La Gandara's imaginary portrait—jet-black hair, almond eyes, rosy cheeks, and a white flower on the lapel—corresponds exactly to Blanche's painting. It is intriguing that Proust would substitute La Gandara for Blanche, especially considering that Blanche would be remembered as the more talented and successful of the two painters (in addition to his society portraits, Blanche painted Stéphane Mallarmé, André Gide, Igor Stravisnky, James Joyce, Henri Bergson, and Paul Valéry). Perhaps it was his fresh relationship with his Venezuelan boyfriend that led Proust to imagine himself sitting for a Mexican painter. Or perhaps he considered the name La Gandara more exotic and more appropriate for inclusion in a novel than the very ordinary Blanche, which means white in French.

Jean Santeuil presents La Gandara's portrait as a symbol of the transformation Jean has undergone since his school days; he has changed from a shy, awkward, and unattractive adolescent to a luminous, attractive, and worldly young man. (Marcel experienced a similar reinvention from his days at the Lycée Condorcet to his life in the salons.) The young Proust associates La Gandara with this ideal world, in which the elegance—and frivolity—of the salons intersected with the intensity of artistic and literary life. Proust had a great affection for the painter, as he told Louisa de Mornand in 1907: "I am overjoyed to know that you will have a magnificent portrait by La Gandara. What delightful hours you must be spending with him: he is so interesting, so marvelously artistic."[17]

When Antonio died in 1917, Proust sent his brother Édouard a heartfelt condolence letter, longer than his usual missives, to express his sadness at losing a friend. By then, he was in financial troubles, and an acquaintance recommended he sell his extra furniture to Édouard, who ran an antiques gallery on Quai Voltaire. Proust rejected the suggestion, fearing that the antiquarian would misinterpret his intentions: "The thought that [Édouard] could believe that I had this sale in mind when I wrote him the condolence letter, and that for this purpose I overstated my kindness, would be so disagreeable to me that I would prefer to make this transaction with another merchant."[18]

Though Antonio de La Gandara was born in Paris, many of his friends viewed him as a foreigner. Repeating the mistake—so common in the belle époque—of referring to Latin Americans as Spaniards, the art critic Camille Mauclair wrote that "though a Spaniard by race, M. Antonio de La Gandara has made himself, in ten years, a considerable place in French art."[19] He was not the only one to associate the painter with Spain. Before acquiring French citizenship in 1895, La Gandara had been required to exhibit in the Spanish section of the salons.[20] Others got the nationality right but exaggerated his foreignness. Alphonse Daudet once described him as "having a Mexican waltz in his eyes" (des yeux de valse mexicaine),[21] and Montes-

Figure P3.4. Manuel de La Gandara in Mexico, ca. 1900. Image courtesy Xavier Mathieu.

quiou penned the following portrait: "Il y avait dans ce mexicain, de la grâce des première Aztèques, unie à la puissance latente du conquérant qu'il allait devenir. Cette dualité se résolvait en un mystère non dénué d'attrait, qui se compliquait de beaucoup d'autres."[22] (There was in this Mexican the grace of the first Aztecs, joined with the latent strength of the conquistador he would become. This duality resolved itself in a mystery, not devoid of charm, complicated by many others.) The count associates the painter with "Les conquérants" and thus suggests a kinship between La Gandara and José-Maria de Heredia. It is striking that the count presents his friend as part Aztec, part conquistador—a description that anticipates Octavio Paz's theory of *mestizaje* and his vision of Mexicans as children of Spaniards and Indians.

La Gandara traveled often, including several trips to the United States, but he never visited Mexico (unlike his brother Manuel, who made the journey in the last years of the century and had himself photographed in a *charro* outfit [fig. P3.4]).[23] In contrast to Heredia or Ramon Fernandez, he never achieved a following in Latin America, though his portraits of the belle-époque would have been a great success in Porfirio Díaz's Mexico. Not even Alfonso Reyes, who was eternally on the lookout for eccentric compatriots, encountered his work during his years at the Mexican embassy in Paris. Roberto Bolaño once wrote about "Mexicans lost in Mexico." La Gandara was a Mexican lost in Paris.

4 Ramon Fernandez
Proust's Mexican Critic

Proust met Ramon Fernandez (1894-1944) during World War I. He was only in his mid-forties, but he was already ill and bed-ridden; Fernandez, in contrast, was a twenty-year-old rising star in Parisian intellectual life (fig. 4.1). It was Proust who sought out the younger man; in 1914 he wrote Lucien Daudet, a mutual friend, to tell him he had "a great desire to meet Fernandez."[1] It is not entirely clear why. Proust had no need to court the critics, and while he was drawn to young, attractive boys—in his last years he even paid waiters from the Ritz to visit him at home so he could bask in the aura of their beauty[2]—he was more interested in Fernandez's mind than in his looks. "His 'physique' is not at all what I find the best in him," he confided to Paul Morand.[3] Proust even wrote Fernandez himself—probably intending it as a compliment—that "it was not a beautiful face, but a beautiful mind that I desired to know in you."[4] He craved the company of smart young men who could engage in interesting conversation. The two became friends, and Fernandez visited him several times during the war. He was one of the last people Proust continued to receive in the final year of his life.

An admirer of Proust since the publication of *Swann's Way*, Ramon welcomed the opportunity to meet the reclusive novelist and found him a sympathetic interlocutor. Around the time of their first meeting, Ramon was working on *Philippe Sauveur*, a novel about a French dandy who discovers his own homosexuality during a stay in London. Ramon asked his new friend to read the manuscript, and Proust obliged, writing him long letters to communicate his impressions. Years later, Ramon would remember that Proust "did not believe—and this was precisely one of the criticisms he levied against my book—that this malady [homosexuality] was found exclusively in the idle sectors of society, in the corrupt bourgeoisie [. . .] He

Figure 4.1. Agence Meurice, press photo of Ramon Fernandez after the award of the Prix Femina, 1931. Département Estampes et photographie, EI-13(2898), Bibliothèque Nationale de France, Paris.

believed that inversion was found in all the social classes"—one of the main themes explored in *Sodom and Gomorrah.*[5]

Ramon Fernandez was born in Paris in 1894. His grandfather had been mayor of Mexico City, and his father, also named Ramón Fernández (with accents), was a diplomat at the Mexican embassy in Paris and close to Porfirio Díaz, the Mexican president deposed in the 1910 revolution. When Ramon was eleven years old, his father died in a riding accident in Mexico. Ramon's mother, Jeanne, a strong-willed woman from the South of France, was a fashion writer and one of the founders of French *Vogue*. She hosted an elegant salon frequented by Reynaldo Hahn, Jean Cocteau, Maurice Rostand, Jean Paulhan, and Lucien Daudet, among others.[6] Ramon's upbringing was thoroughly French: he attended the Sorbonne, followed the seminars of Henri Bergson, studied at Cambridge, and later entered the Collège de France. By his early twenties, he had made a name for himself as a smart critic who was also well versed in contemporary philosophy. He lectured frequently in France and England, where he met T. S. Eliot, who considered him "one of the most promising young men in Paris."[7] He would go on to publish one of the first important critical works on Proust in his *Messages* (1926), as well as monographs on André Gide, Molière, Honoré de Balzac, and George Meredith.

When Ramon met Proust, he had only written articles for newspapers and literary journals, but by the mid-1920s, he would become an influential figure in the Parisian literary world. He wrote for the *Nouvelle Revue Française,* the most prestigious review in France, which counted Gide, Jacques Rivière, and Valery Larbaud among its authors.[8] When Rivière, the editor-in-chief, died in 1925, Ramon became one of the leading contributing editors and used the review as a forum to publish his essays on Proust. In 1927 he launched the *Cahiers Marcel Proust,* a journal devoted entirely to the novelist.

In 1926, Ramon published his first book, *Messages,* a collection of essays that opened with an homage to Rivière and included a crucial chapter on Proust.[9] It was followed by *De la personnalité* (1928), a book that focused on a very Proustian question: the relationship between the work of art and the personality of its author. Coincidentally, Jacques Lacan, then a medical student, was interested in the same issue, and he cited Fernandez as a source in his thesis, "De la psychose paranoïaque dans ses rapports avec la personnalité" (1932). Lacan gave Ramon a copy inscribed, "A Ramon Fernandez, avec qui j'ai médité sur la personnalité, bien avant d'avoir parlé à sa personne. En signe de ma grande sympathie intellectuelle" (To Ramon Fernandez, with whom I meditated on the question of personality, well before I ever spoke to him in person. As a token of my intellectual affinity, Jacques Lacan).[10]

Ramon continued to write monographs on French writers—*La vie de Molière* (1929), *André Gide* (1931)—as well as critical essays. In 1932, he published *Moralisme et littérature,* a collection of his conversations with Jacques Rivière on various subjects, including Proust, and two years later the pamphlet *L'homme, est-il humain?* (1936). He also tried his hand at fiction and wrote several novels, including *Le pari* (1932, winner of the Prix Femina) and *Les Violents* (1935). *Philippe Sauveur* remained unpublished during the author's lifetime. It was considered lost until it surfaced in an attic in the French countryside and was published in 2012 with an introduction by Ramon's son Dominique Fernandez.[11]

In the mid-1930s, Ramon's prolific literary production came to a sudden stop. As political tensions mounted in Europe, and France headed toward another war, the young critic got caught in the whirlwind of prewar politics. He started out as a committed anti-fascist and anti-Stalinist. In 1934, he was

one of the founders of the Committee of Vigilance of Anti-Fascist intellectuals, and he wrote a number of articles against totalitarianism.[12] In 1937, he
veered to the right and joined Jacques Doriot's Parti Populaire Français, an
ultranationalist, anticommunist, and pro-fascist party that would collaborate with the Germans during the occupation. (Incidentally, Doriot had also
switched sides; he had been a member of the French Communist Party before founding his far-right party in 1936.) "He is very nice, Monsieur Ramon
Fernandez, but he does not seem know what he wants," quipped a left-wing
journalist.[13] In 1941, Fernandez, along with Pierre Drieu La Rochelle and
Robert Brasillach, joined a delegation of French intellectuals who traveled
to Weimar, where they were received by Goebbels.[14] He returned to Paris
full of enthusiasm for Nazi Germany and published several articles praising
"the meeting of Maréchal Pétain and Chancellor Hitler" as leading to "a new
reality that could and should make a new Europe."[15] Ironically, it seems to
have been his love of French culture that drew Ramon to the far right. At a
time when Western civilization was under threat, he naïvely chose the party
that most vociferously proclaimed its defense of European culture. This
unfortunate choice put him in the company of other Latin Americans, from
José Vasconcelos to Honorio Delgado, whose admiration for German European culture led them to support Nazism (unlike Borges, who eloquently argued that he opposed Nazism precisely because he was a Germanophile).[16]

Despite his allegiance to Doriot's party, Ramon did not embrace the extreme right's anti-Semitism. In the early thirties, he had been a critic of Céline's anti-Jewish statements, and he renewed his objections in a 1938 article
on *Bagatelles pour un massacre.*[17] During the occupation, his attitude was
more ambivalent. One finds traces of anti-Semitic sentiment in his writings;
at the same time, he championed authors who would have been considered
"degenerate" by the Nazis. He published an homage to Bergson after his
death in 1941, and in 1943 he completed *Proust,* a monograph that summed
up his view on *À la recherche du temps perdu,* a novel that had been a crucial
influence on his conception of literature. Dominique Fernandez, his son
and biographer, considers this last publication, devoted to a half-Jewish,
homosexual writer, an act of defiance against the Germans.[18] Simon Epstein
has summed up Ramon's "French paradox" by labeling him "an anti-racist
collaborator."[19] Marguerite Duras, who lived in the same building as Ramon
and his second wife Betty, and who joined the Resistance during the occupation, admired him despite their incompatible political beliefs. In *L'Amant,*
she recalls their friendship with great affection.

On ne parlait pas de politique. On parlait de la littérature. Ramon Fernandez parlait de Balzac. On l'aurait écouté jusqu'à la fin des nuits. [. . .] Ramon Fernandez avait une civilité sublime jusque dans le savoir, une façon à la fois essentielle et transparente de se servir de la connaissance sans jamais en faire ressentir l'obligation, le poids. C'était quelqu'un de sincère. C'était toujours une fête de le rencontrer dans la rue, au café.[20]

(We didn't talk politics. We talked about literature. Ramon Fernandez used to talk about Balzac. We could have listened to him for ever and a day [. . .] He had a sublime courtesy even in knowledge, a way at once profound and clear of handling knowledge without ever making it seem an obligation or a burden. He was sincere. It was always a joy to meet him in the street or in a café.)[21]

In retrospect, Duras did not see their political views as entirely incompatible.

Collaborateurs, les Fernandez. Et moi, deux ans après la guerre, membre du P.C.F. L'équivalence est absolue, définitive. C'est la même chose, la même pitié, le même appel au secours, la même débilité du jugement, la même superstition disons, qui consiste à croire à la solution politique du problème personnel.[22]

(Collaborators, the Fernandezes were. And I, two years after the war, I was a member of the French Communist Party. The parallel is complete and absolute. The two things are the same, the same pity, the same call for help, the same lack of judgment, the same superstition if you like, that consists in believing in a political solution to the personal problem.)[23]

As the war drew to a close, Ramon's health declined quickly. He slid into alcoholism, suffered from chronic illnesses, and drank himself to death. In 1944, as an allied victory seemed imminent, he died of a stroke in Paris. His premature death—he was only fifty years old—spared him the harsh punishments given to most French intellectuals who collaborated with the Germans. Some, like Robert Brasillach, were sentenced to death; others were sent to prison; and yet others, like Louis-Ferdinand Céline, faced a lifetime of public scorn.

Ramon and Latin American Literature

Ramon Fernandez, like Antonio La Gandara, was born in France. Like Hahn and Heredia, he received a thoroughly French education and went on to become an important figure in French culture—to this day, he is remembered as one of the most important critics of French literature in the twentieth century. But unlike Hahn, Heredia, or Yturri, Fernandez appears to have forgotten the language of his ancestors. After the death of his father, Ramon lost the opportunity to speak Spanish, as he was raised by his mother and no one else in his family spoke the language. When the Mexican writer Alfonso Reyes met him in 1920s, the two corresponded exclusively in French.

Although Fernandez was born and raised in a thoroughly French milieu, he started life as a Mexican citizen. At the time of his birth, his father was an attaché at the Mexican embassy in Paris, and, like all children born to diplomats, he inherited his father's nationality (dual citizenship was not an option at the time). Ramon lived over half of his life as a foreign citizen and did not apply for naturalization until 1927, after he stumbled on a bureaucratic problem on the eve of his marriage to Liliane Chomette. French law dictated that at marriage the wife acquired her husband's nationality, and thus Ramon's bride faced the prospect of losing her French citizenship —and her teaching position along with it. Shortly before the wedding, Ramon wrote to Alfonso Reyes, who was serving as Mexico's ambassador to France, to request his assistance in the naturalization proceedings. "I have always been considered a Mexican citizen by our government as well as by the French," he stressed.[24]

Why had he waited so long to become a French citizen? Did he feel secret sentimental attachment to Mexico? Or was he motivated solely by practical concerns? As a Mexican citizen, he did not have to perform military service, and he avoided the draft during World War I. Nevertheless, living and working in France as a Mexican posed a number of bureaucratic obstacles, and he told Reyes that becoming French had become "a necessary step given my profession."[25]

In *Ramon,* Dominique Fernandez paints a portrait of his father as a man uninterested in his Mexican heritage, who never visited the country of his forebears. "My father," he writes, "never expressed an interest in Mexico. In the heap of articles he wrote, not a single one is devoted to an author from his fatherland."[26] Even if he never wrote an article on the subject, he read the works of Mexican writers, including Alfonso Reyes, who was one of the most widely read Latin American authors at the time. He was interested enough in Reyes's work to invite him to write a piece for the *NRF.*[27] (The review did not run any articles by Reyes, but it did publish a French translation of his *Visión de Anáhuac* in 1927.)[28] It is true, however, that Ramon never included a single Latin American author in the impressive panoply of literary references displayed in his critical essays.

Latin American writers, in contrast, were fascinated by Ramon and regarded him much in the same way that the previous generation had looked upon Heredia—as a distant relative who had conquered the famously impenetrable Parisian literary world. After meeting him in Paris, Reyes urged Ramon to write an autobiographical essay highlighting his connection to Mexico. "Give me the pleasure," Reyes implored from Buenos Aires in 1928,

> of sending me a long autobiographical letter, including all the information you consider appropriate for supplementing your biography. If you could include a few Mexican souvenirs (either direct impressions from your own childhood or family memories) as well as a very brief statement of your position towards philosophy and literature, as you understand it, I could translate your letter. I plan to send *Contemporáneos* a short piece—not at all pretentious but rather warm and friendly—on Ramón Fernández, the French writer from Mexico. Perhaps a photo? Don't say no, I beg you. And don't say *"mañana"*; say "right away."[29]

Ramon never wrote the autobiographical sketch, but he did send Reyes a piece for *Contemporáneos*—an essay on Proust adapted from a chapter in *Messages*. It was translated into Spanish by Xavier Villaurrutia, a young poet associated with the journal, and published as "Notas sobre la estética de Proust" in the March 1930 issue.[30]

The young avant-garde writers who edited *Contemporáneos* were also fascinated by the figure of Ramon Fernandez. Like Reyes, they were intrigued by his Mexicanness, but above all they admired him as a critic who had written on Proust, Gide, and Eliot, the modern figures they revered. In his weekly column for *El Universal Ilustrado*, Salvador Novo—one of the youngest members of the group—reviewed the first issues of the *Cahiers Marcel Proust*, edited by Ramon, and speculated on the identity of his curious conational: "Ramon Fernandez," he wrote "is Mexican, the son or grandson of a politician who served in the Porfiriato and who was thrown out of Mexico by the revolution, for the benefit of French letters. M. Ramon Fernandez does not speak or write Spanish. In this he is like [George] Santayana, the Spaniard who writes and thinks exclusively in English."[31]

Xavier Villaurrutia translated at least two of Ramon's texts into Spanish: the essay on Proust for *Contemporáneos* and a piece on the poetics of the novel for the Guadalajara journal *Bandera de Provincias*.[32] In his preface to this last translation, Villaurrutia noted that "Ramon Fernandez is of Mexican origin, we affirm with a melancholic pride. He has suppressed the accent marks from his name, but nothing can suppress the moral marks that continue to define him as a Mexican."[33] Here Villaurrutia draws attention to a curious detail involving Ramon's acculturation to French society. The critic's father and grandfather both spelled their name, "Ramón Fernández," with accent marks. Ramon was the first in his family to drop the accents, but most Latin Americans—including Reyes—insisted on writing the critic's name with accents. They turned Ramon into Ramón, a small gesture that attests to their desire to claim the French critic as one of their own. Fernandez seems to have had some thoughts on these lost accents; he once gave the title "L'accent perdu" to an article about his visits to Proust.

And it was not only Mexican writers who expressed an interest in Ramon. In 1938, the Argentinean publishing house Sur, directed by Victoria and Silvina Ocampo, published a Spanish version of Ramon's book *L'homme, est-il humain?* (1936) translated by Isaac Ungar. Sur also published an influential literary journal bearing the same name, which regularly featured articles by Borges, Reyes, Octavio Paz, and Roger Caillois. (Caillois moved to Buenos Aires in 1939 and spent two years there as Victoria Ocampo's guest.) In 1937 Borges published a scathing review of *L'homme, est-il humain?* in this journal, accusing the author of seeking controversy for controversy's sake: "El procedimiento polémico (el único procedimiento polémico) de este libro no adolece de mucha complejidad. Se limita, cómodamente, a deformar o simplificar las tesis del adversario para luego probar lo simples y deformes que son."[34] (This book's polemical approach (its only polemical approach) is not very complex. It limits itself, quite comfortably, to deform or to simplify the adversary's theses in order to later prove how simplistic and deformed they are).

But what did Latin American writers make of Ramon's lack of interest in their literatures? Most had mixed feelings. Reyes, for instance, admired Ramon's criticism and his friendship with Proust, but deplored his attitude toward Latin America. In an essay from the 1920s, Reyes recalled with affection the first time he met Ramon Fernandez in Paris. He had just moved to the French capital to take his post at the embassy and found himself living at 44, rue Hamelin, the same building where Marcel Proust spent the last three years of his life. Reyes befriended the concierge, who told him many stories about the eccentric novelist's daily routine and illustrious visitors. Reyes learned that "Proust received frequent visits from Ramón Fernández, a Mexican writer who studied in Paris and was a descendant of President Manuel González's ambassador to France."[35] The concierge's description sparked his interest, and he sought out this mysterious Mexican Proustian, unknown in Mexico.

Later in life, Reyes grew more critical of Ramon. In 1958, he lambasted the critic's conservative ideology. He referred to him as "Ramón Fernández, that French writer who was the son and grandson of Mexicans and—I think—of the fashion designer Mme Fernández, who took the creations of the Maison de France to Madrid." Reyes went on to denounce Ramon's cultural prejudices: "Ramón Fernandez was a subtle man, but in a Freudian slip, so as not be confused with his savage brothers, he had the bad taste—a symptom of his bad faith—to write, somewhere, some pejorative and completely useless sentences about Spanish America."[36]

Reyes was probably referring to a minor comment Ramon made about his Mexican origins in *Moralisme et littérature*. In a conversation with Jacques Rivière on European culture, Ramon told his interlocutor: "You have to trust the experience of a Latin American who sought the meaning of life in Europe, and who managed to penetrate, with the passion of a barbarian [avec des exigences de Barbare], the admired French citadel."[37] This phrase has often been taken out of context, and, as Dominique Fernandez notes, it gave rise to the legend of Ramon as a "half-breed from the Americas."[38]

Ramon probably intended the phrase to be ironic, and we could read it as an attempt to emphasize his passion for European culture. It was the study of this culture that "gave meaning to his life," and he was proud to have "penetrated" into the famously closed Parisian literary world. He understood that his achievements were even more remarkable given his origins. Despite his French upbringing, his command of the language, his studies at the best schools, he was aware that many Parisians saw him as a "barbarian." Indeed, in 1934, one of his readers, in a response to a political article, called him "a foreigner [. . .] [who] is not qualified to judge French reactions nor to appreciate the character, the moral significance and the trend of an event as important as that of the 6th of February [the date when a right-wing protest erupted into violence]."[39] It was the Parisians who had always seen him as a "barbarian," and he was adopting, tongue-in-cheek, the voice and tone of his critics.

Ramon suggests that he, as an outsider, might have a better perspective on European culture than his interlocutor, a native Frenchman: "Rivière ne saurait croire, lui qui est de la cité, à quel point la perfection même de la culture française allège, permet de se passer des problèmes qui tourmentent de moins fortunés réduits à vivre au jour le jour, à s'édifier tant bien que mal."[40] (Rivière would never understand—he who had been born inside the citadel —the degree to which the perfection of French culture alleviates and allows us to overcome the problems which torment those less fortunate ones, reduced to living from hand to mouth and to educate themselves as they can.) Ramon hails the redemptive powers of European civilization and holds himself up as an example: he—a man many would consider a "barbarian"— has reached a more sophisticated understanding of European culture than those who were born in it. It was with irony that he wrote of his *exigences de Barbare,* and it was an even greater irony that this jab at his conservative French readers was read as a slight by his Latin American peers.

Proust and Ramon

While Mexican writers recognized Ramon as one of their own, Proust never considered Ramon exotic or foreign, at least as far as we can tell from their surviving correspondence. He commented on his looks but never on his national origin, and there is no indication that the novelist ever perceived a cultural disparity between himself and the critic. He saw him as a young man who was no different from other intellectuals in the Parisian literary scene. Proust only made the link between Ramon and Mexico once, albeit in an indirect way. In 1918, after he decided to sell his ill-fated Mexican stocks, his broker Lionel Hauser asked Marcel to help him secure a review for his recently published theosophical treatise, and Proust obliged, writing to Ramon and suggesting an article in either *Les Écrits Nouveaux* or *L'Europe Nouvelle,* two journals for which the critic was a correspondent.[41] Proust played the role of a power broker, forging a connection between a Mexican critic and a trader of Mexican stocks. The novelist finally liquidated his ill-fated investment around the time he became closer to Ramon. In the end, criticism proved a better deal than stocks: he lost money with Mexico Tramways but gained literary fame through his Mexican critic.

Ramon wrote a brief chronicle of his friendship with Marcel in a special issue the *NRF* devoted to Proust in 1926. He recalled how, during the Great War, Proust once came to visit him in the middle of the night, braving the threat of German bombardments, with a most unusual request: "I'm about to ask you something very indiscreet, very inappropriate, but which will explain, if not excuse, the bother I'm causing you and which you will no doubt

never forgive." The novelist then went to the point: "Could I ask you, you
who know Italian, to say out loud the Italian translation of *sans rigueur*?" He
explained that "a foreign word that I cannot say correctly gives me a kind of
anxiety. I cannot have the right intuition about it, I cannot possess it, I cannot make it part of myself. I am obsessed by this Italian *'sans rigueur'* which
I had the folly to place in a passage, uninteresting otherwise, in my book.
The phrase, with these words I cannot hear, makes me feel as if I had what
mechanics call a wrench in the works [*un loup*]. It is almost intolerable."[42]
Ramon obliged, pronouncing *senza rigore* with his best Italian accent—
several times, for Marcel demanded an encore. The critic recalls that Proust
"listened, his eyes closed, without repeating the word that resonated in the
depths of his memory, and he thanked me as effusively as if I had just taken
him to visit Balbec's church or Saint Mark's in Venice."[43]

Proust inserted the *senza rigore* spoken by Ramon in a passage devoted
to Odette in *A l'ombre des jeunes filles en fleurs*. This demimondaine has been
banished from Madame Verdurin's salon, where she was once a regular, and
she has taken her revenge by stealing many of her rival's guests.

> Dès la fin d'octobre Odette rentrait le plus régulièrement qu'elle pouvait pour le
> thé, qu'on appelait encore dans ce temps-là le *five o'clock tea,* ayant entendu dire
> (et aimant répéter) que si Mme Verdurin s'était fait un salon c'était parce qu'on
> était toujours sûr de pouvoir la rencontrer chez elle à la même heure. Elle
> s'imaginait elle-même en avoir un, du même genre, mais plus libre, *senza rigore,*
> aimait-elle à dire.[44]

> (By the end of October, Odette would come home as regularly as possible to take
> tea—a ceremony which was still known in those days by the English expression
> "five o'clock tea" because she had once heard it said, and enjoyed repeating,
> that the real origin of Mme Verdurin's salon had been the knowledge in people's
> minds that their hostess could always be found at home at the same time each
> day. She now prided herself on having built up a salon of her own, similar in de-
> sign but freer in spirit, or as she liked to put it, *senza rigore*.)[45]

"Senza rigore" is a musical term, indicating a passage to be played without a strict tempo, but Proust gave it the more general meaning of "without strict rules." Odette prides herself on avoiding the stiffness of Madame
Verdurin's receptions and sees her salon as a more relaxed space, devoid
of protocol. The phrase also illustrates Odette's will to be cosmopolitan by

peppering her sentences with foreign words like the English "five o'clock"
or the Italian *"senza rigore."* The passage paints her pretended cosmopolit-
ism with a grain of irony, suggesting that Odette does not fully master the
words she uses (elsewhere she refers to the style of a piece of furniture as
"moyen-âgeux," medieval-like).[46] Odette uses foreign terms in a rather care-
less way, *senza rigore.*

When Ramon later spotted the Italian phrase in *À l'ombre des jeunes filles
en fleurs,* he was thrilled to see a bit of himself reflected in Proust's novel.
"I understood, much better than after extensive research," he wrote, "that
in Proust's work, which like a living tissue is a mass of nerves, the slightest
word, perhaps even the slightest letter, represents a desire, a concern, an
experience, a memory."[47]

The *senza rigore* episode marks the only time that Proust associated
Ramon with foreignness. Why did Proust think that Ramon, born in France
of a Mexican father, was the right person to intone the cadences of the Italian expression? Dominique Fernandez believes the novelist simply "mixed
up his southern countries" and perceived Mexico and Italy as interchange-
able hot, distant nations. Proust would have thus assumed that a Mexican
would know more about Italian culture than a Frenchman.[48] But there is
another possible explanation. Perhaps, unconsciously, Proust thought of
Ramon as someone who was more relaxed and informal than his peers in
Parisian intellectual circles—a young man *senza rigore*—and thus an apt
spokesman for the little phrase. Later in life, Ramon became famous for
his skill as a tango dancer and his love of fast cars—passions that reveal an
expansive personality entirely devoid of *rigore.*

In any case, Ramon was delighted to find a trace of his late-night conversations with Proust in *À la recherche.* His essay for the *NRF* reveals a sense of
pride at having contributed these two Italian words to Proust's vast novel.
And he was relaxed enough that he did not mind seeing his words placed
in the lips of Odette, one of the least sophisticated characters in the book.
Others might have taken this as a jab, but Ramon's attitude was more open,
senza rigore, and he was pleased to see his phrase uttered by a *cocotte.*

Ramon and Proust's Latin Americans

Ramon was too young to have met Gabriel Yturri or José-Maria de
Heredia—they both died in 1905, when the future critic was an eleven-year-
old boy. He did not have much in common with Yturri, who was gay, from

a modest background, immersed in a rather frivolous literary circle, and mocked as a *rastaquouère* by Parisian society. Ramon was almost his exact opposite—a heterosexual born to privilege who befriended serious novelists and became a pillar of Parisian intellectual life. Despite these differences, Ramon might have liked Yturri. As Dominique Fernandez has shown, though the critic played the role of a Latin Don Juan, he had a fondness for gay artists, wrote on Proust and Gide, and included several "homosexual socialites" among his closest friends.[49]

On the other hand, Ramon would have had much in common with Heredia. Both came from rich Latin American families, were educated in France, spoke accentless French, and rose to the summit of Parisian letters. They were serial seducers with a knack for gambling, and both died relatively young—Heredia in his early sixties, Ramon at fifty. Their work, however, could not have been more different. Heredia only wrote one book of poetry in his lifetime, while Ramon published over a dozen monographs and countless articles. Heredia wrote unforgettable poems and articles about Latin America, whereas Ramon concerned himself exclusively with European writers.

Although Ramon never met Yturri or Heredia, he was close to Reynaldo Hahn, who was a good friend of his mother and a regular at her salon. They, too, shared similar backgrounds and became canonical figures in French culture. They both became French citizens at the age of thirty-three, and they both shared a passion for Proust, though Ramon's interest was platonic and focused on his work. During World War II Ramon and Reynaldo found themselves on opposite ends of the political spectrum: Ramon proclaimed his rightist politics from his tribune at the *NRF,* while Hahn never made a single political statement in print. During the German occupation, Fernandez collaborated with the Vichy government and worked closely with its leaders. Hahn saw himself black-listed as a Jewish composer, spent the war years in exile, and lost several Jewish friends, including the artist and composer Fernand Ochsé, who died at Auschwitz.[50] Though Fernandez objected to the anti-Semitic bent of the Parti Populaire Français, it is surprising that a man who was half-Mexican and had mestizo blood was accepted into the fold of a group of ideologues who preached racial purity.

But their political differences did not affect their friendship, even during the war years. In 1943, Ramon sent Hahn a copy of his *Proust,* and the composer responded with the following letter (published here for the first time):

Monte Carlo
Sept. 43
Mon cher Ramon,

Je vous remercie sincèrement de m'avoir envoyé votre livre sur Marcel.

Non, certes, vous ne "l'avez pas trahi." Vous lui avez rendu un hommage qui compte! Chaque page, chaque phrase atteste votre pitié! C'est un prodige d'*attention,* qui implique l'amour.

Je ne vous dirai pas qu'il m'ait toujours été possible de vous suivre dans vos explications; il m'en eut fallu pour cela une faculté de *perception métaphysique* dont je suis, hélas, tout à fait dépourvu.

[Ça montre que?] certains phénomènes inconscients du génie échappent comme au génie lui-même, à ceux qui ont vécu tant près de lui. C'est mon cas: bien des choses qui, chez Marcel, me paraissaient toutes simples parce que je les avais sans cesse devant les yeux, sont pour vous matière à investigations biologiques, à descriptions minutieuses et révélatrices, qui apportent à l'exégèse "Proustienne" une contribution inappréciable. Je suis sûr que Marcel aurait admiré votre analyse et se serait montré touché de la ferveur dont elle témoigne.

Quant à moi, je vous en reparlerai plus longuement un jour, quand nous nous reverrons—si tant c'est que nous nous revoyions jamais . . . Est-on sûr de rien présentement?

Mille souvenirs,
Reynaldo Hahn[51]

(My dear Ramon:
I sincerely thank you for having sent me your book on Marcel.
No: you certainly did not "betray him"; you have paid him homage in a way that counts! Every page, every phrase certifies your empathy! Your book is a remarkable feat of *attention,* and thus a token of love.

I won't tell you that I could always follow you in your explications; for that I would have needed a skill of *metaphysical perception* that, alas, I don't have at all.

There are certain unconscious phenomena linked to genius that go unnoticed by the virtuoso himself, but also by those who lived so close to him, as is my case. In Marcel there were many things which I considered extremely simple because I had them constantly before my eyes, while for you these constitute a raw matter for biological investigations, for careful and revealing descriptions that are a priceless contribution to the "Proustian" exegesis. I am certain that Marcel would have admired your analysis and that he would have been moved by the fervor it displays.

As for me . . . I'll tell you more when we meet again—if we get to meet again. Can one be certain of anything at present?

A thousand regards,

Reynaldo Hahn)

Proust had been dead for over two decades, but even in the midst of World War II he continued to serve as the intermediary between Ramon and Reynaldo. Hahn's letter reveals an important ideological difference between himself and Ramon. Reynaldo could not separate the personality of an author from his published work—and thus the monumental *À la recherche* remained, for him, the creation of his exceedingly neurotic first lover. Ramon, on the other hand, studied the novel as an autonomous creation, as a work that transcended the personality of its author. Though Ramon knew Proust, his criticism refrained from seeking clues in the novelist's biography, turning instead to philosophical questions, highlighting the links between the ideas presented in *À la recherche* and philosophical concepts. Ramon's conception of literature was close to Proust's. One of the novelist's first works, *Contre Sainte-Beuve,* made an impassioned argument against the nineteenth-century critic Sainte-Beuve's view of literary creation as intertwined with the author's personality. Proust, in contrast, argued that a work of art is the result of a mysterious process that eludes the conscious understanding of its creator and thus has very little to do with the author's personality. "Un livre est le produit d'un autre moi que celui que nous manifestons dans nos habitudes, dans la société, dans nos vices. Ce moi-là, si nous voulons essayer de le comprendre, c'est au fond de nous-même, en essayant de le recréer en nous, que nous pouvons y parvenir." ("A book is the product of a self other than that which we display in our habits, in company, in our vices. If we want to try and understand this self, it is deep inside us, by trying to recreate it within us, that we may succeed.")[52] Ramon presented a similar argument in *De la personnalité* (1928).[53]

Hahn and Ramon would never meet again. The critic died a year after this last exchange, and Reynaldo sent Ramon's mother a condolence letter from Monte Carlo.[54] When the war ended, he returned to Paris, where he continued to see Jeanne Fernandez, who outlived him and died in 1961.

Ramon Fernandez in Key West

Ramon Fernandez was admired by French writers, by Mexican intellectuals, and also by at least one important American poet. In 1934, Wallace
Stevens paid tribute to him in "The idea of order at Key West," a poem that
opens with a mysterious woman singing "beyond the genius of the sea" and
closes with the following apostrophe to the critic:

> Ramon Fernandez, tell me, if you know,
> Why, when the singing ended and we turned
> Toward the town, tell why the glassy lights,
> The lights in the fishing boats at anchor there,
> As the night descended, tilting in the air,
> Mastered the night and portioned out the sea,
> Fixing emblazoned zones and fiery poles,
> Arranging, deepening, enchanting night.
>
> Oh! Blessed rage for order, pale Ramon,
> The maker's rage to order words of the sea,
> Words of the fragrant portals, dimly-starred,
> And of ourselves and of our origins,
> In ghostlier demarcations, keener sounds.[55]

Ever since the poem was published in the October 1934 issue of *Alcestis*,
readers have been intrigued by this curious apostrophe to Ramon. The Italian
literary critic Renato Poggioli wrote Stevens in 1954 asking him to explain the
role played by the French critic in the poem. Stevens responded: "When I
was trying to think of a Spanish name for *The Idea of Order*, etc., I simply put
together by chance two exceedingly common names in order to make one
and I did not have in mind Ramon Fernandez. Afterwards, someone asked
me whether I meant the man you have in mind. I have never even given him
a conscious thought. The real Fernandez used to write feuilletons in one of
the Paris weeklies and it is true that I used to read these. But I did not con-
sciously have him in mind."[56] In another letter, Stevens quipped that "Ramon
Fernandez was not intended to be anyone at all."[57]

Critics have been skeptical of Stevens's denial. James Longenbach has
pointed out that English translations of Fernandez's articles appeared in the
Partisan Review and the *Criterion,* journals that Stevens knew well. Longenbach believes that Stevens would have been especially familiar with Fernandez's open letter to André Gide and with his essay "I Came Near Being

a Fascist" (published before he actually became one) in the *Partisan Review* around the same time that Stevens composed "The Idea of Order at Key West."[58] Longenbach notes that in this text Fernandez confessed "a professional fondness for theorizing, which tends to make one highly susceptible to original 'solutions'" and that this proclamation, combined with his "public announcements of political commitments and conversions," made him "the opposite of Stevens, who recoiled at the idea of associating himself with any group or program that offered 'solutions.'"[59]

But what role does Ramon Fernandez play in "The Idea of Order at Key West"? The main figure in the poem is a singing woman who appears in the first stanza.

> She sang beyond the genius of the sea.
> The water never formed to mind or voice,
> Like a body wholly body, fluttering
> Its empty sleeves; and yet its mimic motion
> Made constant cry, caused constantly a cry,
> That was not ours although we understood,
> Inhuman, of the veritable ocean.[60]

Who is this mysterious singer? And what exactly is her song about? All we know about her is that her singing emerges as the focal event in the poem. The song seems to mimic the roaring of the sea, but we soon learn that the two sounds are completely distinct and that "The song and water were not medleyed sound / Even if what she sang was what she heard." The poet stresses that "it was she and not the sea we heard."

The chief characteristic of the song is that it emanates from the singer, "For she was the maker of the song she sang." The process by which the song is produced, however, remains shrouded in mystery, but the poet expresses a continued desire to discover its workings: "Whose spirit was this? We said, because we knew / It was the spirit that we sought and knew / That we should ask this as often as she sang." Eventually, the poem concludes that the only thing we can know with certainty about the song is that the woman "was the single artificer of the world / in which she sang." Her song is the expression of a creative act that has the power to reshape the environment around her and to command even the natural force of the sea, for "when she sang, the sea, / Whatever self it had, became the self / That was her song, for she was the maker." Moreover, the act of singing brings about a complete, almost mystical fulfillment to the singer, as she reaches a state of pure concentration that the narrator witnesses with awe: "Then we,/As we beheld her striding there alone,/Knew that there never was a world for her/Except the one she sang and, singing made."

At this point it becomes clear that the poem is developing an age-old trope—singing as a metaphor for poetic creation. The description of the woman's song becomes a condensed manifesto of Stevens' aesthetic beliefs. First and foremost, the song teaches the reader that poetry is composed through an enigmatic process—one that escapes even the poet himself. This is the same position championed by Proust in *Contre Sainte-Beuve* and by Ramon Fernandez in *De la personnalité* and other works. As Susan Stewart writes, "the speaker of the poem is at sea looking toward the shore where this figure sings as a siren sings—making a song distinct from, but owing something to, the rhythms and grindings and plungings of the sea and wind. The song is not an imitation of the sea, but a way of making a world in which the song, constructed word by word in sequence and "measured" as music is measured, has its resonance."[61]

It is immediately after this celebration of the mysteries of poetic creation that Ramon Fernandez makes an appearance (though one can also read the poem as if he were on the boat, looking at the shore, in which case he is present from the first stanza, identified by "we"). The narrator challenges him to explain the song's powerful effect on the listeners, an effect that lingers even after the singing has stopped. "Ramon Fernandez, tell me, if you know,/Why, when the singing ended and we turned/Toward the town." The narrator then dares Fernandez to "tell why the glassy lights,/The lights in the fishing boats at anchor there,/As the lights descended, tilting in the air,/Mastered the night and portioned out the sea,/Fixing emblazoned zones and fiery poles,/Arranging, deepening, enchanting night." These are, of course, things that neither Ramon Fernandez nor anyone else can explain. There is no reason why the lights shine with that particular quality against the nocturnal seascape of Key West, just as there is no reason why the song leaves the narrator in a state of heightened perception and sensibility. These experiences, like the creative process hailed in the poem, cannot be elucidated by asking "why"? They are the fleeting illuminations of a contemplative life—the stuff that Stevens's poetry is made of.

The poem presents Ramon Fernandez as the antithesis of the singing woman. She creates, he theorizes; she enthralls the narrator with her song; he leaves him indifferent with his inability to explain. In the end, the song succeeds, creating a powerful effect in those who listen. But Ramon Fernandez fails at explaining the song; he remains silent and cannot respond to the narrator's inquiries.

Longenbach reads the opposition between the singer and Ramon Fernandez as embodying one of the central themes of the poem: the contrast between certainty and uncertainty. Ramon Fernandez, he writes, "might have been certain about the sources of the singer's song, but the only thing Stevens was sure of was that in his certainty, Fernandez would have been wrong."[62] I would go even further and argue that Stevens considered Ramon Fernandez the embodiment of French thought bound by a strict Cartesianism. The inclusion of this critic in the poem stages an opposition between artistic creation—based on experience and sense perception—and a cold, cerebral, intelligence that is limited to asking "why?"

Ramon would not have recognized himself in "The Idea of Order in Key West." Like Stevens, he was fascinated by the mystery of aesthetic creation, and in his conversations with Rivière he argued that "intelligence, even sensitive intelligence, could never exhaust life or art [. . .] by dint of wanting to understand and to feel with exactitude, one destroys in oneself that which it matters most to understand and to feel."[63] The real Ramon, it turns out, would have been as enthralled with the woman's song as the narrator in Stevens's poem. But Stevens did not known this, and he caricatured the French critic as a cerebral intellectual.

In *Ramon,* Dominique Fernandez portrays his father as a man marked by the excesses of a "Southern culture" in which families spoil boys from an early age, indulging their every whim and avoiding any kind of discipline. In the son's view, the passions that marked Ramon's adult life—women, fast cars, gambling—can all be traced back to his southern roots.[64] His son sees Ramon as an archetypal hot-blooded southerner; Stevens, in contrast, makes the critic a representative of a French mode of thought that is too cerebral and too detached from the senses. Character, it seems, is in the eye of the beholder. As for Proust, he considered the young man a serious critic but one with a special connection to the south. He was interested in Ramon's mind and in his criticism (his body, as he repeated twice, did not do much for him). Yet, he saw Ramon as the perfect person to pronounce *senza rigore,* associating him with the sensual world of Italy, musical composition, and southern Europe. As usual, Proust was deft at seeing ambiguities, including those of Ramon Fernandez.

Ramon on Proust

Through the *Nouvelle Revue Française,* Ramon played an important role in disseminating serious scholarship on Proust. In January 1923, he helped Rivière edit a special issue on the novelist featuring the most brilliant critics and writers of the period: François Mauriac, Ernst Robert Curtius, Jean Cocteau, Philippe Soupault, Jacques-Émile Blanche, Léon Daudet, Maurice Barrès, Albert Thibaudet, Edmond Jaloux, Jacques Boulenger, and Paul Valéry.

After the publication of *Swann's Way* in 1913, readers and critics were distracted by the pastime of identifying the models for Proust's characters and comparing the originals to their novelistic versions. Others read the novel for clues about Marcel's sexual life. Even Cocteau, as late as 1952, seemed mostly interested in these biographical questions.[65] Fernandez, in contrast, was one of the first to put Proust's novel in dialogue with philosophical ideals and to elevate Proustian criticism to a theoretical level. His most important contribution in this area is the chapter devoted to Proust in *Messages* (1926), "The Guaranteeing of Sentiments and the Intermittences of the Heart," an essay that paved the way for later studies by intellectuals such as Curtius (1928), Benjamin (1929), Beckett (1931), and Maurois (1931).

Fernandez brushed aside all biographical speculations to apply the method he called "philosophical criticism" (the title of the first chapter in *Messages*). His chapter on Proust focused instead on one concrete problem: the episodes of involuntary memory Proust associates with "the intermittences of the heart," and the psychological and philosophical consequences of this mode of experience. In the novel, past experience can only be fully grasped after it is relived in an episode of involuntary remembrance, as the narrator shows when one of these epiphanies makes him relive the moment of his grandmother's death: "it was only at that instant, more than a year after her funeral, because of that anachronism which so often prevents the calendar of facts from coinciding with that of the feelings,—that I had come to learn that she was dead."[66]

Ramon then asks what kind of theory of personality can be extrapolated from these mnemonic intermittences. He is chiefly interested in relating these episodes to contemporary theories of "spirituality" and to highlighting the role of "moral guarantee and responsibility" in a subjectivity shaped by intermittent recollections.[67] How can an individual, he asks, take responsibility for his past actions and make "spiritual progress" if he can only make sense of the past intermittently, after these involuntary episodes? To re-

solve this problem, he invokes various thinkers who explored the link between memory, volition, and responsibility: Montaigne, Descartes, Alain,
Bergson, and George Meredith. But the main theoretical source is John
Henry Newman (1801-1890), an English cardinal and Oxford-trained theolo-
gian whose *Grammar of Ascent* (1870)—a defense of faith against Cartesian
reason—was a fundamental influence on Ramon's ideas. *Messages* examines
the fundamental incompatibility between Proustian subjectivity and moral
responsibility—"spiritual progress," as theorized by Newman.

Ramon cites previous criticisms of Proust—most notably by the very
Catholic François Mauriac—emphasizing the problem of morality in the
novel, which "does not manifest, from its opening to its conclusion, any
spiritual progress"[68] or offer "an index of maturity."[69] He argues that Proust's
conception of the individual is morally defective, a fault he attributes to the
novelist's psychological troubles: "Marcel Proust suffered from a hypertro-
phied affectivity: now, pleasure and pain felt too strongly destroy the order
of things and draw back to themselves the sentimental values through an
easily conceivable subterfuge. Through the disproportionate resonances
which they are able to ring from the body, they give a false voice to the soul;
in the same way as ventriloquists surprise dumb spectators by making them
speak."[70] He believes that the affective intensity of involuntary memory im-
pairs the subject's capacity for distinguishing between important and trivial
experiences: "Most serious of all is that the preponderance of affective dis-
charges prevents him from distinguishing things from one another through
their value, and consequently from distributing wisely the effort of his intelligence, since the scent of a rose and the scent of a soul alike create for him
an ego and equally justify his aversion or his desire."[71]

In the end, Ramon attributes these problems to a fundamental flaw in
Proust's character: "Proust's defect for me is of a psychological order, it is a
flaw in the machine; hence it *may* be observed independently of any metaphysical assumption."[72] The defect, however, can be fixed. "It is just because
his machine is admirably conceived that the part missing must quickly be
added in order that such a machine may work normally."[73] How, one wonders,
could one add that extra part in order to repair Proust's novelistic machinery?

Ramon was in his early thirties when he wrote this piece, which has not
aged well. In it, we can see a young man's passion for knowledge and intellectual curiosity. His philosophical readings are impressive, and they cover
a wide range of tendencies and historical periods. And in contrast to the
provincialism of critics intent on matching characters to celebrities of the

Faubourg Saint-Germain, Ramon demonstrates an intellectual cosmopolit-
ism that leads him to continental philosophy and English Catholic theology.
He liked ideas, and he distilled, elegantly and masterfully, a theory of subjectivity from the novel's most famous passages.

But his method is surprising when we place it in historical context. He
was writing in the midst of a veritable explosion of avant-garde thought in
Europe. Freud had published his *Interpretation of Dreams* in 1900; Marinetti
his "Manifesto of Futurism" in 1909; Breton his "Manifesto of Surrealism" in
1924. For over two decades, poets, artists and critics had been crafting new
theories of literature and literary criticism. Deeply influenced by Freud, figures from Breton to Bataille had rejected nineteenth-century literary and
critical models, centered on the notion of Cartesian subjectivity, to fore-
ground the role of the unconscious in literary creation. The ego was not
master in his own house, and Proust was one of the first novelists—without
having ever read Freud—to illustrate in great detail the tricks played by
the unconscious through the epiphanies of involuntary memory and other
subterfuges. Amid this veritable revolt against the tyranny of consciousness
and of master narratives, Ramon emerges as a reactionary critic, seeking to
restore the rule of consciousness and harking back to a nineteenth-century
conception of "spirituality." At a time when Freud, Marx, and Nietzsche inspired critics to conceive a new form of literary criticism, Ramon finds shel-
ter in books written by an English Catholic priest.

In contrast to the rebellious surrealists, Ramon appears to have had a
great need for guidance, for a moral compass. (His main criticism against
Proust's novel is that it cannot be used for this purpose.) A decade later, this
need for guidance would lead him to join a far-right party and to collaborate
with the Nazis, who offered him the clearly defined morality he could not
find in Proust's novel. In the end, the clear guidelines for living a responsible
life he found in Cardinal Newman's work did not help him make the right
choice. (One wonders if Proust, with his emphasis on the singularity of individual experience and his rejection of a universal code of ethics, would have
proved a better guide for the kind of "spiritual progress" Ramon desired.)

At one point in this chapter, Ramon alludes to Mexican history in his
critique of Proust's novel. He compares the instability of a subject prone
to mnemonic illuminations to the political situation in Latin America: "[. . .]
if the flights of our sensibility are dependent upon a phenomenon of reminis-
cence, if to be aware of a sentiment we must await the affective spark, which
will enable us to relive integrally an anterior experience, if to understand,

and feel, and desire, and will, we must first undergo an inverted metempsychosis, whereby the useless forms of our past lives, imperious and exclusive, are returned to us, we are no better than those little South American republics which each month change their programmes and their promises with a change of dictators."[74] Ramon probably had in mind the events of the Mexican Revolution, which had ended five years before he wrote this piece. He could have been thinking of his own family—his grandfather, who served as governor of Mexico, and his father, who was Porfirio Díaz's envoy—and their precarious history: close to power one day, political outcasts the next. In his mind, this political instability was a perfect metaphor for the subjective changeability that characterizes the Proustian subject, prone to mnemonic and other unconscious irruptions.

Involuntary memory and social upheavals prove equally unpalatable to Ramon, who did not have much tolerance for revolutions, whether political or mnemonic in nature. He rejected involuntary memory for the same reason he turned his back on the country of his ancestors; they were unstable regions, subject to sudden reversals and alterations. In contrast, he chose France and a type of Cartesianism inflected by Catholic theology—rock-solid terrains he considered impervious to the political and aesthetic insurrections that shook the world during the 1920s. But this binary opposition did not hold. In the 1930s, it was France that descended into political chaos and war, while Mexico entered an unprecedented period of political stability that would last until the 1960s.

Ramon Fernandez would revisit *À la recherche* almost twenty years later, in *Proust,* one of his last works, completed in 1942 and published in 1943. Ramon was now in his late forties and nearing the end of his life, and this book marks a coda to his career by offering a compendium of the key philosophical concepts of literary criticism he had developed over almost three decades of writing.

Unlike the very focused Proust chapter in *Messages, Proust* aims to present an overview of the novel and its contribution to the literary canon and the history of ideas. The book is divided into eight chapters, each devoted to one aspect of the novel. "A vol d'oiseau" (A Bird's Eye View) discusses the larger structure and explains how each of the volumes fits into a larger architecture. "Les personnages et les types" (The Characters and Types) identifies the key figures in the novel—Swann, Françoise, and Charlus, as well as a few other "invisible" and "picturesque" types[75]—and discusses their significance to the Proustian project. Other chapters focus on the major themes in the novel: "Love," "Social Life," "Death," and "Art."

Almost none of the chapters manage to develop an argument as carefully and as eloquently as their author had done in *Messages*. At times the book seems hastily put together, and on countless occasions Ramon cuts corners by quoting himself or transcribing long passages from his earlier texts. Dominique Fernandez attributes these compositional flaws to his father's incessant journalistic and political activity during the Occupation, tasks that left him little time for writing.

Proust argues that *À la recherche* is a novel that, despite its apparently frivolous subject matter, advances a novel theory of subjectivity. Proust transformed "a banal life, a life of the eighth *arrondissement*" into "the most extraordinary and the most significant work of our time."[76] In contrast to *Messages,* with its narrow focus on the writings of Cardinal Newman and the question of moral responsibility, *Proust* asks much larger questions and relates the novelist's ideas to a panoply of philosophical ideas. Plato, Spinoza, Bergson, Freud, Nietzsche, Schopenhauer, Braunschweig, Ortega y Gasset, and many others serve as points of reference. "The *Temps perdu*," the book concludes, "constitutes, in an unexpected manner, a philosophy of knowledge."[77]

Fernandez devotes several pages to analyzing the role of homosexuality in the novel and alludes to the long conversations he had with the novelist on this subject. Proust "attributed a symbolic significance to the meeting between Charlus and Jupien," and he "established an important difference— almost a natural one—between Greek love and modern inversion." If Gide argued for a Platonic view of homosexual love, "Proust would have clearly denied the possibility of an ethical view like the one proposed in *Corydon*." *À la recherche* presents "inversion as an illness [*maladie*]"—a trope decried by Gide—but Ramon shrewdly points out that "so called normal love" is also presented as pathological.[78] "If love is an illness, it is in the pathological forms of love (inversion or sadism) that it will demonstrate most openly its veritable nature."[79] The critic recalls that Proust "affirmed, in writing that the inversion he studied was a sort of generalized social illness [*maladie*] and that *in this form* it carried the mark of our time."[80]

Ramon notes the similarities between Proust's and Freud's theories of sexuality and suggest a Freudian reading of Charlus, whom he considers the most developed character in the novel. "He is a child—a grown, mustachioed child, if we are to believe Freud's theory of the invert's infantile 'fixation'—who wanders through *Lost Time,* with great strides and loud cries, weak, despotic, whimsical, frivolous, intelligent, demented, and damned."[81]

The analysis of homosexuality is among the most developed, but the

book contains dozens of extremely perceptive observations, interpretations, and interrogations that are not elaborated. Each of them could serve
as the subject for an article or a chapter, and they reveal a sharp critic who
had perhaps run out of time to flesh out his ideas. On airplanes: "Unfortunately for us and for him, Proust did not experience flying [. . .] he was
prevented from having this experience by his asthma, which he only knew
from below."[82] On the Great War as a watershed: "*Le Temps perdu* is the
history of the decomposition [*désagrégation*] of a society in the same way
that, for a psychological view, it presents the history of the deconstruction
[*délitement*] of personality."[83] On religion: "Religion and its social function
[. . .] are absent from the *Temps perdu*, and we can conclude that the Proustian conception of society negates religion."[84] On servants: "Though their
profession, servants constitute a sort of masonic sect."[85] On the family
maid: "Françoise is to the servants at Balbec what the duchesse de Guermantes is to the Verdurins";[86] and "Françoise seems taken out of the Middle Ages."[87] On Proust versus Swann: "Proust is saved in timelessness, but
Swann loses himself in lost time [. . .] Swann is a truly elegant man—a dandy
if you will—while Proust wandered through the world as a somnambulist
or a medium in trance. Proust *se sauve,* a verb which in French has a double
sense: he is saved [*se* sauve] spiritually and he flees [*se sauve*] from a society
that threatens to annihilate it. Swann is a man who does not flee, who is
not saved."[88] On time regained: "*Le temps retrouvé* is time reborn and turned
into eternity."[89] On death: "For Proust death is the key factor in the esthetic
conception of life."[90] On the Vinteuil sonata: "To describe the sonata [. . .]
Proust employs neither technical terms nor ideas that are particularly musical; rather, he proceeds through transpositions, equivalences and meta-
phors."[91] In the end, Ramon considers the *Recherche* a work that launches a
new form of literary criticism: "as it unfolds [. . .] it unravels, by the same
movement, its own exegesis."[92]

    Proust also discusses the role of identity in the *À la recherche* and notes
that the novelist "always recognized and stressed the specificity of the Jews,
refusing to dissolve it into the common, neutral traits of the [French] democratic identity. In the same way, he recognized the specificity of homosexuals and even a form of specificity of the aristocracy."[93] Ramon highlights
the novelist's eye for what Kristeva, many years later, would call the quandary of *en être*: "Proust painted all those whom, through a certain existential
condition, are accustomed to a painful concealment [*dissimulation douloureuse*], from servants to abnormal types, and including all snobs, all victims

of humiliation, all *déclassés,* all solitaries, all pariahs."[94] It is striking that this list does not include Latin Americans living in Paris, another group that, as he have seen in the preceding chapters, constitutes a group marked by a cultural specificity. The omission is even more glaring since, elsewhere in *Proust,* Ramon outs himself as a foreigner and relates his own experience to Reynaldo Hahn's.[95] To use his own terms, we can conclude that Ramon's life was marked by a *"dissimulation douloureuse,"* but unlike the novelist, he refused to recognize his own "specificity" and devoted his life to dissolving the marks of his cultural alterity into the "French democratic identity." Proust dissected the peculiarities of Jewish and homosexual identity. Ramon admired the novelist's procedure but could not apply the same analysis to his own identity as a Latin American.

Ramon Fernandez was the only one of Proust's Latin Americans who lived to understand the full impact of *À la recherche du temps perdu* on literary history. Yturri and Heredia died before Proust published the first volume of his novel. Hahn lived to see the extraordinary success of the novel, but he never understood its importance, since he could not separate the work from the life of the person he had known so well. Fernandez was the only one of the four who was a literary critic and who plunged into a critical reading of the novel that highlighted its literary and philosophical importance.

Fernandez was also the only one of the five whom Proust did not see as an exotic foreigner. Reynaldo was "Teutonic and Meridional," Yturri was a Spaniard in the court of Saint-Simon, Heredia was the poet of the Conquest, but Ramon was simply a brilliant young critic. Could Proust have characterized him differently because Ramon was the only one of the group who did not feel a bond to Latin America?

Fernandez came into Proust's life too late to be incorporated into his work, but Proust's novel became a fundamental influence on Fernandez's conception of literature. Even if he was not always sympathetic to the novelist's project, his reflections on Proust's work are the bookends of his career. His first book, *Messages,* grew around a philosophical analysis of the novel, and his last publication, *Marcel Proust,* revisited the topic almost two decades later. Fernandez was also the only one of Proust's friends who helped make his work known in Latin America. Through Alfonso Reyes's efforts, he became the intermediary who first brought Proust to the attention of many Mexican and South American intellectuals. Ramon Fernandez was, and perhaps continues to be, the most Proustian of Mexicans.

Paperolle No. 4

Proust's Spanish

Several characters in Proust's novel speak, or rather pretend to speak, Spanish, though none of them come from Spanish-speaking countries. We never hear the Peruvian or the lascivious characters at Balbec speak their mother tongue, but we do hear others play with Spanish words. Doctor Cottard accompanies his prescriptions of an all-dairy regime with a pun. "Olé olé olé: Spain is in fashion," he tells his students and patients, punning on the French word for "take milk" (au lait) and the Spanish interjection *olé,* usually associated with toreros and bullfights.[1] Elsewhere the narrator muses on how, even after several generations in France, assimilated Latin American families continue to pepper their French with Spanish words. Ironically, it is a mysterious word uttered by Monsieur Verdurin as he schemes to help the bankrupt Saniette that leads the narrator to evoke the use of Spanish. As he tells his plans to Madame Verdurin,

> M Verdurin ajouta un mot qui signifiait évidemment ce genre de scènes touchantes et de phrases qu'ils désiraient éviter. Mais il n'a pu m'être dit exactement, car ce n'était pas un mot français, mais un de ces termes comme on en a dans les familles pour désigner certaines choses, surtout ces choses agaçantes, probablement parce qu'on veut pouvoir les signaler devant les intéressés sans être compris. Ce genre d'expressions est généralement un reliquat contemporain d'un état antérieur de la famille. Dans une famille juive, par exemple, ce sera un terme rituel détourné de son sens et peut-être le seul mot hébreu que la famille, maintenant francisée, connaisse encore. Dans une famille très fortement provinciale, ce sera un terme du patois de la province, bien que la famille ne parle plus et ne comprenne même plus le patois. Dans une famille venue de l'Amérique du Sud et ne parlant plus que le français, ce sera un mot espagnol. Et à la génération suivante, le mot n'existera plus qu'à titre de souvenir d'enfance. On se rappellera bien que

les parents à table faisaient allusion aux domestiques qui servaient, sans être compris d'eux, en disant tel mot, mais les enfants ignorent ce que voulait dire au juste
ce mot, si c'était de l'espagnol, de l'hébreu, de l'allemand, du patois, si même cela
avait jamais appartenu à une langue quelconque et n'était pas un nom propre, ou
un mot entièrement forgé. Le doute ne peut être éclairci que si on a un grand-
oncle, un vieux cousin encore vivant et qui a dû user du même terme. Comme je
n'ai connu aucun parent des Verdurin, je n'ai pu restituer le mot. Toujours est-il
qu'il fit certainement sourire Mme Verdurin, car l'emploi de cette langue moins
générale, plus personnelle, plus secrète, que la langue habituelle donne à ceux qui
en usent entre eux un sentiment égoïste qui ne va jamais sans une certaine
satisfaction.[2]

(M Verdurin added here a word which evidently stood for the kind of emotional
scene and embarrassing phrase which he wanted to avoid. But my informant
could not repeat it to me exactly, for it was not a normal French word, but one of
those terms that are used within families to designate certain things, in particular
annoying things, no doubt because the family wishes to be able to point them out
without the offenders understanding. Such expressions are usually a throwback
to an earlier state of the family in question. In a Jewish family, for example, it
will be a ritual term displaced from its original meaning, perhaps the only word
of Hebrew that the family, now wholly French in its manners, has retained. In a
very strongly provincial family, it will be a term of their provincial dialect, even
though the family no longer speaks dialect and can barely understand it any longer. In a South American family which now speaks only French, it will be a word
of Spanish. And in the next generation, the word will survive only as a childhood
memory. The children will remember that their parents could speak about the
servants waiting at table without being understood by them, using a particular
word, but they cannot tell exactly what the word meant, whether it was Spanish,
Hebrew, German or dialect, or even whether it had ever belonged to any real
language and was not a proper name or simply something invented. The mystery
can be solved only if there is a great-uncle, an elderly cousin still living who must
have once used the word himself. As I never knew any of the Verdurins' relatives, I was never able to supply the exact word. However, it clearly made Mme
Verdurin smile, for the use of this private, personal, secret language instead of the
language of every day gives the users of it a self-centered feeling which is always
accompanied by a certain satisfaction.)[3]

In their Pléiade edition of *À la recherche*, Antoine Compagnon and Pierre-
Édmond Robert relate this passage to Proust's interaction with his Latin

American friends: "Sans doute Proust fait-il des allusions, respectivement
à sa propre famille—maternelle pour 'un terme rituel,' paternelle pour une
expression provinciale venue d'Illiers—et aux familles de Reynaldo Hahn né
au Venezuela, ou d'Albert Nahmias, dont la mère était également originaire
de l'Amérique du Sud."[4] (Proust must certainly be making an allusion to
his own family—his mother's side for "a ritual term" and his father's for a
provincial expression originating in Illiers—and to the families of Reynaldo
Hahn, born in Venezuela, or Albert Nahmias, whose mother was also born
in South America.) Along with Max Daireux, Albert Nahmias was one of
the young Latin American men Proust befriended in Cabourg during the
summer of 1908, male counterparts to the blossoming young girls evoked in
the novel. Proust consulted his new friend on financial questions—he came
from a family of bankers—hired him to type the drafts of his novel (Nahmias
did not have the time or qualifications, so he in turn enlisted the services of
Cecilia Hayward, an English secretary), and even used him as a go-between
in his disputes with Alfred Agostinelli, his chauffeur and unrequited crush.
Nahmias's father was Jewish, and his mother, born Ana Segundo Ballen de
Guzmán, came from a family of Ecuadorian notables.[5]

Nahmias belonged to the circle of Marcel's Parisian friends who had one
Latin American parent and that also included Reynaldo (with a Venezuelan
father), La Gandara (with a Mexican father), Marie de Heredia (with a Cuban
father), Ramon Fernandez (with a Mexican father), and Max Daireaux (with
an Argentinean mother). All of them were children of Franco-Latin American couples who spoke French at home but would have also employed the
kind of Spanish language "relics" evoked by the narrator at the Verdurins'
soirée. Reynaldo and Albert lived in households that were Latin American
and Jewish, and their families would have also used German or Hebrew
terms. Marcel could relate his Latin American friends' linguistic hybridity to
his own experience: we know that his mother used Yiddish and Hebrew
terms at home and in her correspondence.[6]

But why does the narrator compare the Verdurins, who are fully French,
to assimilated foreign families who give away their cultural difference
though the use of linguistic relics? The term used by the Verdurins is part
of a private language—a "secret" language as the narrator calls it—that has
several characteristics. First, it is designed to exclude. Servants do not understand any of it, and children can only decipher it if they have access to
"a great-uncle" or another relative who plays the role of interpreter. The
private language thus separates those who belong to the family from those

who don't. Monsieur Verdurin uses the term to exclude outsiders—including the narrator—from his plans.

The private language is closely linked to pleasure. Madame Verdurin smiles when she hears and understands her husband's secret word, and the narrator comments that the use of such a private language brings a narcissistic pleasure (*un sentiment égoïste*) and a "certain satisfaction" to those who use it. It is also linked to the themes of sadism and cruelty that run through the novel and that are foregrounded in the humiliation of Charlus that precedes this scene. The pleasure derived from a private language stems from marginalizing those who cannot understand. This special language also has the capacity to turn unpleasant matters—its use is usually sparked by the need to refer to *choses agaçantes*—into a pleasurable experience based on cultural and linguistic bonding.

The narrator refers to the mysterious word uttered by Monsieur Verdurin as "a reliquary of an anterior state of the family," a linguistic relic that, like the contents of the unconscious, has survived from the most remote past, and which Freud compared to relics and phylogenetic traits linking the individual to an archaic, collective history. If the fragments of unconscious material found in dreams and slips shed light on an individual past, the linguistic relics described by the narrator expose the forgotten elements in a family history. Here we find Proust's theory of a *cultural unconscious* in which a slip of the tongue sparks the return of an alterity that had been repressed.

Up to this point, the Verdurins seemed to fully belong. They are rich, and they have succeeded in luring the most distinguished artists, writers, and aristocrats to their salon. But in this passage, the narrator suggests that their sense of belonging might be more precarious than it appears. As happens with assimilated Jewish, Latin American, or provincial families, they fit in, but a single word can expose their *otherness*. Ironically, the narrator's comments invite the reader to imagine the Verdurins as provincials (a likely hypothesis), as Jews (less likely), or as Latin Americans (highly unlikely—though if they spoke Spanish, the Verdurins could speak to their Peruvian guest in his native tongue). In the end, the narrator introduces this triple alterity as a sign of the degree to which Madame Verdurin and her husband do not belong; they are as foreign in the world of salons as a family of assimilated provincial, Jewish, Latin Americans.

Surprisingly, the narrator associates the linguistic relics stemming from a family's cultural unconscious with kindness. After reveling in the public humiliation of Charlus, the Verdurins meet in private to help Saniette, and the word in question emerges as they plan an act of generosity. The narrator is surprised by Monsieur Verdurin's unexpected display of empathy, which he interprets as another relic from the family's past: "Une bonté partielle—où subsistait peut-être un peu de la famille amie de ma grande tante—existait probablement chez lui avant que je la connusse par ce fait, comme l'Amérique ou le Pôle Nord avant Colomb ou Peary"[7] ("A partial kindness—in which there subsisted, perhaps, a trace of the family whom my great-aunt had known—probably existed in him before I discovered it through this fact, as America or the North Pole existed before Columbus or Peary."[8]) In contrast to the Freudian unconscious—the seat of destructive impulses, the death drive, and other dark forces—the Proustian cultural unconscious contains a reservoir of empathy springing from a kinder, gentler family past. The narrator compares this inner region to America before the arrival of Columbus. In this analogy the narrator presents himself as a Christopher Columbus of human nature, a discoverer of a vast continent of kindness, while Monsieur Verdurin's psyche plays the role of an inner America (or North Pole), a terra incognita whose discovery ushered in a new worldview. In Proust's world, Latin America can be a state of mind.

In the end, neither the narrator nor reader can grasp the secret word uttered by the Verdurins. Their private linguistic universe remains hermetically sealed to outsiders, and the meaning of the word gets lost in the dark regions of the unknown. Behind this scene, Spanish pulsates—along with other secret languages like German and Hebrew—as the novel's linguistic unconscious, as the repository of a primeval alterity that subverts the Verdurin's sense of belonging. To paraphrase Lacan's famous dictum: for Proust, the unconscious is structured like a Spanish language.

Epilogue

On Wednesday, May 30, 1894, Robert de Montesquiou hosted a lavish garden party at his house in Versailles that brought together an impressive group of aristocrats from the Faubourg Saint-Germain, members of the Académie française, respected artists and poets, young intellectuals, and crowds of socialites. A twenty-two-year-old Marcel Proust was there, taking everything in and making mental notes about the elegant countesses and baronesses he would later describe in his novel. As usual, Gabriel de Yturri was there, making the rounds, greeting every guest, and making sure the day's program unfolded as scheduled; he had just turned thirty-four and had lived with Montesquiou for nine years. The poet José-Maria de Heredia was also there, accompanied by his flirtatious daughters, waiting to hear his poems recited by the actress Julia Bartet. Antonio de La Gandara was there, accompanied by his wife, working the room—and the garden—surveying the various guests who would later become his models. Although his name does not appear in the program, the nineteen-year-old Reynaldo Hahn could have been there—he attended many of the count's parties, where his compositions were often performed. Ramon Fernandez was barely two months old and was most likely at home with his nanny, but his mother, Jeanne, could have been there, accompanied by her diplomat husband, the other Ramón Fernández.[1]

The party at Versailles was only one of many occasions on which Proust's Latin Americans found themselves in the same room. They had many opportunities to cross paths at Madeleine Lemaire's gatherings, at Hahn's recitals, at Heredia's readings, at Jeanne Fernandez's salon, not to mention at the opera, the theater, or any of the public spaces they frequented. There, they were often joined by many other Latin Americans who had made Paris their home—diplomats like Lucio V. Mansilla and Ventura García Calderón, writ-

ers like Rubén Darío and Enrique Gómez Carrillo, socialites like Leonor Anchorena de Uriburu and Eugenia Huichi Arguedas de Errázuriz,[2] and even
exiled ex-presidents like Porfirio Díaz and Antonio Guzmán Blanco. Like the
Jewish artists and intellectuals discussed by Carl E. Shorske in *Fin de siècle
Vienna,* these Latin Americans constituted an important minority in turn-of-
the-last-century France whose presence—and whose contribution to their
adoptive culture—has not been appropriately acknowledged.

The complicated relationship between Proust's Latin Americans and
France recalls the rapport between the narrator and Albertine in the *À la
recherche.* He pursues her; she ignores him. He finally seduces her, but she
remains aloof, a stance that unleashes myriad doubts and insecurities: Does
she love him? Is she being duplicitous? Is her heart elsewhere? Are her dec-
larations of love sincere? And when she responds, the narrator is no longer
sure he wants her anymore. Marcel's Latin American friends experienced
similar doubts and anxiety: they loved France, but did France love them
back? Sometimes she did; often she did not. In the end they were all recognized as important writers and artists, but this respect came at the expense
of their cultural identity, which was forgotten. The subtitle for this book
could have been *Les Latino-américans disparus.*

During their lives, Proust's Latin Americans found themselves in a double bind. In France they were considered exotic foreigners; in their native
countries, they were dismissed for being too French. "Were they really
Latin Americans?" I was often asked as I was writing this book. All five were
Latin Americans in the eyes of the law. They lived a good part of their lives
as foreign residents in France, as citizens of Venezuela, Argentina, Spanish
Cuba, and Mexico. With the exception of Ramon Fernandez, they all identified with the language and culture of their native countries. And all five
exerted a great fascination on Latin American intellectuals, who recognized
them—even if that recognition was neurotically couched as rejection—as
fellow citizens who had found success in Paris.

In the same years that the concept of Latin America gained currency,
these five figures tested the boundaries of Latin American identity. From
the start, "Latin America" was an idealistic construct that incorporated
peoples as diverse as Patagonian Indians and Mexican mestizos, Uruguayan
ranchers and Peruvian coca-planters, Afro-Cuban priests and Guatemalan
Mayas. The concept of a shared identity linking the diverse countries, cultures, and peoples from Tierra del Fuego to the Rio Grande is, by definition,
ample enough to incorporate the experiences of Reynaldo Hahn, Gabriel

Yturri, José-Maria de Heredia, Antonio La Gandara and Ramon Fernandez. These five Latin Americans spent their lives crossing cultures, boundaries, and languages and were able to make themselves at home wherever they went. It was precisely the mobility and fluidity of their cosmopolitan experience that threatened conservative critics in France and Latin America who espoused a monolithic view of cultural identity. If Latin America represents a utopian ideal of an open identity that can accommodate alterity, then these five figures are prototypical Latin Americans.[3]

Taken together, the stories of these five figures paint a very different portrait of Marcel Proust: a Proust who had a Venezuelan lover; a Proust who speculated in Mexican stocks and became embroiled in the ups and downs of the Mexican revolution; a Proust who upheld a Cuban poet as his first literary model; a Proust who enthused about Yturri's parrot hunt in Tucumán; a Proust who narrated Columbus's encounter with the natives; a Proust who learnt by heart Heredia's verses on the Spanish conquistadors; a Proust who fantasized about sitting for a Mexican painter; a Proust who summoned a Mexican critic to his bedside at odd hours of the night.

   Proust's life was framed by France's colonial expansion into Latin America. He was born four years after French intervention in Mexico collapsed; he was in his late twenties when the Panama Affair exploded and laid bare a tangle of corruption stretching from Paris to Central America; and during his thirties and forties, his speculations in Mexican stocks put him in the company of other French investors who scouted global investment opportunities.

   Latin America has been the dark continent in Proustian studies. I hope that by shedding light on Proust's Latin Americans, my readers will experience the same wonder that Heredia attributed to his conquistadors as they saw new stars rise "above the depths of the Ocean." May we also see the rise of a new star: a Latin American Proust.

Notes

Abbreviations

Arsenal: Fonds José-Maria de Heredia, Bibliothèque de l'Arsenal, Paris.

BNF: Département des Manuscrits, Bibliothèque Nationale de France, Paris.

Corr.: Marcel Proust. *Correspondance.* Ed. Philip Kolb. 21 vols. Paris: Plon, 1970–1993.

Harvard: Houghton Library, Harvard University, Cambridge, MA.

Musique: Département de la Musique, Bibliothèque Nationale de France, Paris.

Opéra: Bibliothèque de l'Opéra, Bibliothèque Nationale de France, Paris.

Recherche: Marcel Proust. *À la recherche du temps perdu.* Ed. Jean-Yves Tadié. 4 vols. Paris: Gallimard, Éditions de la Pléiade, 1987–1989.

SL: Marcel Proust. *Selected Letters.* Vol. 1, ed. Philip Kolb, trans. Ralph Manheim, intro. J. M. Cocking. New York: Doubleday, 1983. Vol. 2, ed. Philip Kolb, trans. Terence Kilmartin. New York: Oxford University Press, 1989.

Introduction

1. JMG, "Les Coulisses," *La Lanterne,* Mar. 21, 1899, 3; Philippe Blay, *L'île du rêve de Reynaldo Hahn* (Villeneuve: Presses Universitaires du Septentrion, 2001), 682–85.

2. François Coppée, *Souvenirs d'un Parisien* (Paris: A. Lemerre, 1910), 75–79. Qtd in Miodrag Ibrovac, *José María de Heredia* (Paris: Presses françaises, 1923), 84. Unless otherwise indicated, all translations are by Lorna Scott Fox.

3. *Rastaquouère* was an insult coined in the nineteenth century and directed primarily against Latin Americans. The *Dictionnaire de l'Académie* defines *rastaquouère* as "terme familier, emprunté de l'espagnol et servant à désigner un Personnage exotique qui étale un luxe suspect et de mauvais goût. On dit aussi, par abréviation et plus familièrement: RASTA." Curiously, the Spanish *Diccionario de la Real Academia* defines *rastacuero* as "1. m. Vividor; advenedizo. 2. Com. Am. Persona inculta, adinerada y jactanciosa" and attributes the origin of the term to France, "Del fr. rastaquouère."

4. Rubén Darío, "La evolución del rastacuerismo," *Opiniones* (Madrid: Editorial Mundo Latino, 1918), 126.

5. "Rastaquouère," *Grand dictionnaire universel Larousse du XIXè siècle,* second supplement (Paris: Larousse, 1888).

6. Ibid., 10.

7. André Benhaïm has explored references to foreign cultures in the novel in his article "From Baalbek to Baghdad and Beyond: Marcel Proust's Foreign Memories of France," *Journal of European Studies* 35 (2009): 87-101. Herbert E. Craig has written about the reception of Proust in Latin America, and he also mentions a few of the Latin Americans in Proust's circle in his *Marcel Proust and Spanish America: From Critical Response to Narrative Dialogue* (Cranbury, NJ: Associated University Presses, 2002).

8. André Benhaïm notes that the anecdote about the Singhalese "stages, for the first time in the novel, a non-western character." André Benhaïm, "Proust's Singhalese Song (A Strange Little Story)," *The Strange M. Proust,* ed. André Benhaïm (London: Legenda, 2009), 59.

9. Julia Kristeva, *Strangers to Ourselves* (New York: Columbia University Press, 1991), 183.

10. Julia Kristeva, *Time and Sense: Proust and the Experience of Literature* (New York: Columbia University Press, 1996), 163.

11. Ibid.

12. On General Mancilla, see *Corr.,* 6:350-51. Proust mentions Guzmán Blanco in a letter to Princess Soutzo dated Dec. 25, 1918, *Corr.,* 17:522-23.

13. Arturo Ardao, *Génesis de la idea y el nombre de América* (Caracas: Centro de Estudios Latinoamericanos Rómulo Gallegos, 1980).

14. Sylvia Molloy, *La diffusion de la littérature Hispano-Américaine en France au XXè siècle* (Paris: Presses Universitaires de France, 1972).

15. Proust mentions reading *La cousine Bette* in a letter to Reynaldo Hahn. Proust to Hahn, Sept. 3 or 4, 1896, *SL,* 1:140-41.

16. Honoré de Balzac, "La cousine Bette," *La comédie humaine* (Paris: Gallimard, Bibliothèque de la Pléiade, 1976-1981), 7:210.

17. Ibid., 211.

18. Ibid., 404. Honoré de Balzac, *Cousin Bette,* trans. Sylvia Bellos (Oxford University Press, 1992), 435.

19. Henri Meilhac and Ludovic Halévy, *Théâtre de Meilhac et Halévy,* 8 vols. (Paris: C. Levy, 1900-1902), 5:388.

20. Gaston Jollivet, *Souvenirs de la vie de plaisir sous le Second Empire* (Paris: 1927), 79. See also Charles V. Aubrun, "Rastaquouère et rasta," *Bulletin Hispanique* 57, no. 4 (1955): 430-39.

21. Henri Meilhac and Ludovic Halévy, *La vie parisienne: Pièce en cinq actes* (Paris: Lévy, 1867); Jacques Offenbach, *La vie parisienne* (Berlin: Boosey & Hawkes, 2003), 5.

22. Jacques Offenbach, *La vie parisienne* (EMI Classics, 1976), CD liner notes, p. 19.

23. Ibid.

24. Georges Feydeau, *Un fil à la patte* (Paris: Éditions des Équateurs, 2011), 66.

25. Marcel Arland, preface to Valery Larbaud, *Œuvres* (Paris: Gallimard, Bibliothèque de la Pléiade, 1957), xvi.

26. Valery Larbaud, *Fermina Márquez,* trans. Hubert Gibbs (London: Quartet Encounters, 1988), 2, 44.

27. Molloy, *La diffusion,* 149, 153.

28. Valery Larbaud, *Œuvres,* ed. G. Jean-Aubry and Robert Mallet (Paris: Gallimard, Bibliothèque de la Pléiade, 1957), 1219.

29. *Recherche,* 1:659; 904; 1847. The same expression appears in a different context: Swann urges the narrator to travel and tells him to "partir pour ces délicieuses îles de l'Océanie, vous verrez que vous n'en reviendrez pas." *Recherche,* 2:31; 1:721.

30. *Recherche,* 2:814-15.

31. Marcel Proust, *The Guermantes Way,* trans. Mark Treharne (New York: Penguin, 2005), 525.

32. Ibid., 239.

33. See Daniel Bendahan, *Reynaldo Hahn: Su vida y obra* (Caracas: Italgráfica, 1973).

34. Proust, "Esquisse XXXIX," *Recherche,* 2:916.

35. Proust to his mother, June 15, 1905, *Corr.,* 5:221.

36. Françoise "avait perdu dans le Panama un petit avoir que [ma tante Léonie] lui avait laissé." *Recherche,* 1:387, 1273; 2:889, 1036; 4:777.

37. Proust, "Esquisse XXXII," *Recherche,* 2:1301.

38. On Gomez Carrillo, see Molloy, *La diffusion,* 26.

39. Proust, *Sodom and Gomorrah,* trans. John Sturrock (New York: Penguin, 2002), 227.

40. *Recherche,* 3:832.

41. *Recherche,* 3:1475

42. This scene of bankrupt debauchery takes place in Nissim Bernard's fantasies.

43. *Recherche,* 3:775; Proust, *The Prisoner and the Fugitive,* trans. Carol Clark and Peter Collier (New York: Penguin, 2003), 249.

44. *Recherche,* 2:1475.

45. *Recherche,* 2:523.

46. Roberto Pompeu de Toledo, "Brasil nos grandes livros," *Veja* 1379 (Feb. 15, 1995): 114.

47. Edward Said, *Culture and Imperialism* (New York: Vintage, 1993), 212.

48. Edward Said, *Reflections on Exile* (Cambridge: Harvard University Press, 2000), xv.

49. Diderot and D'Alembert, *Encyclopédie ou dictionnaire raisonnée des sciences, des arts et des métiers* (Paris: Briasson, David, Le Breton, Durand, 1760), 4:297.

50. Immanuel Kant, "Idea of a Universal History with a Cosmopolitan Purpose," *Political Writings* (Cambridge: Cambridge University Press, 1991), 51.

51. Immanuel Kant, "Perpetual Peace: A Philosophical Sketch," *Political Writings* (Cambridge: Cambridge University Press, 1991), 105-6.

52. Kwame Anthony Appiah, *Cosmopolitanism: Ethics in a World of Strangers* (New York: Norton, 2006), 144, 151.

53. See David Damrosch, *What Is World Literature?* (Princeton: Princeton University Press, 2003).

54. See, e.g., Richard Beardsworth, *Cosmopolitanism and International Relations* (Cambridge: Polity Press, 2011); *Cosmopolitanism in Context: Perspectives from International Law and Political Theory,* ed. Roland Pierik and Wouter Werner (Cambridge: Cambridge University Press, 2010), James Brasset, *Cosmopolitanism and Global Financial Reform* (New York: Routledge, 2010); Stan van Hooft, *Cosmopolitanism: A Philosophy for Global Ethics* (Montreal: McGill-Queens University Press, 2009).

55. On Porfirio Díaz's melancholy life in Paris, see Carlos Tello Díaz, *El exilio: Un relato de familia* (Mexico City: Cal y Arena, 1993).

56. Dinesh D'Souza, *Illiberal Education: The Politics of Race and Sex on Campus* (New York: Free Press, 1991); John Beverly, *Against Literature* (Minneapolis: University of Minnesota, 1993).

57. Damrosch, *What Is World Literature?* 4–5.

58. Said, *Culture and Imperialism,* 69.

59. Kristeva, *Strangers to Ourselves,* 40

60. See Gérard Genette, *Figures III* (Paris: Seuil, 1972), 54; Philippe Lejeune, "Les carafes de la Vivonne," *Recherche de Proust* (Paris: Seuil, 1980), 163.

Chapter 1. Reynaldo Hahn

1. "Tout ce que j'ai jamais fait a toujours été grâce à Reynaldo," Feb. 1904, *Corr.,* 4:54.

2. There are several sources, in Spanish, French, and English, for biographical information on Reynaldo Hahn. The best source for Hahn's early years in Venezuela is Mario Milanca Guzmán, *Reynaldo Hahn, caraqueño: Contribución a la biografía caraqueño de Reynaldo Hahn Echenagucia* (Caracas: Biblioteca de la Academia Nacional de Historia, 1989), 21. In French, the most complete study of Hahn's life and work is Phillipe Blay, *L'île du rêve de Reynaldo Hahn: Contribution à l'étude de l'opéra français de l'époque fin-de-siècle* (Villeneuve: Presses Universitaires du Septentrion, 2001). A concise biography is Jacques Depaulis, *Reynaldo Hahn* (Biarritz: Atlantica, 2007). In English, the most recent studies on the Proust-Hahn friendship are in William C. Carter, *Proust in Love* (New Haven: Yale University Press, 2006), and *Marcel Proust: A Life* (New Haven: Yale University Press, 2000).

3. "La mort de Baldassare Silvande" was published in the fall of 1895 in *La revue hebdomadaire.* Proust, *Jean Santeuil* (Paris: Gallimard, Bibiothèque de la Pléiade, 1971), 913, note 2. Reynaldo enthused about the piece to his friends. "I'm happy to announce," he wrote Suzette Lemaire, "that [Marcel Proust] has just written a novella that has astonished me!! It is the most poetic, the most poignant, the truest

work he has written up to now. Ever since the piece was dedicated to me I wait for people to salute me . . . ," Hahn to Lemaire, Oct.-Nov. 1894, Harvard, MsFr 219 (8).

4. Marcel read the poems while Reynaldo played the piano on two occasions: first at Madeleine Lemaire's salon in 1895 and again on April 21, 1897, at a theater in Paris, La Bodinière, as part of an evening that was to be introduced by Stéphane Mallarmé. *Le Figaro* published the following account of the performance: "La dernière séance d'*Une heure de musique moderne,* consacrée aux œuvres de M. Reynaldo Hahn, avait attirée à la Bodinière une assistance des plus élégantes: Mme. La princesse Mathilde, la duchesse d'Uzès, le ministre de Suède et Norvège, et Mme Due; Mme Alphonse Daudet, etc., etc. Après une conférence de M. Mallarmé, on a entendu Mmes Moreno et Horwitz, MM. Risler, Engel, Diaz de Soria, Cortet" (*Le Figaro,* Apr. 24, 1897). Proust had invited Robert de Montesquiou to the event, emphasizing that his poems would be read by the "marvelous" Moreno. See *Corr.,* 2:186. Mallarmé did not make it to the performance, but his introduction was read by Mademoiselle Moreno. His text is reprinted in Mallarmé, *Œuvres complètes* (Paris: Gallimard, Bibliothèque de la Pléiade, 1956), 860-61.

5. This heterogeneous volume included most of the poems, novellas, and short stories—including "La mort de Baldassare Silvande" and *Portraits de peintres*—he had written since 1893. Marcel had carefully planned a luxury edition that was also a window into his glamorous Parisian life: the cover featured watercolors by Madeleine Lemaire, who was famous for her floral drawings; the preface was by Anatole France, one of the authors he esteemed the most; and the volume included the piano score Reynaldo had composed for *Portraits de peintres*. It was a beautiful object, but it proved to be too expensive—it was sold for 13.50 francs, while most books cost three francs—and the sales were meager. Marcel was so traumatized by the fate of his first book—heaps of unsold volumes languished in the publisher's warehouse—that many years later, when he had secured an editor for *À la recherche,* he did everything he could—including offering to pay for the typesetting and printing—so that the book would be offered at a reasonable price. Proust, *Jean Santeuil,* 906-7.

6. Proust describes Cottard arriving at the Verdurins as follows: "Chez Mme Verdurin Cottard assistait maintenant aux réceptions dans un uniforme de colonel de *L'île du rêve* assez semblable à celui d'un amiral haïtien et sur le drap duquel un large ruban bleu ciel rappelait celui des Enfants de Marie." *Recherche,* 4:348.

7. "Ma vie en ce moment est bien ennuyeuse: je n'ai pas de domicile, mes affaires sont disséminées partout, je n'ai pas de domestique," Reynaldo Hahn to Suzette Lemaire, Autumn 1912, Harvard, MsFr 219 (81).

8. JMG, "Les Coulisses," *La Lanterne* (Mar. 21, 1899): 3; Philippe Blay, *L'île du rêve de Reynaldo Hahn* (Villeneuve: Presses Universitaires du Septentrion, 2001), 682-85.

9. Blay believes that "Un Vénézuelien, pensait-on, devait rendre avec puissance une nature dont son pays pouvait lui fournir l'analogie," *L'île du rêve,* 515.

10. Reynaldo told Risler of receiving an anonymous letter telling him "que si je n'étais pas "juif et protégé par les juifs" je serais depuis longtemps "au feu." Je ne suis pas le seul à déchaîner cette haine immonde" (that if I were not "a Jew and protected by the Jews," I should have been sent into action long ago. I'm not the only one who arouses this sickening hatred). Hahn to Risler, Albi, 1914, Musique, LAS 415.

11. Depaulis, *Reynaldo Hahn,* 92.

12. In 1935, André Cœuroy published a scathing article on Reynaldo's music in the right-wing journal *Gringoire.* It was written as a mock ad for "Reynaldose," a remedy against insomnia and poor digestion.

Demandez partout: LA REYNALDOSE HAHN / Rien du pétrole! Ne pas confondre! Ce produit parfait de douceur ne renferme aucune substance irritante ou mordante. Il est bénin, BENIN, BENIN. Entièrement fabriqué avec les essences les plus suaves, il est le résultat d'une formule éprouvée dont nous ne pouvons livrer le secret (*made in France!*), mais dont les composantes principales sont des garanties de valeur (*se méfier des contrefaçons!*): Eau de rose 60% / Grains d'encens 30% Œillet (toutes nuances) 8% / Fleur des pois 2% / Nos derniers flacons—Nos derniers success / Flacon MARCHAND DE VENISE (parfum classique) / Flacon MALVINA (parfum romantique). Les deux flacons, dans un élégant panier à bouteilles, emballage artistique d'Yves Alix. En prime: magnifique chromo 1830 (copie garantie).

André Cœuroy, "La Reynaldose," *Gringoire* (Mar. 29, 1935): 15. Lucien Rebatet was even more violent: "Entré dans la vie parisienne sous le patronage ésotérique de Mallarmé, puis bientôt de toutes les duchesses et comtesses du faubourg Saint-Germain, intime de Proust à qui il souffla de cruelles sottises sur Debussy, Reynaldo Hahn (1875–1947), né au Venezuela d'un père juif allemand, ne faisant aucun mystère de ses mœurs, resta jusqu'à son dernier jour la plus étonnante figure de vieil inverti à perruque, monocle et corset." Lucien Rebatet, *Une histoire de la musique* (Paris: Robert Laffont, 1969), 498–99.

13. In a letter to Suzette Lemaire, for instance, Hahn described himself as "un natif du Venezuela et [. . .] enfant adoptif de la France" (a native of Venezuela [and] an adopted son of France). Hahn to Lemaire, 1897, Harvard, MsFr 219 (38).

14. See Reynaldo Hahn to Jeanne Fernandez, Dec. 20, 1944. Dominique Fernandez private collection.

15. Antoine Bertrand, *Les curiosités esthétiques de Robert de Montesquiou* (Genève: Librairie Droz, 1996), 597.

16. Ibid., 598.

17. Camille Mauclair, "La religion de l'orchestre et la musique française actuelle," *Revue de revues,* Feb. 15, 1900, 376.

18. Jean-Marc Rodrigues, "Genèse du wagnérisme proustien," *Romantisme* 57 (1987): 76.

19. The letters exchanged between Risler and Reynaldo are held in the collec-

tions of the Bibliothèque Nationale's music department, and most have not been published.

20. "Je ne parle pas ici de Wagner lui-même, mais, franchement, des 3/4 des personnes qui vont à Bayreuth, y vont pour y avoir été, comme dirait Alphonse Kaas." Hahn to Risler, 1892, Musique, LAS 157.

21. Hahn to Risler, 1893, Musique, LAS 221.

22. Hahn to Risler, no date, Musique, LAS 312.

23. Hahn to Risler, June 18, 1893, Musique, LAS 227.

24. Mauclair, "La religion," 376.

25. Rodrigues, "Genèse du wagnérisme proustien," 79.

26. Proust to Suzette Lemaire, May 20, 1895, *Corr.*, 1:388-89.

27. Ibid.

28. Hahn to Risler, 1895?, Musique, LAS 309.

29. Hahn to Risler, Feb. 1894, Musique, LAS 278.

30. Proust wrote "Mélomanie" hastily on the back of a letter to Reynaldo during a sleepless night. He conceived it as a playful postscript to a text he had published a few months earlier, "Mondanité de Bouvard et Pécuchet," in *La Revue Blanche* (July-Aug. 1893), in which Flaubert's characters engage in a debate about literature. "Mélomanie" stands out as Proust's first written meditation on Reynaldo Hahn's place in the musical scene. After meeting Reynaldo, he incorporated the debate on Wagner and published an expanded version, "Mondanité et mélomanie de Bouvard et Pécuchet," in his first book, *Les plaisirs et les jours* (1896). See Mireille Naturel, *Proust et Flaubert: Un secret d'écriture* (Amsterdam: Editions Rodopi, 2007), 63-64.

31. Proust to Hahn, Aug. 27, 1894, *Corr.*, 1:182.

32. Naturel, *Proust et Flaubert*, 66.

33. Marcel Proust, *Jean Santeuil* (Paris: Bibliothèque de la Pléiade, 1971), 64.

34. The poem reads: "Où donc ai-je lu, Sainte Vierge!/Dans *L'imparcial*, dans *Le Heraldo*/Où fit ses débuts Daniel Vierge/Qu'espagnol était Reynaldo/Espagnol né dans son Dodo." Proust to Hahn, Dec. 25, 1901, *Corr.*, 2:482. An English translation appears in *The Collected Poems*, ed. Harold Augenbraum (New York: Penguin, 2013), 152-53: "Where then did I read, Holy Virgin!/In the *Imparcial* or in the *Heraldo*/Where Daniel Vierge got his start/That Spanish was Reynaldo/Spanish born in his heart."

35. Proust, *Jean Santeuil*, 64.

36. Hahn to Risler, Jan. 18, 1892, Musique, LAS 103.

37. Hahn to Risler, Jan. 1892, Musique, LAS 105.

38. "Erik Satie me semble le degré le plus bas où puisse descendre la prostitution artistique. Qu'il nous soit le caoutchouc qui nous fera rebondir dans les régions de l'Honneur." Hahn to Risler, Jan.-Feb. 1892, Musique, LAS 106.

39. "S'il voulait, il serait très gentil," he wrote Risler. "Mais il faudrait pour cela qu'il composât moins et qu'il se lavât plus!" Hahn to Risler, 1893, Musique, LAS 252.

40. "C'est un sot prétentieux et non musicien, en somme, insipide, froid." Hahn to Risler, 1892?, *Musique*, LAS 106.

41. "Il m'a paru que l'ensemble de tout le spectacle dénotait une recherche perpétuelle du bizarre, un souci de 'faire laid'"; "Ici, M. Stravinski avait à exprimer des choses si amorphes, des sentiments si rudimentaires[,] qu'il a morcelé son discours plus encore que de coutume, et l'a rendu par moments presqu'insaisissable." Reynaldo Hahn, "La Musique," *Le Journal,* June 2, 1913, 2. Reprinted in *Corr.,* 13:63.

42. Proust to Hahn, Jan. 15, 1914, *Corr.,* 13:62.

43. William Marx, *Les arrière-gardes au XXème siècle: L'autre face de la modernité esthétique* (Paris: Presses Universitaires de France, 2004).

44. Ibid., 11.

45. "Le dieu émerge: il est complètement de couleur bleu, avec des lèvres et des ongles d'argent." See Depaulis, *Reynaldo Hahn,* 84. See also "Album de coupures de presse, *La Fête chez Thérèse, Le Dieu Bleu,*" Opéra, B717.

46. Edward Said, *Orientalism* (New York: Vintage Books, 1978).

47. See Philippe Blay, *L'île du rêve de Reynaldo Hahn* (Villeneuve: Presses Universitaires du Septentrion, 2001).

48. William C. Carter writes that in the correspondence "'moschant,' an obvious corruption of 'méchant' (bad or mean) often indicated homosexual behavior or an individual known or thought to be gay," *Proust in Love,* 36.

49. Proust to Hahn, July 11, 1911, *Corr.,* X: 312.

50. The letter to Zadig is in a letter from Proust to Hahn, after Nov. 3, 1911. *Corr.,* X: 372-73.

51. Carter, *Proust in Love,* 36.

52. Proust to Hahn, Apr. 21, 1906, *Corr.,* 6:71-72.

53. Proust to Hahn, Jan. 29, 1914, *Corr.,* 13:86-87

54. Gérard Genette, *Palimpsests,* 80.

55. Proust to Hahn, May 9-10, 1909, *Corr.,* 9:95.

56. Jacques Lacan, *The Four Fundamental Concepts of Psychoanalysis* (New York: Norton, 1981).

57. Philippe Sollers, *L'œil de Proust* (Paris: Gallimard, 1999), 40.

58. Proust to Hahn, Jan. 29, 1914, *Corr.,* 13:86.

59. F. T. Marinetti, "Technical Manifesto of Futurist Literature," *Critical Writings,* ed. Günter Berghaus (New York: Farrar, Straus and Giroux, 2006), 107.

60. Carter, *Proust in Love,* 36.

61. Several critics have studied Marcel Proust's drawings. See Sibylla Laemmel, "Marcel Proust als Zeichner," *Marcel Proust: Zwischen Belle Epoque und Moderne,* ed. Reiner Speck et al. (Frankfurt: Suhrkamp Verlag, 1999), 155-67; Claude Gandelman, "The Drawings of Marcel Proust," *ADAM International Review* 40 (1976): 21-57; Gandelmann, "L'écrivain comme dessinateur," *Actes du VIIIème Congrès de l'Association Internationale de Littérature Comparée* (Stuttgart, 1980): 881-86; Isabelle Zuber, Luzius

Keller, and Sybilla Laemmel, "Dessin, tableau, texte," *Nouvelles directions de la recherche proustienne* (Paris: Lettres Modernes Minard, 2000): 115–39; Virginie Greene and Caroline Szylowicz, "Le miroir des images: Étude de quelques dessins médiévaux de Proust," *Bulletin d'information proustiennes* 28 (1997): 7–25.

62. Proust to Hahn, Dec. 31, 1907, *Corr.,* 7:327–28. A facsimile of the letter showing the drawing is reproduced in Reiner Speck, *Sur la lecture II* (Cologne: Marcel Proust Gesellschaft, 1996), 74.

63. Proust to Hahn, Dec. 31, 1907, *Corr.,* 7:327–28.

64. At one point, Proust even asked Mâle to recommend which cathedrals he should visit. Proust to Emile Mâle, Aug. 18 [year unknown], qtd in Robert de Billy, *Marcel Proust: Lettres et conversations* (Paris: Éditions des Portiques, 1930), 113; see also *SL,* 2:318.

65. The drawing is reproduced in Philip Kolb, *Lettres à Reynaldo Hahn* (Paris: Gallimard, 1956), 117, and Sollers, *L'œil de Proust,* 42.

66. The entire text accompanying the drawing reads: "Cher Enfant Reynaldo / Que je comble par ce casdeau / Ne croyez pas que je ne fais pas dodo / Parce que je serai allé chemin de fer / Car rentrerai vite me couscher. / Mais si passez devant meson à 9h3/4 / vous pouvez / monter me donner petit bonsjour (9h3/4 matin) / Est-ce que ceci est plus genstil que les derniers / (Prophète de Reims)." Kolb, *Lettres à Reynaldo Hahn,* 105.

67. See Claude Gandelman, "The Drawings of Marcel Proust," *ADAM International Review* 40 (1976): 21–57; and also Gandelmann, "L'écrivain comme dessinateur," *Actes du VIIIème Congrès de l'Association Internationale de Littérature Comparée* (Stuttgart, 1980), 881–86.

68. The titles of works inscribed on the angel's wings include *L'île du rêve* (1898), *La Carmélite* (1902), *Le bal de Beatrice d'Este* (1905), *Chansons grises* (1893), *Portraits de peintres* (1896). This drawing is in the Mante-Proust family collection and is reproduced in Sollers, *L'œil de Proust,* 39.

69. The drawing is reproduced in Kolb, *Lettres à Reynaldo Hahn,* 81, and Sollers, *L'œil de Proust,* 83.

70. See *Corr.,* 1:326, 333, 334.

71. Proust to Hahn, Sept. 16, 1894, *Corr.,* 1:326–27; *SL,* 1:75–76.

72. Hahn to Madeleine Lemaire, no date, 1895, Harvard, bMsFr 219 (4); Hahn to Pierre Lavallée, Sept. 9, 1895. *Corr.,* 7:331.

73. Proust to Hahn, May–June, 1895?, *Corr.,* 1:398.

74. Proust to Hahn, between mid-July and mid-August, 1896, *Corr.,* 2:101.

75. Proust to Hahn, May–June 1895?, *Corr.,* 1:396.

76. Proust to Hahn, May–June, 1895?, *Corr.,* 1:397.

77. Proust to Hahn, Dec. 24, 1911, *Corr.,* 10:388.

78. Carter, *Proust in Love,* 63.

79. Zuber, Keller, and Laemmel, "Dessin, tableau, texte," 134.

80. Sollers, *L'œil de Proust,* 40.

81. This image is published in Kolb, *Lettres à Reynaldo Hahn,* 30, and Sollers, *L'œil de Proust,* 47. The drawing was traced from Émile Mâle, *L'art réligieux du XIIIème siècle en France* (Paris: Librairie Armand Colin, 1902), 56.

82. In his caption to the drawing, Marcel presents the raised hand as a gesture of empathy; Reynaldo exclaims "poor pony!" The visual imagery, however, suggests a more sadistic reading.

83. Sollers writes, "Le dessin en rappelle un autre: 'Le Maître el le Poney' [. . .] le 'petit chevalch' pouvant donc être ce poney auquel Proust s'idéntifie." Sollers, *L'œil de Proust,* 86.

84. The image is in Cahier 16684, p. 7 verso, at the Fonds Marcel Proust, BNF.

85. Claude Gandelman, "The Drawings of Marcel Proust," *ADAM International Review* 394/396 (1976): 51.

86. Proust to Hahn, before Apr. 29, 1912, *Corr.,* 11:120.

87. Proust to Hahn, July 13, 1912, *Corr.,* 11:164-65.

88. See, e.g., Marcel's discussion of his nocturnal schedule in *Corr.,* 2:292-93.

89. Proust to Hahn, after Aug. 18, 1912, *Corr.,* 11:185.

90. Proust to Hahn, after Aug. 19, 1912, *Corr.,* 11:191.

91. After his mother's death, Reynaldo had to move out of the apartment at 9, rue Alfred de Vigny, by the end of June 1912. He moved into Antonie Bibesco's apartment and lived there until at least November 21, 1913 (see *Corr.,* 12:332) and probably until he was mobilized in 1914.

92. "Petit projet de genstil vitrail" is reproduced in Kolb, *Lettres à Reynaldo Hahn,* 74, and Sollers, *L'œil de Proust,* 85.

93. For an alternate translation, see Proust, *Collected Poems,* 148-49.

94. Reynaldo's maid was Marie Martel. She worked for his family and, after the death of his parents, for him. Reynaldo took her with him to the south of France in 1940, and she died during the war. See Depaulis, *Reynaldo Hahn,* 131

95. Marcel makes the first mention of Legras power in a letter to his mother from 1896. See *Corr.,* 2:116-17.

96. Sollers, *L'œil de Proust,* 39-40.

97. Proust to Hahn, early July 1910, *Corr.,* 10:122-24.

98. Ibid. Marcel's full explication of the stained glass reads:

   1. Buncht dans son lit escoute (Clair de lune)
   2. Bunibuls de l'autre côté de la porte joue l'ouverture des *Maîtres-Chanteurs*
   3. Céline à l'autre bout de l'appartement prépare la sole
   4. Bunibuls fasché d'avoir joué s'en va, pressé, disant *On ne m'y reprendra plus*
   5. Buncht ému de la gentilese de Bunibuls pleurse. Une larme est tombée sur le lit, il approche mouchoir de œil où on voit les larmes
   6. À la porte frappent Nicolas et son cousin
   7. À la porte frappe Ulrich

8. Buncht toujours dans le lit approche téléphone d'oreille pour parler Robert

9. Buncht levé se lave ses petites pattes

10. Buncht lit *Marche Nuptiale* et lève les bras en en reconnaissant la beauté

11. Buncht écrit à Bunibuls pour lui dire que *Marche Nuptiale* a génie

12. Le soleil s'étant lévé, Buncht a fermé rideaux et s'est remis au lit

13. L'image de Bunibuls apparaît à l'âme reconnaisante de Buncht qui joint les mains vers Dieu, en actions de grâces de posséder un tel ami

14. L'action de grâces terminée, Buncht envoie avec mains beser à Bunibuls

15. Docteur-médekin aux lunettes dit à Buncht qu'il va mourir

16. Mort de Buncht (cette verrière a beaucoup souffert)

17. On a mis bouquest sur le lit où Buncht mort repose

18. Tombeau de Buncht sur lequel fleurs arbres, aubépines au-dessus et soleil maintenant que ne lui fait plus malch. Et son Bunchtnibuls, avec chapeau haut de forme vient au petit Kimetière présenter son adieu à Buncht.

99. Céleste Albaret, *Monsieur Proust,* trans. Barbara Bray (New York: New York Review of Books, 2003), 230.

100. Proust to Hahn, after Oct. 21, 1922, *Corr.,* 21:515.

101. There are few sources of information on Guy Ferrant. The Bibliothèque de l'Opéra in Paris holds dozens of scores that Reynaldo Hahn dedicated to him. *Le temps d'aimer* includes the following inscription: "à Guy Ferrant affectueux souvenir de RH, 1919-1926" (Opéra &4694). *Ciboulette* bears a similar inscription: "A l'ami vigilant de ce petite ouvrage, à Guy Ferrant, souvenir affectueux de RH, 1919-1923" (Opéra &4718). Philippe Blay takes 1919 as the date when Hahn and Ferrant met, *L'île du rêve,* 204, note 736. A newspaper article from 1937 gives Ferrant's age at the time as "no more than thirty-five," so he was probably born around 1902. (See "Old Songsters are Resurrected in Parisian's Record Collection," *New York Herald Tribune,* Apr. 6, 1937.)

102. See the program for "Le bal de Béatrice d'Este, duchesse de Milan, par Reynaldo Hahn," *La folie Saint James,* May 11, 1923, Opéra, B 728.

103. The libretto specifies that *Ciboulette* is set in 1867. *Swann's Way* opens by narrating the life of Charles Swann during the Second Empire, before the narrator's birth.

104. Reynaldo Hahn, *Ciboulette* (Emi Digital, 1982), libretto, 120-21. Act III, scene 4, track 38.

105. Ibid., 117-19.

106. Friedrich Nietzsche, *The Birth of Tragedy and the Case of Wagner,* trans. Walter Kaufmann (New York: Random House, 1967), 157.

107. Friedrich Nietzsche, *Le cas Wagner: Un problem musical,* trans. Robert Dreyfus and Daniel Halévy (Paris: A. Schultz, 1893).

108. Carmen's aria, "Près de remparts de Séville," *Carmen,* Act I, scene 9.

109. *Ciboulette,* Act III, scene 4, 133.

110. The image of Spain as an exotic other can be seen in the dozens of pejorative

popular expressions that continue to be used to this day. The popular saying "Africa begins at the Pyrenees"—invoked, among others, by Alexandre Dumas—presents Spain as an other so radical that it belongs in another continent, and the expression "Parler français comme une vache espagnole" (To speak French like a Spanish cow) paints the Spaniards as so distant that they belong in the animal kingdom.

111. Nietzsche, *The Birth of Tragedy and The Case of Wagner,* 166.

112. Judith Butler, *Gender Trouble: Feminism and the Subversion of Identity* (New York: Routledge, 1990).

113. Julia Kristeva, *Strangers to Ourselves* (New York: Columbia University Press, 1991), 39.

Paperolle No. 1

1. Philip Kolb published a short survey article on Proust's investments. This is the first study of the novelist's Mexican stocks. See Philip Kolb, "Marcel Proust spécula-teur," *Études proustiennes* 1, Cahiers Marcel Proust, n.s., 6 (1973).

2. Lionel Hauser, *The Three Levers of the New World: Competence, Probity, Altruism* (London: Theosophical Publishing House, 1920), 110.

3. Kolb, "Marcel Proust spéculateur," 179.

4. Jean Yves Tadié, *Marcel Proust* (Paris: Gallimard, 1996), 618–19.

5. Proust to Hauser, May 9, 1909, *Corr.,* 9:93.

6. Proust to Hauser, Sept. 10, 1908, *Corr.,* 8:215; Proust to Hauser, Nov. 1. 1908, *Corr.,* 8:266.

7. Hauser to Proust, May 10, 1909, *Corr.,* 9:97.

8. Proust to Hauser, Apr. 21 or 22, 1910, *Corr.,* 10:76; Proust to Hauser, Nov. 7, 1910, *Corr.,* 10:203.

9. "Conditions Which Govern the Type of Car of City Service: Mexico City," *Brill Magazine* (Mar. 1911): 64–66.

10. Arnaud Yvel, "Courrier de la Bourse," *Le Figaro,* Feb. 2, 1910, 5.

11. Hauser to Proust, Nov. 10, 1910, *Corr.,* 10:206.

12. Hauser to Proust, mid-Sept. 1913, *Corr.,* 12:230.

13. "Amérique Latine," *Le Figaro,* Sept. 13, 1910, 2.

14. "Amérique Latine," *Le Figaro,* Nov. 23, 1910, 2.

15. Arnaud Yvel, "Courrier de la Bourse," *Le Figaro,* Nov. 22, 1910, 3.

16. Arnaud Yvel, "Courrier de la Bourse," *Le Figaro,* Feb. 11, 1910, 4.

17. *Le Figaro,* Dec. 13, 1912, 7.

18. Proust to Hauser, June 1, 1912, *Corr.,* 11:133.

19. Hauser to Proust, Oct. 18, 1912, *Corr.,* 11:230.

20. *Le Figaro,* Nov. 5, 1913, 8.

21. "The Tramways of the City of Mexico," *Tramway and Railway World,* Jan. 15, 1914, 17.

22. Proust to Hauser, July 28, 1914, *Corr.*, 12:276.

23. Ibid.

24. Hauser to Proust, July 30, 1914, *Corr.*, 12:280.

25. Proust to Hauser, Sept. 1915. *Corr.*, 14:218.

26. Proust to Hauser, Sept. 1915, *Corr.*, 14:230.

27. Hauser to Proust, Oct. 30, 1915, *Corr.*, 14:268-69.

28. Proust to Hauser, Sept. 1915, *Corr.*, 14:322.

29. Hauser to Proust, Mar. 26, 1916, *Corr.*, 15:72.

30. Hauser to Proust, May 26, 1916, *Corr.*, 15:122.

31. Hauser to Proust, June 21, 1916, *Corr.*, 15:188.

32. Proust to Hauser, July 17, 1916, *Corr.*, 15:223.

33. Hauser to Proust, July 19, 1916, *Corr.*, 15:227.

34. Proust to Hauser, July 25, 1916, *Corr.*, 15:232.

35. Hauser to Proust, July 27, 1916, *Corr.*, 15:238.

36. Hauser to Proust, Aug. 26, 1916. *Corr.*, 15:273-74.

37. Proust to Hauser, Aug. 27, 1916, *Corr.*, 15:275.

38. Proust to Hauser, Sept. 13, 1916, *Corr.*, 15:292.

39. Hauser to Proust, Nov. 10, 1916, *Corr.*, 15:326.

40. Hauser to Proust, Mar. 17, 1917, *Corr.*, 16:76-77.

41. Hauser to Proust, Feb. 1, 1917, *Corr.*, 16:40.

42. Proust to Hauser, Mar. 17, 1917, *Corr.*, 16:83.

43. Hauser to Proust, Mar. 31, 1917, *Corr.*, 16:87.

44. Proust to Hauser, Apr. 1, 1917, *Corr.*, 16:89-90.

45. Hauser to Proust, May 3, 1917, *Corr.*, 16:115.

46. Barbara Tuchman, *The Zimmermann Telegram* (New York: Viking, 1958).

47. Hauser to Proust, May 3, 1917, *Corr.*, 16:116.

48. Proust to Hauser, after May 3, 1917, *Corr.*, 16:120.

49. Proust to Hauser, June 23, 1917, *Corr.*, 16:167.

50. Proust to Hauser, Feb. 24/25, 1918. *Corr.*, 17:128.

51. Hauser to Proust, Mar. 6, 1918, *Corr.*, 17:135.

52. Hauser to Proust, Apr. 2, 1918, *Corr.*, 17:158.

53. Proust to Hauser, May 15, 1918, *Corr.*, 17:244.

54. Hauser to Proust, Nov. 18, 1918, *Corr.*, 17:474.

55. Hauser to Proust, Oct. 16, 1918, *Corr.*, 17:40.

56. Proust to Hauser, Jan. 9, 1919, *Corr.*, 18:39-40.

57. Proust to Hauser, Nov. 17, 1918, *Corr.*, 17:469.

58. It is not clear whether he actually went through with this plan, although later he did purchase stock in another Mexican oil company, Compañía Mexicana de Petróleos El Águila. Proust to Madame Straus, Dec. 24, 1919, *Corr.*, 18:555.

59. Hauser to Proust, Oct. 20, 1918, *Corr.*, 17:409.

60. Hauser to Proust, Oct. 20, 1918, *Corr.*, 17:409.

232 Notes to Pages 84–87

61. Proust confessed to a friend: "Croisset ne m'ayant pas offert de me loger, je pense vaguement profiter du déménagement forcé pour aller voir Pérouse, Sienne et Pise," qtd in Pierre Barillet, *Les seigneurs du rire: Robert de Flers, Gaston de Caillavet, Francis de Croisset* (Paris: Fayard, 1999), 459.

62. Proust to Hauser, Mar. 4, 1919, *Corr.,* 18:126.

63. Proust to Madame Straus, Dec. 24, 1919, *Corr.,* 18:555.

64. Hauser to Proust, Mar. 30, 1920, *Corr.,* 19:170. Proust paid little attention to this break-up letter, and continued to ask Hauser for advise on potential investments. In March 1921, he asked what he should do with his shares of Mexican Railways (keep them, Hauser advised). Hauser to Proust, Mar. 7, 1921, *Corr.,* 20:121.

65. *Recherche,* 4:218–19.

66. Proust, *The Prisoner and the Fugitive,* trans. Carol Clark and Peter Collier (New York: Penguin, 2003), 604.

67. The two had first met in 1907, when Proust needed a driver to take him to see the sights in Normandy, and Agostinelli, a chauffeur employed by Unic Taximètres—the company owned by Jacques Bizet—offered his services. Proust was smitten with the uniform-clad youth and hired him during each of his visits to Cabourg. He even devoted an article, "Impressions de route en automobile"—later included in *Pastiches et mélanges*—to an excursion they took together to visit the cathedrals in Normandy. In 1913 Agostinelli asked Proust to hire him as a full-time chauffeur, but since he already had one at his service—Odilon Albaret—he proposed to take him in as a private secretary, much to the consternation of his friends.

68. Proust to Émile Straus, June 3, 1914, *Corr.,* 13:228.

69. See Rubén Gallo, "Perversions," *Freud's Mexico: Into the Wilds of Psychoanalysis* (Cambridge: MIT Press, 2010).

70. See Maurice Sachs, *Le Sabbat: Souvenirs d'une jeuneusse orageuse* (Paris: Correa, 1946); Jean Cocteau, *Journal, 1942–1945* (Paris: Gallimard, 1989); Painter, *Marcel Proust* (London: Chatto & Windus, 1989).

71. Proust to Hauser, Apr. 1, 1917, *Corr.,* 16:89.

72. On LeCuziat's brothel, see Laure Murat, "Proust, Marcel, 46 ans, rentier," *La revue littéraire* (May 2005): 82–93. Hauser's office was on rue de l'Arcade in 1909, as mentioned in the correspondence.

73. Mexico Tramways had been nationalized by the government in 1952.

74. This fascination with tramways was not the exclusive domain of Mexican intellectuals. In a passage later cited by Walter Benjamin in one of his essays on Baudelaire, Georg Simmel discussed tramways as elements of a nineteenth-century modernity that privileged the visual over the aural. "Before the development of buses, railroads, and trams in the nineteenth century, people had never been in situations where they had to look at one another for long minutes or even hours without speaking to one another." Georg Simmel, *Soziologie,* 4th ed. (Berlin, 1958), 486. The passage is quoted in Walter Benjamin, "The Paris of the Second Empire in Baude-

laire," *Selected Writings*, vol. 4, *1938-1940*, trans. Edmund Jephcott et al. (Cambridge: Harvard University Press, 2003), 19-20.

75. At 660 francs each, Proust's three hundred shares in Mexico Tramways would now be worth approximately 750,000 Euros. Source: www.insee.fr.

Chapter 2. Gabriel de Yturri

1. Yturri was taken to Portugal by Kenelm Vaughan, an English Catholic priest who had been fundraising in Argentina. In a letter written aboard the *Senegal*, Vaughan told Gabriel's mother, "I expect this voyage to be for his physical as well as moral wellbeing." The plan was to enroll Gabriel at the English College in Lisbon, "whose president, Monsignor Baines, is a close friend of mine." He would remain there for two years, and after this period of "hard work and serious studies [. . .] he will be able to return to his homeland a well educated man, with the skills to embrace some advantageous profession." Vaughan to Genoveva Zurita, Jan. 26, 1881, qtd in Carlos Páez de la Torre, *El argentino de oro* (Buenos Aires: Bajo La Luna, 2011), 28.

2. Montesquiou told his friends he had met Yturri in 1885 at the École des Beaux-Arts during an exhibition of paintings by Delacroix. The young man introduced himself as an admirer of the count's work and expressed such passion for his poetry that he decided to hire him as a secretary. Robert de Montesquiou, *Le chancelier de fleurs* (Paris: La Maison du Livre, 1907), 34. Others, however, told the story of a less distinguished encounter. Yturri started out a tie salesman at Le Carnaval de Venise, a clothing store near La Madeleine, where he was discovered by Baron Jacques Doasan, who took him in as his protégé until the young man left him for Montesquiou in 1885. George D. Painter, *Marcel Proust: A Biography*, 2 vols. (London: Chatto and Windus, 1989), 1:130.

3. Montesquiou, *Le chancelier*, 130.

4. Ibid., 133.

5. Proust to Montesquiou, June 20, 1901, *Corr.*, 2:435.

6. Ilán de Casa Fuerte, *Le dernier des Guermantes* (Paris: Éditions Julliard, 1994), 144.

7. There are several novels with characters based on Montesquiou: Joris-Karl Huysmans turned him into Des Esseintes in *Against the Grain* (1884). Jean Lorrain—a writer who fought a duel with Proust—depicted him in *Monsieur de Phocas* (1901). Proust modeled one of his novel's most memorable characters, the Baron de Charlus, on Montesquiou.

8. Proust to Montesquiou, Apr. 15, 1893, *Corr.*, 1:205-6.

9. "Cher Monsieur, poète et ami," Proust to Yturri, May 13, 1896, *Corr.*, 2:65.

10. See, for instance, Proust to Montesquiou, Aug. 12, 1894, *Corr.*, 1:317; Proust to Yturri, Aug. 14, 1894, *Corr.*, 1:318.

11. Proust to Montesquiou, Apr. 13-20, 1897, *Corr.*, 2:186.

12. "Come with your brother Hahn," the count urged Marcel as he invited him to

a party. Montesquiou to Proust, July 23, 1895, *Corr.,* 1:412. On the double dates, see also Proust to Montesquiou, June 17, 1895, *Corr.,* 1:403; Proust to Montesquiou, Apr. 15–20, 1897, *Corr.,* 2:186; Proust to Montesquiou, Apr. 21, 1899, *Corr.,* 2:284.

13. Léon Daudet mocked Yturri's accent: "Le connté a dit . . . Écoutez la parole merrveillouse qui vient dé tomber des lèvres du connté . . . admirable, positivement étrange et admirable," parodied Léon Daudet in *L'entre-deux-guerres* (Paris: Nouvelle Imprimerie Nationale, 1915), 91. Painter gives some English renditions of these linguistic eccentricities in "Mossou le Connte; I was ze secretary of ze Baron Doasan," Painter, *Marcel Proust,* 1:130.

14. Proust to Yturri, Oct. 1899, *Corr.,* 2:363; the comment on "grace and erudition" appears in a letter to Montesquiou about 'La chasse aux perroquets [The parrot hunt],'" a prose piece written by Yturri and reprinted by the count in his volume *Roseaux pensants.* Proust to Montesquiou, Jan. 13, 1894, *Corr.,* 1:272.

15. Proust's dedication reads: "À M Gabriel de Yturri, en souvenir de mon admiration profonde pour une éblouissante 'Chasse au Perroquet' et pour l'extrême et rare subtilité de son esprit," 1896, *Bibliothèque de Robert de Montesquiou* (Paris: Librairie de Maurice Escoffier, 1923), 2:87.

16. Páez de la Torre, *El argentino,* 73–77.

17. "Or, Gabriel de Yturri était à mon avis, fort supérieur, pour l'intelligence et la sensibilité, à son supercoquentieux patron [. . .] derrière ces pétarades, qui faisaient la joie des assistants, guettait un œil clair, observateur et froid. Ce singulier garçon est demeuré pour moi une énigme vivante." Daudet, *Entre deux guerres,* 91.

18. Ibid., 91–92.

19. "Ce singulier garçon est demeuré pour moi une énigme vivante." Ibid., 91.

20. "Une avance d'une centaine de francs pour dépenses indispensables," Verlaine to Yturri, Aug. 21, 1893, BNF, NaFr, 23057, f. 33.

21. "De m'avancer un billet de cinquante francs qui me permît d'attendre les 1rs jours de mars." "Les gens qui me donnent de l'argent sont lents, lents! Enfin je fais appel à tous bons cœurs!" he quips in another missive; "aussi vous serais-je obligé de quelque avance d'argent immédiate par la poste au 39 (et non au 37) Rue Descartes," Verlaine to Yturri, Jan. 24, 1894, BNF, NaFr, 23057, n47.

22. Verlaine to Yturri, Dec.[?] 4, 1895, BNF, NaFr, 23057, n75.

23. Verlaine to Montesquiou, Dec. 30, 1895, *Correspondance de Paul Verlaine,* ed. Adolphe van Bever (Paris: Albert Messein, 1929), 3:243.

24. Verlaine to Yturri, May 1, 1894, BNF, NaFr, 23057, n52.

25. Paul Verlaine, *Œuvres completes* (Paris: Vanier, 1901), 3:206.

26. The Spanish critic Juan Valera once complained about the proliferation of Carmens, Amaëguies, and other stereotypical voluptuous Spanish women in French literature: "Doña Sabina, la marquesa de Amaegui, Rosita, Pepita y Juanita y otras heroínas de versos, siempre livianos y tontos a menudo, compuestos por Víctor Hugo y Alfredo de Musset, son fuera de España el ideal de la mujer española, de

facha algo gatuna, con dientes de tigre, ardiente, celosísima, materialista y sensual, ignorante, voluptuosa y devota, tan dispuesta a entregarse a Dios como al diablo, y que lo mismo da una puñalada que un beso. La Carmen, de Mérimée, es el prototipo de estas mujeres, y no se puede negar que está trazado de mano maestra." Juan Valera, "Sobre el concepto que hoy se forma de España," *Obras completas* (Madrid: Aguilar, 1958), 2:737–51. I thank William Marx for this reference.

27. Mina Curtis, *Other People's Letters: In Search of Proust, A Memoir* (Canada: Helen Marx Books, 2005), 167.

28. Casa Fuerte, *Le dernier des Guermantes,* 142.

29. Philippe Jullian, *Robert de Montesquiou: Un prince 1900* (Paris: Perrin, 1965), 161.

30. Ibid., 110.

31. Rubén Darío, "La evolución del rastacuerismo," *Opiniones* (Madrid: Editorial Mundo Latino, 1918), 126.

32. Ibid., 125.

33. Darío to Montesquiou, June 13, 1902. This unpublished letter reads: "Monsieur et cher maître, Je suis vraiment désolé de ne pouvoir accepter votre aimable invitation, étant obligé de partir inopinément pour Londres. Des mon retour, j'aurais l'honneur et le plaisir de vous faire une visite. Je vous prie d'agréer, Monsieur et cher Maître, l'expression de mes sentiments respectueux. Rubén Darío." BNF, NaFr, 15052, 99.

34. *Recherche,* 3:211.

35. JMG, "Les Coulisses," *La Lanterne,* Mar. 21 1899, 3; Philippe Blay, *L'île du rêve de Reynaldo Hahn* (Villeneuve: Presses Universitaires du Septentrion, 2001), 682–85.

36. Darío, "La evolución del rastacuerismo," 128.

37. Groussac, *El viaje intellectual: Impresiones de naturaleza y arte* (Buenos Aires: Ediciones Simurg, 2005), 105–6.

38. Ibid., 106–9.

39. Hugo Foguet, *Pretérito Perfecto* (Buenos Aires: Planeta, 1992), 59.

40. "Tucumán está presente en mi obra como una fatalidad," *La Gaceta* (Nov. 19, 2006); Hernández evokes the many myths that circulated about Yturri: "Me pareció interesante porque sobre Iturri se han escrito versiones diferentes. Se dice que era hijo de una chola y un cura y que era hijo de gente muy tradicional de Yerba Buena y también que era un hombre hermoso, una especie de Ganímedes. El mismo Groussac llegó a decir que se fue a Bs As como prestigiditador y no se supo más de él hasta que reapareció en París." "No hay arte más regional que la poesía," *Los Andes* (Mendoza, Argentina), June 24, 2001, accessed at www.losandes.com.ar/notas/2001/6/24/cultura-15524.asp.

41. Juan José Hernández, "Gabriel Iturri," *Cantar y Contar: poemas y retratos* (Buenos Aires: Bajo la Luna Nueva, 1999), 51–52.

42. Proust changed the original title "Fête chez Montesquiou à Neuilly" to "Dans les *Mémoires* de Saint-Simon" in *Pastiches et mélanges*. In this chapter, I use the origi-

nal title. Proust, "Dans les *Mémoires* de Saint Simon," in *Contre Sainte-Beuve* (Paris: Gallimard, Bibliothèque de la Pléiade, 1971), 49.

43. Proust, "Fête chez Montesquiou à Neuilly: Extrait des Mémoires du duc de Saint-Simon," *Le Figaro,* Jan. 4, 1904.

44. Montesquiou to Proust, Feb. 21, 1909, *Corr.,* 9:42. On this episode, see also William Carter, *Marcel Proust: A Life* (New Haven: Yale University Press, 2000), 464.

45. Proust, *Contre Sainte-Beuve,* 43.

46. "Robert de Montesquiou-Fezensac [. . .] répondit par cet admirable apophtegme qu'il descendait des anciens comtes de Fezensac, lesquels sont connus avant Philippe-Auguste, et qu'il ne voyait pas pour quelle raison cent ans—c'était le prince Murat qu'il voulait dire—devraient passer avant mille ans." Ibid., 49.

47. Jean Milly, *Les pastiches de Proust* (Paris: Librairie Armand Colin, 1970), 229.

48. Ibid., 232.

49. Proust, *Contre Sainte-Beuve,* 360–65.

50. Reprinted as "Robert de Montesquiou 'le souverain des choses transitoires'" in Proust, *Contre Sainte-Beuve,* 405–11.

51. Ibid., 51.

52. Ibid., 49–50.

53. Proust mentions Yturri's Argentine origins in several letters. In one, he mentions reading a chronicle Yturri wrote during the single visit he made to Tucumán in 1890. Proust to Montesquiou, Jan. 13, 1894, *Corr.,* 1:272.

54. Proust, *Contre Sainte-Beuve,* 49.

55. Montesquiou, *Le chancelier,* 44, 49.

56. Proust to Reynaldo Hahn, Dec. 25 1901, *Corr.,* 2:482; Marcel Proust, *The Collected Poems,* ed. Harold Augenbraum (New York: Penguin, 2013), 152–53.

57. Gérard Genette, *Palimpsests: Literature in the Second Degree,* trans. Channa Newman and Claude Doubinski (Lincoln: University of Nebraska Press, 1997), 85.

58. See the photo "Père," in which Robert de Montesquiou had his father—his père—dressed like a priest—a père. BNF, NaFr, 15039, f. 126. Most of these photos are in the same volume.

59. See, e.g., Eve Kosofsky Sedgwick, *Epistemology of the Closet* (Berkeley: University of California Press, 1990).

60. Proust to Montesquiou, Dec. 13, 1895, *Corr.,* 1:451–52.

61. Painter, *Marcel Proust,* 1:130.

62. "I was sad to hear," Proust wrote Montesquiou on Mar. 13, 1904, "that Monsieur de Yturri was very ill [. . .] I am under the impression that he is one of those condemned men who are never executed and that he will soon get his reprieve and live to spend many unhoped-for and happy days. I remember several years ago now my poor Papa had found him very ill. And you see how he recovered. I believe he would be wrong to worry, and so would you." Proust to Montesquiou, Mar. 13, 1904, *Corr.,* 4:90; *SL,* 2:31–32.

63. Proust to Yturri, June 29, 1905, *Corr.,* 5:271.

64. Proust to Montesquiou, June 29, 1905, *Corr.,* 5:270.

65. Adrien Proust and A. Matthieu, *L'hygiène des diabétiques* (Paris, 1899). See *Bibliothèque de Robert de Montesquiou* (Paris: Librairie de Maurice Escoffier, 1923), 1:71.

66. Proust to Montesquiou, Mar. 13, 1904, *Corr.,* 4:90; *SL,* 2:31–32: "il y a plusieurs années mon pauvre papa l'avait trouvé très mal." See also Paul Morand, *Journal d'un attaché d'ambassade, 1916–1917* (Paris: Gallimard, 1996), 184. "[Proust] nous raconte que Montesquiou demande au Dr. Proust un consultation pour Iturry [*sic*], son ami, son secrétaire, con commensal, son inséparable de vingt ans. Le docteur répond: 'Son cas est mortel, ne le lui dites pas.—Il faut que je le lui disse, répond Montesquiou, il a des tas de commissions à faire pour moi.'"

67. Montesquiou, *Le chancelier,* 188.

68. Montesquiou to Proust, Nov. 13–17, 1905, *Corr.,* 5:369.

69. One biographer notes the shock with which Montesquiou's family received the news about the count's funeral plans: "This man from such humble origins, a foreigner, born in Tucuman, Argentina, who owed his *particule* [. . .] to the protection of his master—how did he come to be chosen over the funerary statues at the Château de Courtanvaux as a companion for the next life?" Marthe Bibesco, *Le Confesseur et les poètes* (Paris: Grasset, 1970), 165.

70. Proust to Montesquiou, July 9, 1905, *Corr.,* 5:290.

71. "Ce qui me touche, dans la façon dont vous m'en parlez, c'est que vous me parlez de lui, et non de moi, comme font la plupart, qui me parlent de lui par rapport à moi, au lieu de me parler de moi, par rapport à lui, ce qui, je le répète, m'émeut cent fois plus." Montesquiou to Proust, Aug. 1905, *Corr.,* 5:321.

72. "J'aime à imaginer, entre vous et lui, des correspondances mystérieuses. Son ingénieux dévouement d'outre-tombe cherche et trouve sans doute à se loger dans des esprits et des cœurs, qu'il dispose à me comprendre mieux, et à m'aimer davantage." Ibid., 321–22.

73. The book bore the subtitle "twelve stations of friendship," and its chapters included a meditation on various philosophical visions of friendship; a biographical sketch of Yturri, including his childhood in Argentina; fragments of Yturri's letters to Montesquiou; transcriptions of the condolences sent to the count by writers, artists, and aristocrats, including Marcel Proust, Reynaldo Hahn, Anna de Noailles, Pierre Loti, Anatole France, and many others; and a chapter on the marble basin, described as Yturri's favorite object. The volume featured two photographs: one of a forty-something, elegantly dressed Yturri, and another depicting the angel of silence at his tomb. The count had one hundred copies printed and bound in brown leather, to be distributed among "those friends who have kept, like him, the faithful memory of the departed friend." Emile Berr, *"Le chancelier de fleurs," Le Figaro,* June 1907. In BNF, NaFr, 15151, f. 44.

74. Montesquiou, *Le chancelier,* 105.

75. "Ces lettres, elles sont des centaines; il faut les presser, les pressurer, pour en extraire, avant l'extinction, la sève obscure de l'encre, la suavité du sentiment, la saveur du génie. Je dis: avant l'extinction; car je le répète, ensuite, il n'y aura plus qu'a faire brûler, a laisser s'éteindre. Des indiscrets ne viendraient plus qu'y chercher des fautes d'orthographe et des imperfections de nature. C'est pourquoi, si l'on y réfléchit avec sagacité, il serait plus que puéril, coupable, aux yeux des amateurs de belles âmes, de déplorer la dessiccation de tels gulf-streams d'écriture. La correspondance est fungible; elle appartient au groupe, efficace entre tous, des vénérables choses qui périssent par, et après l'usage." Montesquiou, *Le chancelier,* 40–41.

76. "Je conserverai les enveloppes vides. Fuies d'où s'est envolé—et pour ne revenir jamais!—ce que le Poëte a appelé 'divins oiseaux du cœur.'" Montesquiou, *Le chancelier,* 41.

77. Proust to Hahn, Dec. 31, 1906, *Corr.,* 7:22.

78. "Cher Monsieur, Je suis allé au cimetière et j'ai longuement contemplé la tombe qui produit, ainsi que vous me l'avez dit, une impression de mystère et de silence tout à fait saisissante. La couleur de la pierre, la forme à la fois mystique et libre de la stèle, la noblesse sombre du marbre, et enfin l'expression et la beauté de cette statue singulière imposent la méditation le recueillement et pourtant dégagent quelque chose de chaleureux. On reconnaît dans cet arrangement singulier la main de l'artiste et le cœur de l'ami tout ensemble. Quand les arbres auront leurs feuilles et que le printemps épandra autour de ce site funèbre sa majestueuse ariste, *votre œuvre* acquérira encore plus de signification et de profondeur. Je suis heureux de l'avoir admirée et, m'identifiant aux sentiments de votre âme, je suis certain que *le mort* n'aurait pas pu désirer une plus affectueuse et plus magnifique sépulture. Votre dévoué Reynaldo Hahn." Hahn to Montesquiou, no date, BNF, NaFr, 15152, f. 10.

79. Casa Fuerte, *Le dernier des Guermantes,* 224.

80. Montesquiou to Proust, Mar. 23, 1907, *Corr.,* 7:117; *SL,* 2:266; Montesquiou to Proust, Mar. 25, 1907, *Corr.,* 7:118; *SL,* 2:267; Montesquiou to Proust, Apr. 19, 1907, *Corr.,* 7:145–46; *SL,* 2:278–79.

81. Proust to Montesquiou, June 27, 1908, *Corr.,* 8:156; *SL,* 2:383.

82. Proust to Hahn, early July 1908, *Corr.,* 8:163; *SL,* 2:386.

83. Montesquiou to Proust, early July 1908, *Corr.,* 8:162–63.

84. Montesquiou included an excerpt from Proust's article in the chapter "Images et Empreintes," *Le chancelier,* 143–44; Proust's condolence letter is reproduced on p. 246; Montesquiou's responses to Proust are on pp. 274–75.

85. Proust to Montesquiou, early July 1908, *Corr.,* 8:165–67.

86. "C'est un grand livre que vous m'avez donné, un portrait qui vivra et où l'avenir ne cherchera moins le portrait involontaire du peintre que le portrait voulu du modèle. Yturri par Montesquiou qui ne veut être que le portrait d'Yturri, mais est d'autant plus un Montesquiou subjectif grâce à son objectivité. On ne se livre

que quand on s'oublie. C'est en parlant d'un autre que vous avez dit vos plus beaux secrets." Proust to Montesquiou, early July 1908, *Corr.,* 8:169.

87. "C'est au cours de mon habitation au quai d'Orsay que je fis la connaissance de mon cher Yturri, qui partagea ma vie vingt ans, que je ne cesse de regretter, et dont je bénis toujours la mémoire." Montesquiou, *Les pas effacés* (Paris: Editions du Sandre, 2007), 2:112.

88. Casa Fuerte, *Le dernier des Guermantes,* 186.

89. Painter, *Marcel Proust,* 2:40.

90. *Recherche,* 3:98.

91. Proust, *Sodom and Gomorrah,* trans. John Sturrock (London: Allen Lane, 2002), 103.

92. "Esquisse LXVIII: Les Homosexuels," *Recherche,* 3:973.

93. "Yturri est un peu Morel un peu Jupien." Jean-Yves Tadié, *Marcel Proust* (Paris: Gallimard, 1996), 544.

94. *Recherche,* 3:255.

95. Proust, *Sodom and Gomorrah,* 261.

96. *Recherche,* 3:257.

97. Proust, *Sodom and Gomorrah,* 262.

98. *Recherche,* 3:306.

99. Proust, *Sodom and Gomorrah,* 312.

100. *Recherche,* 3:399.

101. Proust, *Sodom and Gomorrah,* 405.

102. *Recherche,* 3:476.

103. Proust, *Sodom and Gomorrah,* 482.

104. *Recherche,* 3:421.

105. Proust, *Sodom and Gomorrah,* 427.

106. *Recherche,* 3:450; Proust, *Sodom and Gomorrah,* 456.

107. *Recherche,* 3:448.

108. Proust, *Sodom and Gomorrah,* 455.

109. Proust, *Finding Time Again,* trans. Ian Patterson (London: Allen Lane, 2002), 128.

110. *Recherche,* 4:283; *Finding Time Again,* 11.

111. Ibid., 3:348. The French original reads: "'lé coupé', dit, en contrefaisant l'accent rastaquouère, Cottard." John Sturrock translates the passage as "'Me ter-rump you,' said Cottard putting on his vulgar rich foreigner's voice." *Sodom and Gomorrah,* 354.

112. *Recherche,* 3:452:

Tandis que Morel me parlait, je regardais avec stupéfaction les admirables livres que lui avait données M. de Charlus et qui encombraient la chambre. Le violoniste ayant refusé ceux qui portaient "Je suis baron, etc.," devise qui lui semblait insultante pour lui-même comme un signe d'appartenance, le baron, avec l'ingéniosité sentimentale où se complaît l'amour malheureux, en avait varié d'autres, provenant d'ancêtres, mais commandés au relieur selon les circonstances d'une mélancolique amitié. [. . .] trouvant trop verte la grappe qu'il ne pouvait atteindre, feignant de n'avoir pas recherché ce qu'il n'avait pas obtenu, M. de Charlus disait dans l'une: "*Non mortale quod opto.*"

(As Morel was talking I was gazing in amazement at the splendid books that M. de Charlus had given him and which were cluttering the room. The violinist having refused those that bore "I belong to the Baron" and the like, a device he found insulting to himself, as signifying possession, the Baron, with that sentimental ingenuity in which an unhappy love takes pleasure, had varied it by others, originating with his forebears, but ordered from the binder's according to the circumstances of a melancholy affection [. . .] and, finding the bunch of grapes he had been unable to reach too green, and pretending not to have been seeking for what he had not obtained, in one of them M. de Charlus had said: "*Non mortale quod* opto.") (*Sodom and Gomorrah,* 459).

A note in the Pléiade edition of *Sodome et Gomorrhe* adds that this was an approximate transcription of Charles de Lorraine's motto: "non est mortale quod opto," which in turn was adapted from Ovid's *Metamorphoses* 2:56, "Sors tua mortalis; non est mortale quod optas" (your destiny is that of a mortal; you ambition that of an immortal). *Recherche* 3:1597, n. 7.

113. *Recherche,* 3:419.

114. Ibid., 3:422.

115. Proust, *Sodom and Gomorrah,* 428.

116. *Recherche,* 3:420.

117. Proust, *Sodom and Gomorrah,* 426.

118. Ibid., 3:713.

119. Proust, *The Prisoner and The Fugitive,* trans. Carol Clark (London: Allen Lane, 2002), 190.

120. We can see Yturri's literary gifts in two stories included in *Le chancelier de fleurs*: "La chasse aux perroquets" and "Le pain assassin." In the first, Yturri recounts his only trip back to Tucumán in 1890, including a day spent in the countryside hunting parrots. The second narrates a visit to the Isle of Noirmoutier, a remote island off the coast of Brittany, where he learned of a peasant woman who had died after baking bread while ill. These stories—with their eye for exotic details and picturesque scenery—recall the novels of Pierre Loti, the nineteenth-century travel writer who published novels about Turkey and Japan, as well as the remote French regions of Brittany and the Basque Country.

Paperolle No. 2

1. *Recherche,* 3:775.

2. Proust, *The Prisoner and the Fugitive* (New York: Penguin, 2003), 249.

3. Luis Loayza, "Vagamente dos peruanos," *El sol de lima* (Mexico City: Fondo de Cultura Económica, 1993), 53–58.

4. Fernando Iwasaki Cauti, "En busca de un tipo perdido," *Hueso húmero* 35 (Dec. 1999): 153–59.

5. Manuel Mujica Láinez to Carlos Páez de la Torre, Oct. 10, 1981, qtd in *El canciller de las flores* (Tucumán: Ediciones del Gabinete, 1992), 111–12. This is a provocative hypothesis, but Montesquiou, as we saw, correctly identified Gabriel Yturri's birthplace as Tucumán in *Le chancelier de fleurs.*

6. Philippe Jullian, *Robert de Montesquiou: Un prince 1900* (Paris: Librairie Académique Perrin, 1965), 262.

7. Proust to Paul Souday, May 11, 1921, *Corr.,* 20:259.

8. *Recherche,* 3:1475.

9. Luis Alberto Sánchez, *La literatura peruana: Derrotero para una historia cultural del Perú,* (Lima: P. L. Villanueva Editor), 1975.

10. Proust to Gaston Gallimard, early Jan. 1920, *Corr.,* 19:43–44; Proust to Edmond Jaloux, Feb. 1920, *Corr.,* 19:131–32.

11. Proust to Gaston Gallimard, early Jan. 1920, *Corr.,* 19:43–44.

12. Lionel Hauser to Proust, May 3, 1917, *Corr.,* 16:116.

13. W. A. Mozart, *Così fan tutte,* Act I, scene 15. I thank Efraín Kristal for this reference.

Chapter 3. José Maria de Heredia

1. José María de Heredia, "Discours de réception à l'Académie française," *Les trophées* (Paris: Librairie Alphonse Lemerre, 1926), 225–26.

2. Jean-Paul Goujon, ed., *Dossier secret Pierre Louÿs-Marie de Régnier* (Paris: Christian Bourgois, 2002), 93.

3. Marie de Heredia to Proust, June–July 1895, *Corr.,* 1:403.

4. Robert de Billy, ed., *Marcel Proust: Lettres et conversations* (Paris: Éditions des Portiques, 1930), 76.

5. Proust to Marie de Heredia, Aug. 30–Sept. 4, 1895, *Corr.,* 20:611.

6. Proust to Madame Henri de Régnier [Marie de Heredia], May 27, 1922, *Corr.,* 20:233.

7. Jean-Yves Tadié, *Marcel Proust* (Paris: Gallimard, 1996), 262.

8. Proust, *Contre Sainte-Beuve,* (Paris: Gallimard, Pléiade, 1971), 363. The soirée featured piano works by Léon Delafosse, a pretty blond boy who had become Mon-

tesquiou's protégé after Proust introduced him to the count. Proust notes that "this time [Delafosse] played some melodies he himself has composed based on poems by Robert de Montesquiou." In addition to Heredia, the poetry recital included works by Verlaine, Coppée, Montesquiou, and Desbordes-Valmore.

9. Proust, "Robert de Montesquiou, le Souverain des Choses Transitoires," *Contre Sainte-Beuve*, 407.

10. Jacques Patin, "J-M de Heredia et Robert de Montesquiou: Lettres inédites," *Le Figaro*, Supplément Littéraire, Jan. 5, 1929, 1-2.

11. On the tensions between Montesquiou and the Heredias, see Antonie Bertrand, *Les curiosités esthétiques de Robert de Montesquiou* (Geneva: Droz, 1996), 214. After their falling out, Lucien Daudet mocked Heredia in a letter to Montesquiou: "José Maria de Heredia: Jesus Maria quel charabia," qtd in Bertrand, *Les curiosités*, 460. See also Robert de Montesquiou, *Les pas effaces: Mémoires*, 2 vols. (Paris: Éditions du Sandre, 2008), 2:120-22.

12. Proust, *Contre Sainte Beuve*, 450-51.

13. Proust, "Un dîner en ville," *Jean Santeuil: Précedé de Les plaisirs et les jours*, ed. Pierre Clarac (Paris: Gallimard, Bibliothèque de la Pléiade, 1971), 102.

14. "Je sais aussi des lettrés dont toute l'émotion se passe à se dire: 'C'est la fin de la langue française,' à remarquer que l'Académie a accueilli tel mot, à dire que Heredia a adhéré au vers libre." Proust, *Jean Santeuil*, 631.

15. See, e.g., Proust to Montesquiou, Mar. 6, 1905, in which Proust quotes Heredia's verse "Entends-tu le pipeau qui chante sur ses lèvres," *Corr.*, 5:67. Proust quotes from "Les conquérants" in letters to Léon Hauser (Apr. 1, 1917, *Corr.*, 16:89), Mme. De Lude (July 28, 1918, *Corr.*, 17:324), and Albert Thibaudet (July 3, 1920, *Corr.*, 19:342).

16. Proust to Henri de Régnier, Apr. 14, 1920, *Corr.*, 19:214.

17. *Recherche*, 2:107.

18. Marcel Proust, *In the Shadow of Young Girls in Love* (London: Allen Lane, 2002), 328.

19. Dominique Bona, *Les yeux noirs: Les vies extraordinaires des sœurs Heredia* (Paris: Lattès, 1989), 147, 246.

20. José María de Heredia, *Les trophées* (Paris: Librairie Alphonse Lemerre, 1926), 111.

21. "The Conquerors," *Les trophées: The Sonnets*, trans. Henry Johnson (New Haven: Yale University Press, 1910), 111.

22. Heredia's verses "Ils regardaient monter en un ciel ignoré/Du fond de l'Océan des étoiles nouvelles" sparked a lively controversy. Some scholars argued that the image was historically inaccurate, since Columbus did not cross into the southern hemisphere on his first trip; Heredia's defenders countered that the poem condensed the various trips taken by Columbus to the Americas and thus included passages into the South. See Miodrag Ibrovac, *José-Maria de Heredia* (Paris: Presses françaises, 1923), 336. See also Max Henríquez Ureña, "Las nuevas estrellas de Heredia," *Romanic Review* 9 (1918): 112-14.

23. These poems appear on the following pages in *Les trophées*: "Jouvence," 212; "Le tombeau du conquérant," 113; "Carolo Quinto Imperante," 114; "L'ancêtre," 115; "A un fondateur de ville," 116; "Une Carthage neuve au pays de la fable," 117; "Au même," 117; "A une ville morte," 118.

24. "La Détresse d'Atahuallpa: Prologue: Les conquérants de l'or," was first published in *Le Parnasse contemporain* (Paris: Lemerre, 1869), 369-95.

25. Ibrovac, *José-Maria de Heredia*, 276.

26. Jorge Orlando Melo, *Historia de Colombia: El establecimiento de la dominación española* (Bogotá: Presidencia de la República, 1996), 139.

27. Anthony McFarlane, *Colombia Before Independence: Economy, Society, and Politics under Bourbon Rule* (Cambridge: Cambridge University Press, 1993), 17-18. See also Melo, *Historia de Colombia*, 113-21. See also María del Carmen Gómez Pérez, *Pedro de Heredia y Cartagena de Indias* (Seville: Escuela de Estudios Hispano-Americanos, 1984).

28. Simone Szertics, *L'héritage espagnol de José-Maria de Heredia* (Paris: Klincksieck, 1975), 28-29.

29. Rubén Darío, "Lo que queda de Heredia," *Obras completas*, 4 vols. (Madrid: Afrodisio Aguado, 1950), 1:403-12; Enrique Gómez Carrillo, "Los trofeos," *Literatura extranjera: Estudios cosmopolitas* (Paris: Garnier, 1894), 301-8; Amado Nervo, "A Don José María de Heredia," *Poemas* (Paris: Librería de la Viuda de C. Bouret, 1901), 59-60; Pedro Henríquez Ureña, "Las nuevas estrellas de Heredia," *Romanic Review* 9 (1918): 112-14.

30. Enrique Díaz Canedo, "José María de Heredia y las influencias españolas," *Letras de América* (Mexico City: El Colegio de México, 1944), 202-3.

31. Manuel Sanguily, "José María de Heredia no es un poeta cubano," *Hojas Literarias* 1, no. 2 (Aug.-Dec. 1893): 46-47.

32. Ibid., 83.

33. Heredia, "Discours de réception à l'Académie française," *Les trophées*, 219-20.

34. Marcel Proust, "L'éclipse," *Contre Sainte-Beuve*, 325.

35. Ibid., 326.

36. Ibid., 327.

37. Ibid., 327.

38. "A few days after my departure [to Hispaniola] the Indians rebelled and refused to bring them the accustomed food. The admiral had the *caciques* summoned and told them that he was astonished at this discontinuance of supplies, since they knew very well that he had come there at God's command. He said that God was very annoyed with them and would show His anger that night by signs that would appear in the heavens. That night there was an eclipse of the moon, which was almost completely obscured, and the Admiral told them that the cause of this was God's anger with them for no longer supplying him with food. They believed him and in great fear promised always to bring him food, which in fact they did, until the ship which I had sent with provisions arrived." Diego Méndez, "Account by Diego

Méndez of Certain Incidents on Christopher Columbus's Last Voyage," *The Four Voyages of Christopher Columbus,* ed. and trans. J. M. Cohen (London: Penguin, 1969), 304.

39. Washington Irving, *The Life and Voyages of Christopher Columbus* (London: John Murray, 1830), 315–16.

40. Washington Irving, *Vie et voyages de Christophe Colomb,* trans. G. Renson (Paris: Librairie Internationale, 1864). The eclipse is discussed on pp. 173–74.

41. Proust, "L'éclipse," 327.

42. "Cette page fournit un document sur la réception de la geste du navigateur par un bourgeois d'âge scolaire. Dans le monde politiquement stable qui était celui de la Troisième République, ne mettant guère en doute ses valeurs, un jeune homme héroïse une figure de père, de savant, de chef. [. . .] Muni d'une culture humaniste le lycéen voit en Christophe Colomb un nouvel Énée dominant une tempête, un Ulysse faisant triompher l'astuce et l'éloquence sur la force brutale. Le besoin d'admirer une autorité raisonnable se lit aisément dans 'L'éclipse.'" Marie Miguet-Ollagnier, *Gisements profonds d'un sol mental: Marcel Proust* (Besançon: Presses Universitaires de Franche-Comté, 2003), 16.

43. Alice L. Conklin, *A Mission to Civilize: The Republican Idea of Empire in France and West Africa, 1895–1930* (Stanford: Stanford University Press, 1998), 1–2. See also Dino Costantini, *Mission civilisatrice: Le rôle de l'histoire coloniale dans la construction de l'identité politique française* (Paris: La Découverte, 2008).

44. Daniel-Henri Pageaux, "Szertics (Simone), *L'héritage espagnol de José-Maria de Heredia,* Paris, Klincksieck, 1975" (book review), *Revue belge de philologie et d'histoire* 58, no. 3 (1980): 736–39.

45. Jean-Pierre Rioux, *Nationalisme et conservatisme: La ligue de la patrie française, 1899–1904* (Paris: Editions Beauchesne, 1977), 14–15.

46. Ibid.

47. François Coppée, *Souvenirs d'un Parisien* (Paris: A. Lemerre, 1910), 75–79. The comment also appears in François Coppée, "Souvenirs sur les Parnassiens," *Chroniques artistiques, dramatiques et littéraires, 1875–1907* (Paris: Presses de l'Université de Paris-Sorbonne, 2003), 112.

48. On Heredia and the Dreyfus Affair, see Michel Drouin, *L'Affaire Dreyfus: Dictionnaire* (Paris: Flammarion, 2006), 201, 465.

49. Arsenal, 13547, f 57. The complete text of this unpublished letter reads:

Mon cher ami, En signant, avec nos confrères de l'Académie, le manifeste de la Ligue de la Patrie Française, j'ai tout d'abord voulu protester hautement contre l'abominable campagne menée contre l'armée, et, me mettant, au-dessus de la déplorable et incompréhensible affaire qui divise le pays, tenter, en dehors de toute politique, un essai d'apaisement et de conciliation, bref, faire simplement œuvre de bon Français.

Mes idées et mes sentiments n'ont pas varié. Mais la Ligue me semble avoir singulièrement dévié. Ses derniers actes me paraissent aller tellement à l'encontre du premier manifeste auquel j'avais adhéré de si grand cœur que je ne saurais en accepter la responsabilité. J'ai donc le vif regret de vous prier de ne plus me compter au nombre des adhérents à la Ligue. J'espère bien, mon cher Lemaître, que cette détermination qui, je vous l'avoue, me coûte infiniment à prendre, n'altérera en rien les sentiments de cordiale amitié qui nous unissent depuis si longtemps. JM de Heredia.

50. One of the most readable accounts of Maximilian's adventures in Mexico is Joan Haslip, *The Crown of Mexico: Maximilian and His Empress Carlota* (New York: Holt, Rinehart and Winston, 1971), 56-65, 117-19.

51. Qtd in Maron J Simon, *The Panama Affair* (New York: Charles Scribner's Sons, 1971), 25.

52. Ibid., 5, 33.

53. Ibid., 50-71.

54. Wolfred Nelson, "The Panama Canal," *Harper's Weekly*, May 18, 1885, 430.

55. Ibid.

56. Simon, *Panama Affair*, 70-81.

57. Ibid., 254.

58. Jeanne Proust-Weil to Marcel Proust, Aug. 14-15, 1900, *Corr.*, 2:403.

59. *Recherche*, 1:1273.

60. "Esquisse IV," *Recherche*, 1:1036.

61. Proust, *Jean Santeuil*, 579-618.

62. Szertics, *L'héritage espagnol*, 167; Ibrovac, *José-Maria de Heredia*, 320, n. 1.

63. Heredia, "Les conquérants de l'or," *Les trophées*, 177.

64. William H. Prescott, *History of the Conquest of Peru* (London: Richard Bentley, 1846), 175.

65. Heredia, *Les trophées*, 178.

66. Prescott, *History*, 175.

67. Heredia, *Les trophées*, 178.

68. Qtd in Szertics, *L'héritage espagnol*, 149.

69. See Walter Mignolo, *The Idea of Latin America* (New York: Blackwell, 2005), 51; see also Arturo Ardao, *Génesis de la idea y el nombre de América Latina* (Caracas: Centro de Estudios Latinoamericanos Rómulo Gallegos, 1993), and Arturo Ardao, *América Latina y la latinidad* (México: Universidad Nacional Autónoma de México, 1993).

70. Heredia, "En Patagonie," *Le Journal*, Nov. 23, 1900, 1. Reprinted in Henry de La Vaulx, *Voyage en Patagonie* (Paris: Hachette, 1901).

71. Ibid.

72. Ibid.

73. Ibid.

74. Ibid.

75. Ibid.

76. Ibid.

77. Ibid.

78. The unfinished translation of *Don Quixote* is in Arsenal, Ms 13546, f. 110ss.

79. These sonnets were first published in the Havana papers *El Fígaro* and *Social* in 1903. Heredia's manuscript letter, including the poems, is part of the collection of the Museo Heredia, archived in the house where José María Heredia y Heredia was born in Santiago de Cuba. The poems are reprinted in Szertics, *L'héritage espagnol,* 237–38. The poems also appear in *Œuvres poétiques de José-Maria de Heredia* (Paris: Les Belles Lettres, 1984), 2:194–95, 311.

80. Daniel Heller-Roazen, *Echolalias: On the Forgetting of Language* (New York: Zone Books, 2005).

Paperolle No. 3

1. Xavier Mathieu, *Antonio de La Gandara: Un témoin de la belle époque* (Paris: Éditions Librairie des Musées, 2011), 47, 92–93.

2. Edgar Munhall, *Whistler and Montesquiou: The Butterfly and the Bat* (New York: Frick Collection, 1995), 13.

3. Ibid., 152.

4. The portrait is in the collection of the Musée d'Azay-le-Ferron, Tours, France.

5. Musée d'Orsay, RF 1977 210, AM 1974 138, Paris.

6. Robert de Montesquiou, *Le chancelier de fleurs* (Paris: La Maison du Livre, 1907), 137–38.

7. Munhall, *Whistler and Montesquiou,* 39.

8. Ibid., 125.

9. Marcel Proust, "Huit lettres inédites à Maria de Madrazo," *Bulletin de la Société des Amis de Marcel Proust* 3 (1956): 31.

10. Montesquiou, *Le chancelier,* 261.

11. Ibid., 147.

12. The dinner, on May 24, 1897, was reported in *Le Gaulois.* Jean-Yves Tadié, *Marcel Proust* (Paris: Gallimard, 1996), 354–55.

13. Marcel Proust, *Contre Sainte-Beuve* (Paris: Gallimard, Bibliothèque de la Pléiade, 1971), 362.

14. Marcel Proust, *Jean Santeuil* (Paris: Gallimard, Bibliothèque de la Pléiade, 1971), 675.

15. Marcel Proust, *Jean Santeuil,* trans. Gerard Hopkins (New York: Simon and Schuster, 1956), 715.

16. Tadié, *Marcel Proust,* 175–78.

17. Proust to Louisa de Mornand, Apr. 1907, *Corr.,* 7:144.

18. Proust to Madame Catusse, Nov. 23, 1917, *Corr.,* 16:313.

19. Camille Mauclair, *L'art decoratif: Revue mensuelle d'art contemporain* (Dec. 1901): 86. Mathieu, *Antonio de La Gandara,* 276.

20. Mathieu, *Antonio de La Gandara,* 214.

21. Albert Flament, *Le bal du pré Catalan* (Paris: Fayard, 1946), 137.

22. Robert de Montesquiou, *Professionnelles beautés* (Paris: Juven, 1905), 113-21.

23. Mathieu, *Antonio de La Gandara,* 52.

Chapter 4. Ramon Fernandez

1. Proust to Daudet, June 6, 1914, *Corr.,* 13:353-55.

2. See Camille Wixler, "Proust au Ritz: Souvenirs d'un Maître d'hôtel," *ADAM International Review* 294-96 (1976): 14-20.

3. Proust to Morand, May 29, 1917, *Corr.,* 16:145-46.

4. Proust to Ramon Fernandez, Apr. 17, 1918, *Corr.,* 17:204-7.

5. Ramon Fernandez, *Proust* (Paris: Grasset, 1979), 86.

6. For a description of Jeanne Fernandez's salon, see Maurice Rostand, *Confession d'un demi-siècle* (Paris: Jeune Parque, 1948), 167-70.

7. Eliot to Richard Aldington, Nov. 24, 1924, *The Letters of T.S. Eliot* (London: Faber and Faber, 2009), 2:541-42.

8. Alban Cerisier, *Une histoire de la NRF* (Paris: Gallimard, 2009), 269.

9. Ramon Fernandez, *Messages* (1926; Paris: Grasset, 2009).

10. Jacques Lacan, *De la psychose paranoïaque dans ses rapports avec la personnalité* (Paris: Librairie E. Le François, 1932). The copy of this book inscribed to Ramon Fernandez is in Dominique Fernandez's private collection.

11. Ramon Fernandez, *Philippe Sauveur* (Paris: Grasset, 2012).

12. Simon Epstein, *Un paradoxe français: Antiracistes dans la collaboration, antisémites dans la Résistance* (Paris: Albin Michel, 2008), 239.

13. "Dédié aux salopards: Petite chronique des bons Français," *Le Droit de Vivre,* June 19, 1937.

14. Dominique Fernandez, *Ramon* (Paris: Grasset, 2008), 16, 651; Epstein, *Un paradoxe français,* 239-40.

15. Ramon Fernandez, "Le devoir des clercs," *La Gerbe,* Nov. 7, 1940.

16. Jorge Luis Borges, "Definition of a Germanophile," *Selected Non-Fictions,* ed. Eliot Weinberger (New York: Viking, 1999), 203-6.

17. Epstein, *Un paradoxe français,* 239.

18. Dominique Fernandez, "Une longue amitié," preface to Ramon Fernandez, *Proust* (Paris: Grasset, 1979), 8-9.

19. Epstein, *Un paradoxe français,* 239-41.

20. Marguerite Duras, *L'amant* (Paris: Éditions de Minuit, 1984), 84-85.

21. Marguerite Duras, *The Lover* (New York: Harper Perennial, 2006), 72.

22. Duras, *L'amant*, 84-85.

23. Duras, *The Lover*, 73.

24. Ramon Fernandez to Alfonso Reyes, Mar. 7, 1927, *Biblioteca de México* 23-24 (1995): 23.

25. Ibid.

26. "Quoi qu'il en soit, mon père ne s'est jamais intéressé au Mexique. Dans la masse d'articles qu'il a écrits, on n'en trouverait pas un seul consacré à un auteur de son pays paternel." Dominique Fernandez, *Ramon*, 62-63.

27. Ramon Fernandez to Alfonso Reyes, Nov. 5, 1925, *Biblioteca de México* 23-24 (1995): 22-23.

28. Alfonso Reyes, *Vision de l'Anahuac (1519)*, trans. Jeanne Guérandel (Paris: Editions de la Nouvelle Revue Française, 1927).

29. Ramon Fernandez to Alfonso Reyes, Nov. 5, 1925, *Biblioteca de México* 23-24 (1995): 22-23.

30. Ramon Fernandez, "Motivos: Notas sobre la estética de Proust," *Contemporáneos* 22 (Mar. 1930): 269-79.

31. Salvador Novo, "Estanteria," qtd in *Biblioteca de México* 23-24 (1995): 36.

32. Ramon Fernandez, "Poética de la novela," trans. Xavier Villaurrutia, *Bandera de Provincias* 7 (Aug. 1929).

33. Ibid.

34. Jorge Luis Borges, "*L'homme, est-il humain?*" *El Hogar* (Mar. 5, 1937). Reprinted in Borges, *Textos cautivos: Ensayos y reseñas en* El Hogar (Barcelona: Tusquets, 1986), 102-3.

35. Alfonso Reyes, "VII: La última morada de Proust," *Obras completas*, 26 vols. (Mexico: Fondo de Cultura Económica, 1960), 12:67.

36. Reyes, "Cuaderno de lecturas," *Obras completas* 8:216.

37. Ramon Fernandez, *Moralisme et littérature* (Paris: Éditions R. A. Corrêa, 1932), 89.

38. Dominique Fernandez, *Ramon*, 293-94.

39. Ramon Fernandez, "I Came Near Being a Fascist," *Partisan Review* 4 (Sept.-Oct. 1934): 23.

40. Ibid., 89.

41. Marcel Proust to Lionel Hauser, May 29, 1918, *Corr.*, 17:263-66.

42. Ramon Fernandez, "L'accent perdu," *Nouvelle Revue Française* 112 (Jan. 1923): 106.

43. Ibid.

44. *Recherche*, 1:584.

45. Marcel Proust, *In the Shadow of Young Girls in Flower*, trans. James Grieve (London: Allen Lane, 2002), 170.

46. Odette refers to a piece of furniture as "de l'époque." When Swann wants to know which period, she replies "que c'était moyen-âgeux. Elle entendait par là qu'il

avait des boiseries." *Recherche,* 1: 240. Edward J. Hughes believes that this and other passages on Odette's bad taste "simultaneously consolidates Swann's discursive power and mesmerizes him." *Proust, Class, and Nation* (Oxford: Oxford University Press, 2011), 98.

47. Ramon Fernandez, "L'accent perdu," 106.

48. Dominique Fernandez, "Une longue amitié," 10.

49. Fernandez, *Ramon,* 143.

50. See the letter from Reynaldo Hahn to Jeanne Fernandez, Dec. 20, 1944, Dominique Fernandez private collection.

51. Reynaldo Hahn to Ramon Fernandez, Sept. 1943, Dominique Fernandez private collection.

52. Marcel Proust, *Contre Sainte-Beuve* (Paris: Gallimard, Bibliothèque de la Pléiade, 1971), 221-22; Marcel Proust, *Against Sainte-Beuve and Other Essays,* trans. John Sturrock (New York: Penguin, 1994), 12.

53. Ramon espoused a position close to Proust's and insisted on the separation between an author's personality and his published work. "Les signes que combine l'artiste peuvent être identiques, *en tant que signes,* à ceux de la personnalité, mais à la différence de ces derniers ils se trouvent associés à des ensembles qui n'ont que peu ou point de rapport avec la conduite de l'artiste." Ramon Fernandez, *De la personnalité* (Paris: Sans Pareil, 1928), 141.

54. Reynaldo Hahn to Jeanne Fernandez, Dec. 20, 1944, Dominique Fernandez private collection.

55. Wallace Stevens, "The Idea of Order at Key West," *Collected Poems* (New York: Knopf, 1990), 129.

56. *The Letters of Wallace Stevens,* ed. Holly Stevens (Berkeley: University of California Press, 1966), 823.

57. Ibid., 798.

58. Ramon Fernandez, "I Came Near Being a Fascist," *Partisan Review* 4 (Sept.-Oct. 1934): 19-25.

59. James Longenbach, *Wallace Stevens: The Plain Sense of Things* (New York: Oxford University Press, 1991), 161-62.

60. Stevens, *Collected Poems,* 129.

61. Susan Stewart, personal communication, Apr. 13, 2012.

62. Longenbach, *Wallace Stevens,* 162.

63. Ramon Fernandez, *Moralisme et littérature,* 90.

64. Dominique Fernandez, *Ramon,* 65.

65. Jean Cocteau, *Les passé défini* (Paris: Gallimard, 983), 308-9.

66. Ramon Fernandez, *Messages,* trans. Montgomery Belgion (New York: Harcourt, Brace and Company, 1927 [1926]).

67. Ibid., 200.

68. Ibid., 194.

69. Ibid., 204.

70. Ibid., 212-13.

71. Ibid., 213-14.

72. Ibid., 214, n. 10.

73. Ibid., 220.

74. Ibid., 200-201.

75. Ramon Fernandez, *Proust*, 202.

76. Ibid., 19.

77. Ibid., 278.

78. Ibid., 87.

79. Ibid., 105.

80. Ibid., 107

81. Ibid., 200.

82. Ibid., 122.

83. Ibid., 168.

84. Ibid., 175.

85. Ibid., 186.

86. Ibid., 187.

87. Ibid., 188.

88. Ibid., 179.

89. Ibid., 215.

90. Ibid., 234.

91. Ibid., 250.

92. Ibid., 268

93. Ibid., 204.

94. Ibid., 207.

95. Ramon makes this observation after noting an improbable coincidence; he and Reynaldo both used the word *trance* to describe Proust's working method: "On voudra bien remarquer que la comparaison ou l'impression d'une transe est venue spontanément sous la plume d'un vieil ami comme Reynaldo Hahn et sous celle d'un étranger, comme moi-même." Ibid., 116.

Paperolle No. 4

1. "Cela vous plaira, puisque l'Espagne est à la mode, ollé! ollé!" *Recherche,* 1:489; "Milk, that's the thing! You'll like that, because Spain is fashionable these days—*olé au lait!*" *In the Shadow of Young Girls in Love,* trans. James Grieve (New York: Penguin, 2003), 72.

2. *Recherche,* 3:829.

3. Proust, *The Prisoner, the Fugitive,* trans Carol Clark and Peter Collier (London: Allen Lane, 2002), 300-301.

4. *Recherche,* 3:1770, n. 1.

5. *Corr.,* 9:218; 10:394; 13:304; 16:413.

6. Evelyne Bloch-Dano, *Madame Proust: A Biography,* trans. Alice Yaeger Kaplan (Chicago: University of Chicago Press, 2007), 195.

7. *Recherche,* 3:830.

8. Proust, *The Prisoner and the Fugitive,* 302.

Epilogue

1. Marcel Proust, *Contre Sainte-Beuve* (Paris: Gallimard, Bibliothèque de la Pléiade, 1971), 362.

2. Eugenia de Errázuriz (1861–1942) was the daughter of a Chilean silver magnate. She was painted by Jacques-Émile Blanche in 1890. See *Jacques-Émile Blanche, Peintre (1861–1942),* exhibition catalogue (Rouen: Musée des Beaux-Arts, 1997–98), 98.

3. Edward W. Said, *Freud and the Non-European* (New York: Verso, 2004).

Index

Académie des Canaques, 138-40
Académie Française, 1, 22, 103, 134-35,
  139-40, 147-48, 154, 167, 172
Against Sainte-Beuve (Proust), 24, 199, 202
Against the Grain (Huysmans), 22, 90
Agostinelli, Alfred, 86, 213, 232n67
Aimé (headwaiter at the Grand Hotel), 15
À la recherche du temps perdu (Proust), 4-5,
  10, 16, 26, 34, 41, 43, 46, 65, 87, 96, 109,
  121, 128, 130, 141-42, 149, 188, 196, 199,
  207-10, 212, 217, 221n29, 239n112
Albaret, Céleste, 62
Albertine, 85, 86
Albertine disparue (Proust), 85;
Alembert, Jean le Rond d', 17
À l'ombre de jeunes filles en fleur (Proust), 142,
  195-96
Alzire (Voltaire), 10
Amaéguis, Marquise of, 101
Amant, L' (Duras), 188
Amiens Cathedral, 46-47
Anchorena de Uriburu, Leonor, 176, 217
André Gide (Fernandez), 18, 200, 208
Apollinaire, Guillaume, 36
Appiah, Anthony, 18
Arendt, Hannah, 173
Argencourt, Count, 4
Argentina, 12, 74, 109, 162, 172
Argentino de oro, El (Páez de la Torre), 105
Aristophanes, 60
Armas, Augusto de, 147
arrière-garde, 36-37, 43-44
Art religieux du XIIIème siècle en France,
  L' (Mâle), 46
Atahualpa, 146

Aubervilliers, 65
Auschwitz, 197
Aztecs, 146, 183
Azuela, Mariano, 10

Bacardí y Moreau, Emilio, 168
Bagatelles pour un massacre (Céline), 188
Bakst, Léon, 37
Balbec, 13-15, 209, 211
Balboa, Vasco Núñez de, 158-59
Ballets Russes, 26, 37
Balzac, Honoré de, 6, 8-9, 16, 19, 70, 102,
  187, 189
Bandera de Provincias, 191
Bank of Mexico, 75
Banville de, Théodore, 134
Barnet, José, 147
Barrès, Maurice, 204
Bartet, Julia, 140
Bataille, Georges, 206
Baudelaire, Charles, 29
Bayreuth, 30
Bazar de la Charité, 141
Beckett, Samuel, 23, 72, 204
Beethoven, 32
Benhaïm, André, 220nn7-8
Benjamin, Walter, 2, 204
Bergson, Henri, 23, 182, 186, 188, 205, 208
Bernhardt, Sarah, 176, 180
Berry, Walter, 83-84
Beverly, John, 19
Bhabha, Homi, 16
Bibesco, Prince Antoine, 57
Bibesco, Prince Emmanuel, 6
Bible of Amiens, The (Ruskin), 46, 179

Bibliothèque de l'Arsenal, 161, 168
Bizet, Georges, 68-70
Bizet, Jacques, 68
Blanche, Jacques-Émile, 176, 181, 204
Blanco, Antonio Guzmán, 217
Bloch, 5, 142
Blum, Léon, 139
Bobadilla, Emilio, 147
Bodinière, La, 96
Bohl de Faber, Cecilia, 168
Bolaño, Roberto, 184
Boldini, Giovanni, 176
Bolívar, Simon, 162, 167
Borges, Jorge Luis, 10, 103, 188, 192
Boulenger, Jacques, 204
Boulevard Haussmann, 56-57, 84
Bouvard et Pécuchet (Flaubert), 32-33
Bourget, Priory of Le, 49
Brasillach, Robert, 188-89
Brasseur, Jules, 7
Brazil, 7-9, 15-16, 74
Brésilien, Le (Meilhac and Halévy), 7
Breton, André, 206
Brill Magazine, 75
Bucharest, 25
Buenos Aires, 3, 97, 191-92
Buñuel, Luis, 87
Butler, Judith, 71

Caballero, Fernán, 168
Cabourg, 213
Cahiers Marcel Proust, 187, 191, 197-98
Caillois, Roger, 192
Calderón, Ventura García, 132-33, 216
Cambremer, Madame de, 123
Cambridge, 186
Canaquadémie, 138-40
Caraman-Chimay, Élisabeth de, 176
Carmélite, La (Hahn), 47, 63-64
Carmen (Bizet), 68-70, 101
Carnaval de Venise, 90
Caro, Miguel Antonio, 147
Carranza, Venustiano, 80-83
Carrillo, Enrique Gómez, 133, 147, 217
Cartagena de Indias, 145-146
Carter, William C., 39, 50, 226n48
Casa Fuerte, Ilan de, 6, 93, 102, 118, 120, 123, 130
Casas, Bartolomé de las, 146

Case of Wagner, The (Nietzsche), 69-71
Castiglione, Comtesse de, 65
Castilla del Oro, 158
Cavalcanti, Alberto, 63
Céline (maid), 60
Céline, Louis-Ferdinand, 188-89
Central America, 10-11
Cervantes, Miguel de, 19, 168
Chafirete, El, 86-87
chancelier de fleurs, Le (Montesquiou), 97, 117-19, 177, 179, 237n73, 238n75
Chansons grises (Verlaine), 66
Charles V, 145
Charlus, Baron de, 4-5, 14, 86, 90, 107, 121-32, 127, 141, 207-8, 214-15
Chile, 12, 74, 163
China, 37
Chomette, Liliane, 190
Ciboulette (Hahn), 21, 29, 63-71
Ciboulette (Hahn character), 65-69, 71; as Conchita Ciboulero, 67-70
Cioran, Emil, 72
Cipango, 37, 144
Civil War, 154
Clermont-Tonnerre, Élisabeth de, 108
Cocteau, Jean, 29, 37, 186, 204
Cœuroy, André, 29
Colegio Nacional de Tucumán, 103
Collège de France, 186
Colombia, 145, 155, 157, 162
Columbus, Christopher, 144, 149-51, 215
Committee of Vigilance of Anti-Fascist intellectuals, 188
Compagnon, Antoine, 212
Compañía Mexicana de Petróleos El Águila, 85
Conchita Ciboulero, 67-70
Condé, Maryse, 19
Conklin, Alice L., 153
"conquérants, Les" (Heredia), 81, 149, 151-52, 174, 183
conquérants de l'or, Les (Heredia), 142-46, 149, 152, 155, 158-59, 174
Contemporáneaneos, 191
Contre Sainte-Beuve (Proust), 24, 199, 202
Coppée, François, 2, 134, 154
Corneille, Pierre, 99
Cortés, Hernán, 82
Corydon (Gide), 208
Così fan tutte (Mozart), 133

Cottard, 15, 26, 211, 223n6

cousine Bette, La (Balzac), 6

Crédit Industriel, 78

Criterion, The, 200

Croisset, Francis de, 64-65, 69, 84

Cuba, 12, 147-48, 154, 161-62

Cuban-Spanish-American War, 88, 142, 154, 161

Culebra mountains, 155-56

Culture and Imperialism (Said), 20

Curtius, Ernst Robert, 204

Daireaux, Max, 6, 213

Damrosch, David, 20

Darién, 146

Darío, Rubén, 3, 102-3, 147, 217, 235n33

Daudet, Alphonse, 98-101, 182

Daudet, Léon, 98, 122, 204

Daudet, Lucien, 185-86

Degas, Edgar, 154

de Gaulle, Charles, 29

De la Personnalité (Fernandez), 187, 199, 202

"De la simplicité de Robert de Montesquiou" (Proust), 109

Delgado, Honorio, 188

Delibes, Léo, 37

Descartes, René, 205

Diaghilev, Serge, 37

Díaz, Porfirio, 9, 19, 75-79, 184, 186, 207, 217

Diderot, Denis, 17-18

Diesbach, Ghislain de, 129

dieu bleu, Le (Hahn), 37

Díez Canedo, Enrique, 147

"dîner en ville, Un" (Proust), 141

Dominican Republic, 145

Don Quixote (Cervantes), 168

Dorado, El, 58-59

Doriot, Jacques, 188

Dreyfus, Robert, 69

Dreyfus Affair, 6, 11, 13-14, 149, 154

Drieu La Rochelle, Pierre, 188

D'Souza, Dinesh, 19

Du côté de chez Swann (Proust), 27, 34, 185, 204

Duparquet, 65-67

Duras, Marguerite, 35, 188

"éclipse, L'" (Proust) 149-53, 174

École des Chartes, 147

École du Louvre, 176

Écrits nouveaux, Les, 194

Egypt, 74

Eiffel, Gustave, 155, 158

Eliot, T. S., 20, 23, 36-37, 186, 191

Epstein, Simon, 188

Errázuriz, Eugenia de, 217, 251n2

Escamillo, 69

Europe nouvelle, L', 194

Faffenheim-Munsterburg-Weinigen, Prince, 4

Faguet, Émile, 107

Faubourg Saint-Germain, 11, 97, 102, 108, 110, 114, 130, 205

Fermina Marquez (Larbaud), 9-10

Fernandez, Dominique, 187-88, 190, 193, 196-97, 203, 208

Fernandez, Ramón, 2, 3, 23, 184, 192, 204, 213, 185-210, 249n53. Works by: *André Gide,* 187, 200, 208; *L'Homme, est-il humain?,* 187, 192; "I Came Near Being a Fascist," 200-201; *Marcel Proust,* 210; *Messages,* 187, 191, 204-5, 207-8, 210; *Moralisme et littérature,* 187, 193; *Le Pari,* 187; *De la Personnalité,* 187, 199, 202; *Philippe Sauveur,* 185, 187; *La vie de Molière,* 187; *Les violents,* 187

Ferrant, Guy, 63- 65, 229n101

"Fête chez Montesquiou à Neuilly" (Proust), 99, 106-10, 114, 120

"fête littéraire à Versailles, Une" (Proust), 140, 180

Feydeau, Georges, 8, 15, 102

Feyder, Jacques, 63

Figaro, Le, 43, 75-77, 80, 106-7, 130, 141

fil à la patte, Un (Feydeau), 8

Fil des Étoiles (Satie), 34, 35

Finding Time Again (Proust), 88

Flaubert, Gustave, 32, 106

Flers, Robert de, 64-65, 69

Foguet, Hugo, 104

Folie Saint James, La, 63

Fortuny, Mariano, 179

France, Anatole, 180

Françoise, 67, 158, 207, 209

Franco-Prussian War, 134

Franz Josef (emperor of Austria), 154

Frasquita, 69

French Communist Party, 188-89

Freud, Sigmund, 5, 18, 41, 62, 206, 208, 214
Frick Collection, 102
Futurism, 43

Gandelman, Claude, 54
Gautier, Théophile, 29
Genet, Jean, 70
Genette, Gérard, 110
Germany, 28, 30, 46, 71, 188
Gide, André, 186-87, 191, 197
Giotto, 36
Godoy, Armand, 147
Goebbels, Joseph, 188
Goethe, Johann Wolfgang von, 19, 155
Goldsmith, Kenneth, 39
Gómez Carrillo, Enrique, 13, 147
Gonards Cemetery, 115
Goncourt, Edmond de, 103, 106
Goncourt, Jules de, 106
González, Manuel, 193
Goursat, Georges (Sem), 93, 111
Grammar of Ascent (Newman), 205
Grand Hotel de Balbec, 15, 132
Great War, 149, 194, 209
Greffulhe, Comtesse de, 101, 108, 120
Groussac, Paul, 103-5
Guatemala, 12
Guermantes, 14, 65, 131, 209
Guermantes, Duc de, 13
Guermantes, Duchesse de, 11, 65, 68
Guiche, Duc de, 108
Gutiérrez Nájera, Manuel, 87
Guzmán Blanco, Roberto, 6, 9, 12

Hahn, Carlos, 12
Hahn, Maria, 23, 179
Hahn, Reynaldo, 1-3, 6, 12, 16, 18, 20-21, 24,
    25-72, 222n2, 224n10, 238n78;
    langasge moschant, 39-44, 46-7; friend-
    ship with Montesquiou and Yturri, 90,
    95-103, 110, 117-19; and Heredia, 140, 147;
    and La Gandara, 176; and Ramon Fernan-
    dez, 186, 189-90, 197-99, 210, 213. Works
    by: La Carmélite, 47, 63-64; Ciboulette, 21,
    29, 63-71; Le dieu bleu, 37; L'île de rêve, 26,
    28, 37, 64; Journal d'un musicien, 44; Nau-
    sicaa, 63; Ô mon bel inconnu, 29, 63; "Le
    souvenir d'avoir chanté," 63
Halévy, Daniel, 69, 229n107

Halévy, Ludovic, 7
Hapsburg, Franz Josef von (emperor of
    Austria), 154
Hapsburg, Maximilian von (emperor of
    Mexico), 154-55, 164
Harper's Weekly, 156
Hauser, Lionel, 73-89, 133, 141, 142, 194
Hayward, Cecilia, 213
Helleu, Paul, 180
Henri IV, 99
Henríquez Ureña, Pedro, 147
Heredia, Hélène de, 138
Heredia, José-Maria de, 1-3, 6, 16-18, 20,
    22-24, 134-75, 217-18; in Proust's letters to
    Hauser, 81; friendship with Montesquiou
    and Yturri, 103; and La Gandara: 183-84;
    and Ramon Fernandez, 189-191, 196-97,
    210, 242n22, 245n49. Works by: "Les
    conquérants," 81, 149, 151-52, 174, 183; Les
    conquérants de l'or, 142-46, 149, 152, 155,
    158-59, 174; Les trophées, 136, 143, 145-46,
    151, 167, 171; Sonnets et eaux-fortes, 152
Heredia, José María Heredia y, 134, 137, 161,
    168, 171-73
Heredia, Louise de, 138
Heredia, Marie de, 138, 140, 213
Heredia, Pedro de, 145, 172
Heredia Archive, 161, 168
Hernández, Juan José, 104, 105, 235n40
Historiettes (Tallemant des Réaux), 99
Hitler, Adolf, 188
Hœntschel, Georges, 180
Holland, 74
Homme, est-il humain?, L' (Fernandez), 187, 192
Hotel Ritz (Paris), 57, 111
Houville, Gérard d', 140
Huerta, Victoriano, 22, 80
Hugo, Victor, 25
Huysmans, Joris-Karl, 22, 90, 95, 233n7

Ibrovac, Miodrag, 146
"I Came Near Being a Fascist" (Fernandez),
    200-201
"Idea of order at Key West, The" (Stevens),
    200-201, 203
Île de rêve, L' (Hahn), 26, 28, 37, 64
Illusion Travels by Streetcar (Buñuel), 87
Inca Empire, 146, 159
India, 37

Indochina, 174
Interpretation of Dreams, The (Freud), 206
In the Shadow of Young Girls in Flower
   (Proust), 142, 195-96
Ionesco, Eugène, 23, 72
Irrigua, General, 8-9
Irving, Washington, 151
Isthmian Canal Bill, 157
Iwasaki, Fernando, 129

Jaloux, Edmond, 204
Jamaica, 149
Japan, 37, 144
Jardin d'Acclimatation, 4
Jean Santeuil (Proust), 26, 141, 158, 180, 182
Jewish identity, 4, 6, 25, 27, 29, 71
Jollivet, Gaston, 7
Journal d'un musicien (Hahn), 44
Joyce, James, 10, 19, 20, 36, 182
Juan Soldado (Fernán Caballero), 168
Juárez, Benito, 155
Jullian, Philippe, 102
Jupien, 86-87, 122, 132, 208

Kaas, Alphonse, 30, 225n20
Kahlo, Frida, 87
Kant, Immanuel, 17-18
Key West, 200, 202
Kolb, Philip, 74
Kristeva, Julia, 3, 5, 17-18, 23, 72, 209

Lacan, Jacques, 41, 187, 215
Laemmel, Sybilla, 50
La Fontaine, Jean de, 99
La Gandara, Antonio de, 6, 23, 176-84, 213
La Gandara, Édouard de, 180, 182
La Gandara, Manuel de, 184
Lakmé (Delibes), 37
langasge moschant, 39-44, 46-7
Larbaud, Valery, 9, 10, 187
Lavallée, Pierre, 50
League of Nations, 17
Leconte de Lisle, Charles, 134, 142, 147
Le Cuziat, Albert, 87
légende du Parnasse contemporain, La (Catulle
   Mendès), 152
Légion d'honneur, 28
Legras powder, 59
Lemaire, Madeleine, 25, 34, 44, 50, 140

Lemaire, Suzette, 25, 30-31, 44
Lemaître, Jules, 154
Lemoine Affair, 107
Lemoine, Henri, 107
León, Juan Ponce de, 145
Léonie, 13, 158
Lesseps, Ferdinand de, 155-58
Life and Voyages of Christopher Columbus
   (Irving), 151
Ligue de la Patrie Française, 154
Lillas Pastia, 69
livre des sonnets, Le 152
Loayza, Luis, 129
Lobre, Maurice, 180
London, 25, 80-81, 83
London County and Westminster Bank, 83-84
London Theosophical Publishing House, 74
Longenbach, James, 200
Lorrain, Jean, 92, 95
Loti, Pierre, 37
Louis X (Louis the Headstrong; king of
   France), 50
Louis XIII (king of France), 99
Louis XIV (king of France), 107
Louis XV (king of France), 110
Louÿs, Pierre, 139-40, 154
Lully, Jean-Baptiste, 29, 70
Lycée Condorcet, 182

Madeleine, Place de la, 87
Madero, Francisco I., 22, 77-78
Madrazo, Fréderic de, 37, 180
Madrazo, Raimundo de, 179
Madrazo y Ochoa, Federico de, 37, 180
Mâle, Émile, 46-53, 119
Mallarmé, Stéphane, 182
Manet, Édouard, 154, 157
"Manifesto of Futurism" (Marinetti), 43, 206
"Manifesto of Surrealism" (Breton), 206
Mansilla, Lucio, 6, 133, 216
Mapuche Indians, 163, 165
Marcel Proust (Fernandez), 210
Marie, Charles, 158
Marinetti, Filippo Tommaso, 36, 43, 206
Martel, Marie, 228n94
Marx, Karl, 206
Marx, William, 36, 44
Massenet, Jules, 25, 29, 33, 36, 69, 70
Mathilde, Princess, 138, 141

Mauclair, Camille, 182
Mauriac, François, 204-5
Maurois, André, 204
Maurras, Charles, 154
Meilhac, Henri, 7
Meistersinger, Die (Wagner), 30, 63
Melo, Jorge Orlando, 146
"Mélomanie de Bouvard et Pécuchet"
    (Proust), 32-33, 225n30
Mémoirs (Saint-Simon), 107-10, 114, 131
Menchú, Rigoberta, 19
Mendès, Catulle, 152
Meredith, George, 23, 187, 205
Mérope (Voltaire), 10
Merovingians, 95
Messages (Fernandez), 187, 191, 204-5, 207-8,
    210
Metamorphoses (Ovid), 126
Métra, Olivier, 65
Mexican Campaign, 6, 154-55
Mexican Revolution, 22, 78-79, 81, 86, 88,
    186, 207
Mexico, 73-89, 162, 174, 191, 193-94
Mexico City, 75, 78, 86, 88-89
Mexico Tramways Company, 75-89
Michelet, Jules, 107
Milly, Jean, 108
Mistral, Frédéric, 154
Molière, 187
Molloy, Sylvia, 6, 10
Monaco, 29
Monet, Claude, 157
monja alférez, La, 168
Montaigne, Michel de, 205
Monte Carlo, 29, 63, 199
Montès de Montéjanos, Henri, 7
Montespan, Madame de, 131
Montesquiou, Count Robert de, 1-2, 22, 33,
    90-127, 134, 140, 176-77, 180, 183, 233n2,
    233n7, 237n69; *Le chancelier de fleurs,* 97,
    117-19, 177, 179, 237n73, 238n75; *Parcours
    du rêve au souvenir,* 140
Montesquiou, Count Thierry de, 102
Moralisme et littérature (Fernandez), 187, 193
Morand, Paul, 185
Morel, Charlie, 6, 122, 123, 125, 128
Mornand, Louisa de, 176, 182
"mort de Baldassare Silvande, La" (Proust),
    26, 113, 222n3

Mortemart, Madame de, 128-31
Mortemarts, 131-32
Mourmelon, Vice-count of, 64-65
Mozart, Wolfgang Amadeus, 32
Mujica Láinez, Manuel, 130
Musée d'Orsay, 176
Museum of Natural History (Paris), 162, 165

Nahmias, Albert, 213
Napoléon Bonaparte (Taine), 141
Napoleon III, 6, 154-55
National Socialism, 29, 72, 206
Naturel, Mireille, 32
Nausicaa (Hahn), 63
Nazi Germany, 29, 72, 206
Nervo, Amado, 147
Neuburger, Léon, 73
Newman, John Henry Cardinal, 205-8
New Panama Canal Company, 157
Nietzsche, Friedrich, 69-70, 208
Nijinsky, Vaslav, 37
Nissim Bernard, 14-15, 132
Noailles, Anna de, 92, 108, 176
Nordlinger, Marie, 6, 179
Norpois, 11, 85-86
Notre Dame, 51-52
nouveaux messieurs, Les (Feyder), 63
"Novela del tranvía" (Gutiérrez Nájera), 87
Novo, Salvador, 86-87, 191
NRF (*Nouvelle Revue Française*), 23, 36, 187,
    195-97, 204

Ocampo, Silvina, 192
Ocampo, Victoria, 192
Ochsé, Fernand, 29, 197
"Ode to Niagara" (Heredia y Heredia), 134,
    172
Odette, 4-5, 195-96, 248n46
Offenbach, Jacques, 7-9, 15, 16, 29, 70, 102
Ollagnier, Marie Miguet, 152-53, 244n42
Ô mon bel inconnu (Hahn), 29, 63
Opéra Comique, 28, 37
Ortega y Gasset, José, 208
Orvilliers, Princess, 4
Ovid, 126, 173

Pacific Ocean, 159
Páez de la Torre, Carlos, 104-5
Painter, George D., 121, 129

País, El, 137, 161
Palais Rose, 130
Palimpsests (Genette), 110
Palos de Moguer, 143-44
Panama, 6, 12-13, 88, 145, 155-61, 218
Panama Affair, 6, 12-13, 88, 155-57, 159, 218
Panama Canal, 155-57
Panamistes, 157
paperolles, 21, 124
Parcours du rêve au souvenir (Montesquiou), 140
Pari, Le (Fernandez), 187
Parnasse conteporain, Le, 134
Parnassian movement, 134-36, 140, 152, 171, 173-74
Parole in libertà (Marinetti), 43
Parsifal (Wagner), 30
Parti Populaire Français, 188, 197
Partisan Review, 200-201
Pascal, Blaise, 99
pastiche, 99, 111-14
Pastiches et mélanges (Proust), 10, 106
Patagonia, 163-67
Paulhan, Jean, 186
Pavillon des Muses, 112
Pavillon Montesquiou, 113
Paz, Octavio, 183, 192
Peary, Robert, 215
Pécuchet, 32-33
Penhoët, 10
Perloff, Marjorie, 39
Peru, 12, 82, 133, 145
Peruvian (anonymous character), 128-33
Pétain, Philippe, 188
Petróleos de México, 84
Philippe Sauveur (Fernandez), 185, 187
Picasso, Pablo, 23, 36
Pissarro, Camille, 157
Pizarro, Francisco, 145, 158
plaisirs et les jours, Les (Proust), 33, 96, 140, 223n5
Plato, 60, 208
Poggioli, Renato, 200
Pompadour, Madame de, 90, 93
Ponce de León, Juan, 145
Popelin, Claudius, 145
"Portraits de musiciens" (Proust), 33
"Portraits de peintres" (Proust), 26, 33, 96, 223n4

"Portraits de peintres et de musiciens" (Proust), 140
Pound, Ezra, 36
Prescott, William H., 159
Pretérito perfecto (Foguet), 104
Prisonnière, La (Proust), 23
Professionnelles beautés (Montesquiou), 115
Proust, Adrien, 115
Proust, Marcel, articles: "De la simplicité de Robert de Montesquiou" (Of the Simplicity of Robert de Montesquiou) 109; "L'éclipse" (The Eclipse) 149-53, 174; "Fête chez Montesquiou à Neuilly" (A Party at Montesquiou's in Neuilly), 99, 106-10, 114, 120; "Mélomanie de Bouvard et Pécuchet" (Melomania of Bouvard and Pécouchet), 32-33, 225n30; "La mort de Baldasarre Silvande" (The Death of Baldasarre Silvande), 26, 113, 222n3; "Portraits de musiciens" (Portraits of Musicians), 33; "Portraits de peintres" (Portraits of Painters), 26, 33, 96, 223n4; "Portraits de peintres et de musiciens" (Portraits of Painters and Musicians), 140; "Un dîner en ville" (A Dinner in Town), 141; "Une fête littéraire à Versailles" (A Literary Fête at Versailles), 140, 180
Proust, Marcel, books: *À la recherche du temps perdu* (In Search of Lost Time), 4-5, 10, 16, 26, 34, 41, 43, 46, 65, 87, 96, 109, 121, 128, 130, 141-42, 149, 188, 196, 199, 207-10, 212, 217, 221n29, 239n112; *À l'ombre de jeunes filles en fleur* (In the Shadow of Young Girls in Flower), 142, 195-96; *Albertine disparue* (Albertine Is Gone), 85; *Contre Sainte-Beuve* (Against Sainte-Beuve), 24, 199, 202; *Du côté de chez Swann* (Swann's Way), 27, 34, 185, 204; *Jean Santeuil*, 26, 141, 158, 180, 182; *Pastiches et mélanges* (Pastiches and Mélanges), 10, 106; *Les plaisirs et les jours* (The Pleasures and the Days), 33, 96, 140, 223n5; *La Prisonnière* (The Prisoner), 23; *Sodome et Gomorrhe* (Sodom and Gomorrah), 140, 186; *Le temps retrouvé* (Finding Time Again), 88
Proust, Marcel, *langasge moschant*, 39-44, 46-47
Proust, Robert, 60, 139
p'tite Lili, La (Cavalcanti), 63

Quai d'Orsay, 90
Quai Voltaire, 182
Querqueville, 12

Ramon (Dominique Fernandez), 190, 203
Rastacuero, Íñigo, 3
rastaquouère, 2-3, 6-7, 9, 14, 102-3, 124,
    130-31, 197, 219n3
Réaux, Tallemant des, 99
Rebatet, Lucien, 29
Reflections on Exile (Said), 17
Régnier, Henri de, 106, 139-40, 142
Reinach, Baron Jacques de, 155-57
Renan, Ernest, 107
Renoir, Auguste, 154
Réveillon, 25
Réveillon, Henri de, 26
Revue Bleue, La, 152
Reyes, Alfonso, 10, 23, 184, 190-93, 210
Rheims Cathedral, 48
Risler, Édouard, 30-35, 44, 71
Rite of Spring, The (Stravinsky), 35-36
Rivière, Jacques, 36, 187, 193, 204
Roazen, Daniel Heller, 173
Robert, Pierre-Édmond, 212
Rodin, Auguste, 157
Romania, 84
Roosevelt, Theodore, 157
Rostand, Maurice, 186
Rothschild Bank, 73-74
Rouvier, Maurice, 159
Rue de l'Arcade, 87
Rue de la Victoire, 82
Rue du Cirque, 50
Rue du Commandant Marchand, 57
Rushdie, Salman, 19
Ruskin, John, 4, 6, 46-47, 179
Russia, 79
Russian Revolution, 79

Said, Edward, 16-17, 20
Saint-Cloud, 107
Saint-Lazare railway station, 87
Saint-Loup, Robert de, 142
Saint-Saëns, Camille, 29, 32, 36, 69
Sainte-Beuve, Charles Augustin, 24
Saint-Simon, duc de, 106-10,
Salles, Adolphe, 158
Sanguily, Manuel, 147

Saniette, 215
Santayana, George, 191
Santiago de Cuba, 134, 168
Santo Domingo, 149
Satie, Erik, 25, 34-35
Scherbatoff, Princess, 4
Scholl, Aurélien, 3
Schopenhauer, Arthur, 31, 208
Schorske, Carl E., 217
Schubert, Franz, 32
Second Empire, 65
Sedgwick, Eve Kosofsky, 113
Segundo Ballén de Guzmán, Ana, 213
Segura, Diego Méndez de, 151
Sem, 93, 111
Serbia, 74
Sesame and the Lys (Ruskin), 46, 179
Sevigné, Madame de, 36, 99
Sierra, Justo, 147
Sodome et Gomorrhe (*Sodom and Gomorrah*;
    Proust), 140, 186
Solar, Alberto del, 176
Sollers, Philippe, 41, 51, 59
Sonnets et eaux-fortes (Heredia), 152
Son of the Stars, The (Satie), 34, 35
Sorel, Albert, 154
Soto, Hernando de, 145
Soupault, Philippe, 204
Southern Sea, 159
Soutzo, Hélène, 83-84
"souvenir d'avoir chanté, Le" (Hahn), 63
Spain, 9, 69-70, 74, 101, 109, 148-50, 174,
    229n110
Spinoza, Baruch, 208
Stein, Gertrude, 39
Stevens, Wallace, 200-203
Strangers to Ourselves (Kristeva), 3, 23, 72
Straus, Geneviève, 68
Stravinsky, Igor, 35-36, 182
Suez Canal, 142, 155
Sur (Argentinean publishing house), 192
Swann, 5, 121, 126-27, 141, 207, 209
Swann's Way (Proust), 27, 34, 185, 204
Switzerland, 74
Symposium (Plato), 60

Tadié, Jean-Yves, 74, 121-22
Tahiti, 37
Taine, Hippolyte, 141

Tannhäuser (Wagner), 29
"Technical Manifesto of Futurist Literature" (Marinetti), 43
temps retrouvé, Le (Proust), 88
Théâtre des Variétés, 64
Théâtre du Châtelet, 37
Thibaudet, Albert, 204
Thief's Journal, The (Genet), 70
Third Republic, 107, 153-54
Three Levers of the New World, The: Competence, Probity, Altruism (Hauser), 74
Tierra del Fuego, 163
Time and Sense: Proust and the Experience of Literature (Kristeva), 4-5
Todorov, Tzvetan, 23
Tounens, Antoine (King of Patagonia), 163-65
Tramway and Railway World, The, 78
trophées, Les (Heredia), 136, 143, 145-46, 151, 167, 171
True History of the Conquest of New Spain (Bernal Díaz del Castillo), 168
Tucumán, 1, 22, 90, 97, 103-5, 115
Tunisia, 74
Turkey, 74

Ungar, Isaac, 192
Unheimlich, 5
United States, 74, 79-84, 154-57
Universal Ilustrado, El, 191
Universal Panama Interoceanic Canal Company, 155
Uruguay, 162

Valéry, Paul, 182, 204
Valparaíso, 3
Vargas Llosa, Mario, 129
Vasconcelos, José, 188
Vaughan, Kenelm, 90, 233n1
Venezuela, 1, 12, 25, 213
Veracruz, 80, 88
Verdi, Giuseppe, 33

Verdurin, Madame, 5-6, 14-16, 22-23, 128-30, 195, 211-12, 214
Verdurin, Monsieur, 211-12, 214-15
Verdurins, 4, 6, 26, 34, 132, 209, 212-13, 215
Verlaine, Paul, 65, 99-101, 109, 176
Versailles, 112, 115
Vésinet, Le, 130
Vichy, 197
vie de Molière, La (Fernandez), 187
vie parisiènne, La (Meilhac and Halévy), 7
Villaurrutia, Xavier, 191-92
Villeparisis, Madame de, 11
Vinteuil, Mademoiselle de, 34, 55
Violents, Les (Fernandez), 187
Visión de Anáhuac (Reyes), 190
Vivonne, 24
Vogue, 186
Voltaire, 10
Voyage en Patagonie (de La Vaulx), 162-68

Wagner, Richard, 29-30, 32-34, 36, 60, 63, 70-71, 81
Walkyria (Wagner), 33
Wegener, Otto, 93
Weil, Jeanne, 158
Weimar, 188
Whistler, James McNeill, 12, 102, 176
Whitman, Walt, 10
Wilson, Woodrow, 81, 84
World War I, 4, 28, 42, 78-79, 88, 185, 190
World War II, 2, 13, 23, 197, 199

Yaqui Indians, 146
Yerba Buena, 90
Yturri, Gabriel de, 1-3, 6, 16-20, 22, 24, 90-127, 129, 210, 240n120; and Heredia, 136, 147; and Ramon Fernandez, 190, 196-97; and La Gandara, 176-80
Yvel, Arnaud, 75, 77

Zayas, Antonio, 147
Zimmermann Telegram, 82